DEVELOPING DIRECTORS
Building an effective boardroom team

Latest titles in the McGraw-Hill Training Series

CAREER DEVELOPMENT AND PLANNING
A Guide for Managers, Trainers and Personnel Staff
Malcolm Peel   ISBN 0-07-707554-4

SALES TRAINING
A Guide to Developing Effective Salespeople
Frank S. Salisbury   ISBN 0-07-707458-0

CLIENT-CENTRED CONSULTING
A Practical Guide for Internal Advisers and Trainers
Peter Cockman, Bill Evans
and Peter Reynolds   ISBN 0-07-707685-0

TRAINING TO MEET THE TECHNOLOGY CHALLENGE
Trevor Bentley   ISBN 0-07-707589-7

IMAGINATIVE EVENTS Volumes I & II
Ken Jones   ISBN 0-07-707679-6 Volume I
                   ISBN 0-07-707680-X Volume II
                   ISBN 0-07-707681-8 for set of Volumes I & II

LEARNING THROUGH SIMULATIONS
A Guide to the Design and Use of Simulations in Business and Education
John Fripp   ISBN 0-07-707588-9

MEETINGS MANAGEMENT
A Manual of Effective Training Material
Leslie Rae   ISBN 0-07-707782-2

WORKSHOPS THAT WORK
100 Ideas to Make Your Training Event More Effective
Tom Bourner, Vivien Martin
and Phil Race   ISBN 0-07-707800-4

TRAINING FOR PROFIT
A Guide to the Integration of Training
Philip Darling   ISBN 0-07-707785-7

THE HANDBOOK FOR ORGANIZATIONAL CHANGE
Strategy and Skill for Trainers and Developers
Carol A. O'Connor   ISBN 0-07-707693-1

MANAGING THE TRAINING PROCESS
Putting the basics into practice
Mike Wills   0-07-707806-3

RESOURCE-BASED LEARNING
Using Open and Flexible Resources For Continuous Development
Julie Dorrell   ISBN 0-07-707692-3

FACILITATION
Providing Opportunities For Learning
Trevor Bentley   ISBN 0-07-707684-2

Details of these and other titles in the series are available from:

The Product Manager, Professional Books, McGraw-Hill Book Company Europe,
Shoppenhangers Road, Maidenhead, Berkshire SL6 2QL, United Kingdom.
Telephone: 0628 23432. Fax: 0628 770224

Developing Directors

Building an effective boardroom team

Colin Coulson-Thomas

McGRAW-HILL BOOK COMPANY

London · New York · St Louis · San Francisco · Auckland
Bogotá · Caracas · Lisbon · Madrid · Mexico · Milan
Montreal · New Delhi · Panama · Paris · San Juan · São Paulo
Singapore · Sydney · Tokyo · Toronto

Published by
McGRAW-HILL Book Company Europe
Shoppenhangers Road, Maidenhead, Berkshire SL6 2QL, England.
Telephone: 0628 23432
Fax: 0628 770224

British Library Cataloguing in Publication Data
Coulson-Thomas, Colin
    Developing Directors: Building an
    Effective Boardroom Team.—(McGraw-Hill
    Training Series)
    I. Title II. Series
    658.4

ISBN 0-07-707590-0

Library of Congress Cataloging-in-Publication Data
Coulson-Thomas, Colin.
    Developing directors: building an effective boardroom team/
    Colin Coulson-Thomas.
        p.   cm.—(McGraw-Hill training series)
    Includes bibliographical references and index.
    ISBN 0-07-707590-0
    1. Directors of corporations. 2. Corporate governance.
    I. Title.   II. Series.
    HD2745.C653   1993
    658.4'22—dc20   93-8542
                                                                        CIP

12345 CL 96543

Typeset by Book Ens Limited, Baldock, Herts.
Printed and bound in Great Britain by Clays Ltd, St Ives plc.

To Margaret

Contents

Series preface

Training and development are now firmly centre stage in most organizations, if not all. Nothing unusual in that—for some organizations. They have always seen training and development as part of the heart of their businesses—but more and more must see it that same way.

The demographic trends through the nineties will inject into the marketplace severe competition for good people who will need good training. Young people without conventional qualifications, skilled workers in redundant crafts, people out of work, women wishing to return to work—all will require excellent training to fit them to meet the job demands of the 1990s and beyond.

But excellent training does not spring from what we have done well in the past. T&D specialists are in a new ball game. 'Maintenance' training—training to keep up skill levels to do what we have always done—will be less in demand. Rather, organization, work, and market change training are now much more important and will remain so for some time. Changing organizations and people is no easy task, requiring special skills and expertise which, sadly, many T&D specialists do not possess.

To work as a 'change' specialist requires us to get to centre stage—to the heart of the company's business. This means we have to ask about future goals and strategies, and even be involved in their development, at least as far as T&D policies are concerned.

This demands excellent communication skills, political expertise, negotiating ability, diagnostic skills—indeed, all the skills a good internal consultant requires.

The implications for T&D specialists are considerable. It is not enough merely to be skilled in the basics of training, we must also begin to act like business people and to think in business terms and talk the language of business. We must be able to resource training not just from within but by using the vast array of external resources. We must be able to manage our activities as well as any other manager. We must share in the creation and communication of the company's vision. We must never let the goals of the company out of our sight.

In short, we may have to grow and change with the business. It will be hard. We shall not only have to demonstrate relevance but also value for money and achievement of results. We shall be our own boss, as accountable for results as any other line manager, and we shall have to deal with fewer internal resources.

The challenge is on, as many T&D specialists have demonstrated to me over the past few years. We need to be capable of meeting that challenge. This is why McGraw-Hill Book Company (UK) Limited have planned and launched this major new training series—to help us meet that challenge.

The series covers all aspects of T&D and provides the knowledge base from which we can develop plans to meet the challenge. They are practical books for the professional person. They are a starting point for planning our journey into the twenty-first century.

Use them well. Don't just read them. Highlight key ideas, thoughts, action pointers or whatever, and have a go at doing something with them. Through experimentation we evolve; through stagnation we die.

I know that all the authors in the McGraw-Hill Training Series would want me to wish you good luck. Have a great journey into the twenty-first century.

ROGER BENNETT
Series Editor

About the series editor

Roger Bennett has over 20 years' experience in training, management education, research and consulting. He has long been involved with trainer training and trainer effectiveness. He has carried out research into trainer effectiveness, and conducted workshops, seminars, and conferences on the subject around the world. He has written extensively on the subject including the book *Improving Trainer Effectiveness*, Gower. His work has taken him all over the world, and has involved directors of companies as well as managers and trainers.

Dr Bennett has worked in engineering, several business schools (including the International Management Centre, where he launched the UK's first masters degree in T&D) and has been a board director of two companies. He is the editor of the *Journal of European Industrial Training*, and was series editor of the ITD's *Get In There* workbook and video package for the managers of training departments. He now runs his own business called The Management Development Consultancy.

Acknowledgements

I would like to thank my research collaborator Alan Wakelam of Exeter University, my Adaptation colleague Susan Coulson-Thomas, and both the Institute of Directors and the Rank Xerox corporate transformation team for their encouragement, help and support.

I am especially grateful to the many directors who have participated in surveys I have designed and the various activities and programmes I conduct for directors and boards. Their candour and willingness to share their views is much appreciated.

Over a period of years I have served upon several boards in both the private and public sectors. At most of the board meetings I have attended I have learned something from my fellow directors. I apologize for not doing justice to the many insights I have gained from them.

Becoming and remaining an effective director is a never-ending task, but a challenging and satisfying one. My hope is that this book will encourage more people to pursue a directorial career of active learning.

Colin Coulson-Thomas, 1993

1 Introduction

Directors under the spotlight

Is your company led by an effective board composed of a united team of competent directors with complementary skills? Does the board add value to the efforts of management? Is the board an instigator of change or a bystander? Is it a source of vision, drive and purpose or a 'rubber stamp'? How committed is the board to the achievement of corporate objectives?

These are important questions, because in many companies no one is consciously focusing upon the competence of the board or the effectiveness of its members; yet, at the same time, a growing burden of legal duties and responsibilities is being placed upon the shoulders of directors.

The performance of boards has become a matter of public concern on both sides of the Atlantic, and elsewhere. In the UK the 'Cadbury Committee' has been reviewing the financial aspects of corporate governance, while in the US a subcouncil of a presidential council inquiry into competitiveness is examining 'corporate governance and financial markets'.

The situation and directorial frustrations

Many directors are frustrated. Lorsch and MacIver suggest that directors may often be pawns rather than the potentates of popular imagination.[1] In practice, rather than being all powerful, a board can fall under the control of a powerful chief executive officer (CEO), or become a 'self-perpetuating oligarchy'.

The meetings of some boards are cursory rituals rather than arenas of challenge and deliberation leading to the decisive resolution of major issues. The key decisions may be taken elsewhere, or outcomes may be virtually guaranteed even before the board has assembled.

Many directors are unclear as to their directorial duties and responsibilities. One UK study by PRO NED and the Stock Exchange has found that, once appointed, only a third of non-executive directors are given written clarification of their roles and responsibilities.[2] Against this background, it is not surprising that chairmen are often dissatisfied with the quality of directorial contributions, even though they share some responsibility for this situation.

The overwhelming majority of directors will have received little if any preparation for their boardroom roles,[3] and there is often confusion between the respective roles and responsibilities of the board and of management. Where assessment of directors occurs it tends to be in terms of the managerial or 'departmental' performance of executive directors rather than their contribution to the board.[4]

Although routes to the boardroom are generally hidden, the qualities sought in new directors are rarely made explicit and it is not easy for people to prepare themselves for a directorial role. Many directors and boards refuse to acknowledge the need for director and board development, and those wishing to initiate development activity at board level should be under no illusions concerning the magnitude of the challenge they face.

Directorial attitudes and behaviour

The challenge, in the case of many boards, is: (i) to change the attitudes, awareness, perspective, focus, approaches and priorities of the directorial team; and (ii) to remedy the deficiencies of particular members who may be reluctant to acknowledge that these deficiencies exist.

In order to bring about desired changes, the existing situation needs to be understood. Consider the following comments from a small selection of directors:

As a non-executive director I feel on the periphery. I don't really know enough about the business to become involved.

There is mutual suspicion between executives and non-executives. We need to be much clearer about each others' roles.

There is little debate. The chairman keeps an eye on the clock. It's a matter of pride for him to finish by 3.30 pm.

We are swamped with information and don't have time to really understand it. It's never quite what we want . . . The jargon is baffling.

There are some bright people around the table [but] . . . we do not really gel as a team.

You sometimes sense the atmosphere . . . there are suspicions, hostilities, hidden agendas . . . people still pursue their departmental interests.

Even from such a small sample of views, it will be seen that there are several distinct matters to address, and they may be interrelated. No amount of development activity is likely, by itself, to overcome all the various factors that are inhibiting board effectiveness. Nevertheless, it is hoped that this book, and particularly its exercises, will identify those areas in which the greatest contribution can be made.

The attitudes and behaviour of directors are of more than an academic interest, as their consequences can be profound, and the impacts are likely to be felt beyond the boardroom. For example, directorial attitudes and behaviour can have an important influence on corporate morale. Many managers will take a cue from the role model behaviour of members of the board. It is difficult to be forceful, challenging and positive when the directors are uncertain, hesitant and inhibited.

Inconsistencies between the words and the actions of directors can undermine confidence and respect, and lead to disillusion and despair.[5]

Inadequate boards　There is little satisfaction with the performance of boards. This is not a new or even a recent phenomenon. Twenty years ago Mace found that many US boards did not question management or play a significant role in the formulation of strategy.[6]

Many boards fail to give their companies a sense of purpose, a compelling vision, or a distinctive reason for existence. Without a clear vision and mission, a company is rudderless.

Charles Lowe, formerly deputy chairman of Blue Arrow Employment Group, believes that:

to be successful, a board must first set its objectives; the most brilliant individual managers operating in the most buoyant economic circumstances and with access to unlimited finance will be totally ineffective unless it knows what it wants to do. In short, it must have a mission.

Some boards pursue their own interests, and devote inadequate attention to the interests of shareholders and other stakeholders. Others are perceived as a burden rather than as an enabler. Divisions in the boardroom can lead to a lack of direction and can undermine morale throughout an organization.

A recent survey has found that three-quarters of chairmen believe the effectiveness of their companies' boards could be improved.[4] Another study, of companies in crisis situations, has revealed an apparent link between corporate decline and board inadequacy and ineffectiveness.[7]

A common failing of many boards is that they put considerable effort into the crafting of strategy, and then devote inadequate attention to turning aspiration into achievement.[5] Such boards need to devote more attention to 'making it happen'. Left to themselves managers may not be focused, equipped, empowered or motivated to cope.

According to Peter Morgan, director general of the Institute of Directors (IOD):

A shared vision and sustained commitment in the boardroom is vital if outcomes are to match expectations. There is little point creating an excellent strategy which is not implemented.

The directors determine whether or not a company survives and thrives. The extent to which the board liberates or constrains the energies and talents of the people of a company is determined by the competence of the directors, and how effectively they work together as a team.

Many chairmen are not satisfied with the performance of their boards, and few boards operate satisfactorily as a team. In many companies the board—particularly in terms of its commitment—is a barrier to change rather than a facilitator of change.[8]

Harold Geneen, reflecting upon the boards of Fortune 500 companies following his retirement from ITT, has concluded: '95 percent are not fully doing what they are legally, morally and ethically supposed to do. And they couldn't, even if they wanted to.'[9]

Directorial perceptions of the problems

Many board members are sufficiently alert and perceptive to recognize the existence of problems, even though they may not agree, or accept, that development activities might have a role in addressing them. Consider the following comments on the effectiveness of individual boards:

We used to work well . . . I thought the balance was about right. [But] . . . it is different now, . . . the market we are in has changed. We are no longer as effective . . .

As soon as we encountered . . . difficulties people started looking to protect their own interests. . . . It was all how their reputations would be affected [not] what they could do to help save the company. . . . In adversity you learn who puts in and who takes out.

They are good people. As individuals, most are outstanding. But we haven't become a team. . . . They are in their own space. There is no group feeling.

A fish rots from the head down . . . I've never forgotten that. The learning organization is 'pie in the sky' if the board is brain dead.

Why should we necessarily be effective? What have we actually done over the past year, or in recent years, to actually examine our effectiveness, let alone increase it?

To be credible as a contributor to the development of directors and boards, it is necessary to understand, share and see problems from a directorial perspective. Hence, during the course of this book we shall turn occasionally to the comments of experienced directors. While it has been necessary to be selective, it is hoped that sufficient background is given to enable the 'directorial arena' to be understood.

Aims and scope

This book examines the development of competent directors, and the building and maintenance of a coherent, purposeful and productive boardroom team. It explores preferences regarding activities and approaches, and sources of development advice and services. It will also consider inhibitors of, and barriers to, development, before attempting some conclusions and presenting some recommendations concerning how boardroom effectiveness might be improved by appropriate formal and informal development activity.

The book is aimed at members of boards, and those with an interest in providing them with development counselling, advice and support. For easy use the book is divided into three parts:

Part One will explore the qualities of a competent director, the know-ledge and skills a director ought to possess, and the characteristics of an effective board.

In Part Two we shall consider the route to the boardroom and how directors are selected and prepared, then turn our attention to how they should be prepared. Having looked at the development of individual directors, we shall examine the development of the board as a team. Finally, we shall consider the evaluation of directorial contributions and board effectiveness, and the question of 'next steps'.

For those less familiar with directors and boards, Part Three is included by way of background and introduction. We shall examine the nature of the development challenge, the function of the board, the duties and responsibilities of the director, and the distinction between direction and management. An understanding of these issues is the foundation upon which director development should be built. We shall also see that boards vary in type, size, composition and structure, and can change over time.

In the course of the book we shall make certain discoveries:

- Directors have training and development needs that are distinct from those of managers, yet many corporate training and development programmes do not reach into the boardroom. Directors are left to 'pick it up' in the course of their duties.
- While some modification might be required in the context of each company, it is possible in general terms to profile a competent director and an effective board. The broad knowledge and skills that are required in the boardroom can also be identified.
- There is some consensus concerning what makes a good director, and the criteria that are used in selecting directors. However, these criteria are rarely understood by managers, and in many companies they are not taken into account in career planning.
- Only a small minority of directors appear to receive any formal preparation for their boardroom roles. A wide gulf exists between how directors *are* prepared for their boardroom roles, and how they *could* and *should* be prepared.
- Inadequate attention is given to evaluating personal effectiveness in the boardroom, and the performance of the board as a whole. In many companies there is an urgent need for action, the board representing 'the last training frontier'.

The role of the board, and the creation of an effective board that is able to complement, and add value to, management in the development and adaptation of a business to meet changing customer requirements is the subject of another book, 'Creating Excellence in the Boardroom,' which appears in McGraw-Hill's Henley Management Series.[8]

The evidence

Both books draw upon a programme of questionnaire and interview surveys that I conducted which examine the function, size and composition of boards, as perceived by directors themselves (see Bibliography, Section l). The surveys cover the frequency of board meetings, the criteria used in selecting board members, the contributions expected from board members, how the effectiveness of individual directors is assessed, how effectively they work as a team, the requirement to remain up to date, and professional development preferences.

Over 1000 individual directors have participated in the research programme, and over two-thirds of these are the chairman, the chief executive officer (CEO) or the managing director of a company. As a consequence of the findings, nine distinct categories of services have been developed to improve the performance of both individual directors and boardroom teams. These are available from selected professional associations and other specialist organizations.

A selection of the views of survey participants, as expressed in interviews or in response to open-ended questions in questionnaires, is given in this and other chapters of the book. These illustrate the range of situations, circumstances and viewpoints that can be encountered.

Applicability of the findings

The reader might feel that the conclusions need to be treated with some caution in view of the very small fraction of the total population of directors surveyed. However, the pattern and consistency of responses suggest that a significantly larger sample would not necessarily have led to different conclusions.

The boards covered by the surveys are representative of the total population of companies. The replies to most of the questions that were posed in the course of the surveys do not appear to be significantly influenced by company size or status. Hence, the findings are thought to be applicable to a wide range of boards.

A project undertaken by Adaptation Ltd for the UK's Department of Employment to develop an induction programme for new Training and Enterprise Council (TEC) directors, and a recent survey of NHS Authority members and Trust directors,[10] suggest that many of the findings are also applicable to the governance of a wide range of public sector organizations.

While the organizations participating in the surveys cited in section 1 of the Bibliography are primarily based in the UK, they include a mix of companies with headquarters elsewhere in Europe, and also in the US and Japan. As far as the role of the board, the attitudes of directors, and certain key boardroom issues are concerned, a degree of consensus was found across the participants, irrespective of 'corporate nationality'. A study by Demb and Neubauer of 71 directors serving on boards in eight countries has also found certain common features that appear to be broadly independent of the local legal framework.[11]

Understanding the people

A board is composed of people. The key to successful director development is understanding the people and personalities involved. How they come together and interact in the context of the boardroom will determine the extent to which the board could be described as a collection of individuals, a group, a community or a team.

The motivations of directors, why they have sought to become directors, and what they think of their colleagues represent the soil from which teamwork must grow. Why have the members of the board of your company accepted a board appointment? What do they really think and feel?

The nature and extent of directorial commitment could be of some importance to a chairman, or to a CEO charged with transforming a company. A crisis situation can test the resolve of a board. In adversity, undercurrents and conflicts can come to the surface. Exercise 1.1 suggests some questions that could be asked to assess the motivation and commitment of the individual members of the board.

Exercise 1.1: Know your boardroom colleagues

Some people are easier to get to know than others. There may be one or two members of the board, perhaps non-executive directors, who could be asked to assess colleagues. Where confidentiality is assured, a chairman might be willing to encourage all directors to give honest answers to particular questions. In other cases you may need to make your own assessment of the following:

1 How important is board membership for each of your colleagues (or each director, if you do not consider them to be 'colleagues')?
2 What does board membership mean for each of them?
3 Who among your boardroom colleagues most and least enjoy being a director and why?
4 Who among them stand to gain the most and the least from remaining a director?
5 Who among your boardroom colleagues are the most and least protected against the consequences of company failure?
6 Who among them care the most and the least about the various stakeholders in the business?
7 Who among the members of the board are the most and least committed to the long-term future of the company?
8 What value does each member of the board really add by virtue of being a director?
9 Who among the board members could the company most and least afford to lose?
10 Who among your boardroom colleagues would be the most and least difficult to replace if they ceased to be directors?
11 Who among them would be most and least missed if they ceased to be directors?

The questions of Exercise 1.1 represent a long list, and some could be more relevant than others in the context of a particular company and its board. Remember that the purpose of the exercise is to enable you to assess how much you know about the members of the board in terms of 'who they really are'.

The questions of Exercise 1.1 should be put tactfully to the individual directors. Their purpose is to help establish a rapport, and a sense of what might possibly be achieved with a particular group of people over a period of time. Too much should not be expected too soon. There should be no hint of interrogation in this or any other exercise in the book.

Probing motivations and seeking to understand what board membership means to people can cause them to 'clam up'. Some may refuse to answer. In other cases, it may be more productive to raise questions relating to motivation and commitment during the course of informal conversations. The nature and pattern of reactions may reveal something of the atmosphere and ethos of the board, the extent to which there is openness and trust, and the degree to which individual board members feel secure.

It may take some time to assemble a brief profile of each director. If you find you do not understand the directors or 'what makes them tick', and you have not established sufficient trust for them to confide in you, then you should reconsider whatever timetable you have established for director development, in order to allow an openness and rapport to be established.

Comparing different profiles could allow gaps of perspective, a lack of motivation, or incompatibilities of personality to be identified. It may be possible to discover some root causes of certain problems that have given concern. For example, the motivations and approaches of certain directors may not be compatible with those of the chairman or CEO.

If you are a director, or are at director level, compare you own reactions to those of your colleagues. Also reflect upon the way in which their responses differ from, or confirm, your own prior assumptions.

Understanding the team

Once some 'feel' has been obtained for the individual members of the board, the next step is to assess how they interact and interrelate as a group. The culture and chemistry of the board is a critical determinant of its dynamics and effectiveness.

Members of the board need to understand each other's drives and motivations if they are to work well together as a team, especially in circumstances in which a shared vision and a common and sustained commitment is needed to bring about fundamental change.

Members of the board may be reluctant to submit themselves to formal and psychological tests—hence, the suggestion of starting with some informal exploration of what board membership means for each individual. Exercise 1.2 assumes that members of the board have been asked to consider their own personal reasons for agreeing to serve upon a board. The appointment of a new director, and the need to effect introductions, could be used as an opportunity to initiate a discussion along the lines of that suggested.

Exercise 1.2: Getting to know each other

In most companies the directors would be reluctant to disclose and discuss their thoughts and answers to all of the questions of Exercise 1.1. However, the chairman could initiate a formal or informal discussion along the following lines:

1 Which questions were the easiest and the most difficult to answer?
2 Which questions made you think the most, and why?
3 Which questions were the most relevant, and why?
4 Did you feel any of the questions were particularly sensitive or 'near the bone'?
5 What sort of answers to the questions about us as a board would our senior managers have given?
6 What do our company's managers really think about us as a board?
7 Are our managers justified in their views of us as a board?
8 What did you most learn from the exercise about yourself and your colleagues?
9 In what ways have you changed your view of the board?
10 How committed do you feel we are as a board? For example, are we more or less committed than other boards?
11 What can we learn from the exercise as a board?
12 Is there anything that we should do differently as a board?

The responses to Exercise 1.2 will reveal much about how open members of the board are prepared to be with each other. The board that is prepared to be honest and frank is more likely to identify obstacles and barriers to its own effectiveness.

The questions in the checklist at the end of this particular chapter have been phrased in such as way that they could also be put directly to individual directors. If you are not a member of the board, think about how members of the board might respond to each of them.

Where discussion is stilted, or the atmosphere of the boardroom does not encourage sharing and trusting, some of the later exercises in this book could be used to initiate debates on subjects other than the immediate priorities on the boardroom agenda. These can sometimes result in more reflection and may stimulate the consideration of broader issues.

We shall see in the next chapter that there are many obstacles to director and board development. It is important to be realistic and practical concerning what can be achieved, and to avoid promising what cannot be delivered.

Every board is different. It is not suggested that anyone should mechanically work through and use all the exercises suggested in this book, or even the majority of them. At all times, focus upon the particular board that concerns you. When deciding what is relevant and what might be of value, carefully consider the board's role, composition and situation, and the challenges and opportunities it faces.

Finally, do not forget the business development needs of the company. As Peter Morgan of the IOD has pointed out: 'the greatest service a company can perform for any community is to survive and thrive.'[12]

Checklist

1 Is your company led by a united team of competent directors?
2 How important is your membership of the board in your scale of personal priorities?
3 What does board membership mean for you in terms of self-image and your status and standing in the community?
4 To what extent is your membership of the board a burden or a joy?
5 What do you gain from your membership of the board?
6 How would it effect your life if you ceased to be a member of the board?
7 If the company failed, how concerned would you be?
8 How protected are you from the consequences of company failure?
9 How much do you really care about the various stakeholders in the business?
10 How committed are you to the long-term future of the company?
11 What value do you really add as a director?
12 What would the company lose, and what would be missed within the boardroom, if you ceased to be a director?
13 If you ceased to be a director, which if any of the other directors would you continue to keep in touch with as a friend?

Notes and references

1 Jay Lorsch and Elizabeth MacIver, *Pawns or Potentates: The Reality of America's Corporate Boards*, Harvard Business School Press, 1989.
2 PRO NED, *Research into the Role of the Non-Executive Director*, PRO NED, 1992.
3 Colin Coulson-Thomas, *Professional Development of and for the Board*, IOD, 1990.
4 Colin Coulson-Thomas and Alan Wakelam, *The Effective Board: Current Practice, Myths and Realities*. An Institute of Directors discussion document, 1991.
5 Colin Coulson-Thomas, *Transforming the Company: Bridging the Gap between Management Myth and Corporate Reality*, Kogan Page, 1992.
6 Myles Mace, *Directors: Myth and Reality*, Division of Research, Graduate School of Business Administration, Harvard University, 1971.
7 Stuart Slatter, *Corporate Recovery: Successful Turnaround Strategies and their Implementation*, Penguin Books, 1984 and 1987.
8 Colin Coulson-Thomas, *Creating Excellence in the Boardroom*, McGraw-Hill, 1993.
9 Harold S Geneen, 'Why directors can't protect the shareholders', *Fortune*, **17** (September 1984), 28.

10 Colin Coulson-Thomas, *Development Needs of NHS Authority and Board Members*. An Adaptation Ltd report prepared on behalf of the NHS Training Directorate, July 1992.

11 Ada Demb and F-Friedrich Neubauer, *The Corporate Board: Confronting the Paradoxes*, Oxford University Press, 1992.

12 Peter Morgan, *Why an Institute of Directors?* Lecture to the Cardiff Business Club, 3 February 1992, p. 11.

PART ONE

Competent directors and effective boards

2 The competent director

What is a competent director? Programmes to improve the effectiveness of the board and the contributions of individual directors could be based upon foundations of sand if an attempt is not made to define the qualities of the competent director.

Evidence from Canada,[1] the US,[2] and the UK[3] suggests that many directors are not competent to undertake their onerous duties and responsibilities. Their assessment should be approached with respect and an open mind, rather than awe and deference.

In this chapter we begin to examine the competence of directors. In the next chapter we shall look in greater depth at the specific knowledge and skill requirements, before turning to the effectiveness of boards. In practice, directorial competence and board effectiveness are generally interrelated, and both will need to be addressed by an integrated development programme:

- The competence requirements of individual directors can derive from what is needed to complement the qualities and attributes of colleagues, and improve the operating dynamics of the boardroom team.
- The effectiveness of the board in turn can be enhanced or constrained by the strengths or limitations of the individual members.

Personalities may jar rather than gel. Much will depend upon the extent to which individuals are compatible, and bring out the best in each other, when they are brought together in the confines of the boardroom.

Deficiencies of knowledge and skills are likely to be just one cause of a gap between expectations and performance. Attitudes, motivation and commitment often have a significant influence and impact. A lack of time and inadequate information can also prevent directors from making a fuller contribution.[4]

The exercises in this chapter are designed to identify those competences and requirements which are particularly relevant to the circumstances of a particular board.

Directorial competences

Directors need, at least, to understand the role and function of the board, their legal duties and responsibilities, and the essence and distinctive nature of direction (see Part Three). Directors themselves identify perspective, strategic awareness and personal qualities such as integrity as key attributes of the competent director.[5,6]

When directors are asked to describe 'what makes a good director?', certain terms such as awareness, judgement, common sense, vision, wisdom, honesty, tact and communication skills frequently recur.[7] The following are a selection of typical responses to the question of the qualities that distinguish a competent director:

Vision, acumen, and leadership.

Breadth of vision, conceptual thinking, strategic awareness.

Strategic awareness, perspective, breadth, customer focus.

Business/commercial awareness, and strategic awareness.

Ability to contribute to strategic direction and governance.

Particular importance may need to be attached to 'focus upon the customer'.[5,8] Many people become so engrossed in departmental or functional concerns that they lose touch with the requirements of customers.

Addressing the particular

Beyond the above 'core', what is required can depend very much upon the situation, circumstances, context and aspirations of the particular company. It can also depend upon the particular role an individual is expected to play in the boardroom. For example, Jonathan Charkham, formerly head of PRO NED, believes that: 'In the appointment of a non-executive director, it is the person who counts, with his qualities, experience and character.'[9]

In the case of the competences of executive directors with departmental responsibilities, the distinction between direction and management needs to be thought through in respect of each function. For example, Dieter Scholz, a senior director with Coopers & Lybrand believes: 'The IT director is someone who has the brief to translate practical IT developments into business advantage for his or her organization. By contrast, an IT manager will be mainly concerned with the efficient delivery of IT services.'

A competent director needs to be a team player whose attributes complement the qualities of the existing members of the boardroom team. A person who is appropriate in one context might not be suitable in a different situation.

The qualities of existing members of the board need to be taken into account when new directorial appointments are made. Dr Ingram Lenton, chairman of Compass Group plc, believes the: 'starting point . . . is to seek to supplement, to advantage, that body's existing qualities.'

Exercise 2.1 could be used to encourage the members of a board to identify the competence requirements that particularly relate to its own situation and circumstances. Where the board is able to commit the time—for example, by going away for a day—Exercises 2.1, 2.2 and 2.3 could be undertaken in succession.

Exercise 2.1: Selecting directorial competences

Draw up a list of directorial competences derived from the function of the board. (If necessary, before attempting this exercise, review: (a) the purpose of the company; (b) the function of the board; (c) the duties, responsibilities and accountabilities of directors and (d) the key requirements of stakeholders.)

[Complete the initial list of competences.]

Do not be concerned with the length of the list. (The purpose of this exercise is to help determine what is really important.) Then address the following issues and questions:

1 Are there other competence requirements that have derived from the particular situation, circumstances and context of the company?
2 Are there additional and specific competence requirements that derive from: (a) the particular 'make up' or membership of the boardroom team; or (b) the perceived deficiencies of individual directors?
3 Has the ethical dimension been addressed?
4 Are all the listed competences 'directorial' rather than 'managerial'? (Managerial deficiencies should not be ignored. It may be necessary to address them by means of appropriate management development, but the focus of this exercise is upon directorial competences.)

Grouping and categorizing competences

Eventually, the various competences that have been identified as especially relevant for a particular board may need to be grouped in order that they can be addressed by appropriate development activity. There is not a correct approach to competence categorization, but the following groups illustrate the diversity of directorial attributes and qualities.

- Personal qualities such as integrity, wisdom, authority, judgement, 'leadership', courage, independence, a positive outlook, tact and diplomacy.
- Awareness of the business environment and of what constitutes value to customers. (Awareness of developments in the business environment should include ethical and environmental considerations.)
- A sense of accountability to stakeholders, and a willingness to put responsibility to the company above self-interest.
- Vision, and a strategic perspective that should embrace the totality of the company's operations, situation and context.
- Business acumen and sound commercial judgement.

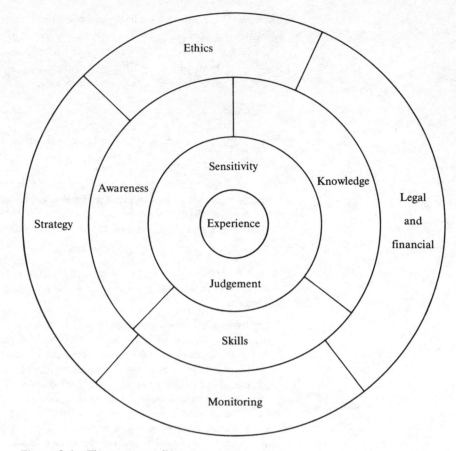

Figure 2.1   The competent director

- Knowledge of relevant legal and financial issues and requirements. (Particular knowledge is required of the role of the board, and of the legal duties and responsibilities of directors.)
- Understanding of the structure and operation of the board, effective boardroom practice, and boardroom matters such as the succession, assessment and remuneration of directors.
- Skills in such areas as decision making and teamwork in a boardroom context, strategy determination, formulating and achieving objectives, organizing and motivating people, and the monitoring of performance.
- Experience of relevance to the particular corporate context.
- Ethical awareness and sensitivity to the attitudes and values of others.

The relationships between various elements of directorial competence that have been identified are shown schematically in Figure 2.1. Each of these areas may need to be addressed.

Some competence categories may appear sharper and more relevant than others. Ethical awareness might seem vague and ill-defined, but qualities such as integrity, courage and adherence to principle in the face of challenge and temptation can save a company, while others founder or later 'come unstuck'.

Personal standards of conduct and behaviour are vital in individuals who are expected to act and behave as role models. 'Steve' Shirley, founder director of FI Group plc, believes 'integrity is essential and those who question what it means surely do not have it'.

To Peter Morgan, director general of the IOD, integrity means that 'contracts are honoured, conflicts of interest are avoided, behaviour is ethical, fiduciary obligations are discharged, and the law is obeyed'.[10] A board cannot afford to be without integrity.

Reviewing competences

The board itself will not necessarily be the best judge of its own competence requirements. Much will depend upon the board's understanding of its accountabilities, the distinction between direction and management, and the extent to which it is honest and self-aware.

The job of defining directorial competences is normally best done by the board itself, assisted by one or more experienced and independent facilitators. In the interests of openness and objectivity, some boards prefer to use the services of an external facilitator—that is, someone who does not have a role within the company.

As an example of an approach that could be adopted, the companion book, *Creating Excellence in the Boardroom*, presents a list of competences derived from various aspects of the function of the board.[11]

If remedial action is to follow, the members of the board must have confidence in the process that is used to define director competences. It is also important that generalization is avoided. The aim should be to identify the 'vital few' qualities or attributes that are especially relevant in the context of a particular board, and its vision, values, goals and objectives.

Those who are given the task of identifying and defining directorial competences should be aware of the distinction between direction and management. Experience of developing management competences could actually be a disadvantage. Rather than re-tread desired 'management' qualities as 'director' competences, the distinct development requirements of directors should be addressed.

Exercise 2.2 takes further the work of Exercise 2.1. It requires the members of the board to prioritize the competence requirements that have been identified. To do this they may need to be categorized and grouped.

<hr>

Exercise 2.2: Prioritizing directorial competences

The exercise should begin with a list of competence requirements that has emerged from a review along the lines of that suggested in Exercise 2.1.

(Prioritize and assess the initial list of competences.)

1 Which of the competences that are listed are the most important? (Distinguish between those that are considered to be: (a) essential; (b) desirable; and (c) nice to have.)
2 Are certain competences more or less important for some directors than for others?
3 What, if anything, do the (a) essential and (b) desirable competence requirements have in common, or suggest? (Is there a pattern?)
4 Can they be grouped or categorized? (For example, are the requirements personal qualities, or dependent upon knowledge, or experience, etc ?)
5 What can be learned from the fact that some competences are ranked more highly than others? (What do the rankings reveal about the situation of the company and the state of the board?)

<hr>

Treading carefully

It is advisable not to 'jump in with both feet' when assessing the qualities and competences of board members. Many directors are suspicious of suggestions and moves to formally define detailed directorial competences. It may be advisable to have an initial discussion in order to determine how much enthusiasm for, and commitment there is likely to be to, the definition and development of directorial competences.

The following views, all of which have been expressed by experienced directors, could be used as a basis for discussion:

I genuinely believe that good directors are born and not made. Direction is all about personal qualities.

Direction is really about tapping inner qualities. Trappings can be picked up at a finishing school. Jargon can be picked up at a business school. What have any of these things to do with being a good director?

People with every qualification and competence known, and great track records, can make lousy directors. . . . Some good directors lose their touch. How do you know if you are not there? How can you test these things other than in the boardroom?

An argument for developing director competences is that if we don't someone else will. I would hate to see the emergence of a director competence bandwagon.

Our board is unique. We need our own competences, not a standard list.

If the opinions stated so far appear 'negative', consider the following 'more encouraging' viewpoints.

I would use a list of director competences tomorrow if I thought the job could be done. I would distrust a long list, but a short list that focused on what is different about being a director could be helpful.

A list might help me clarify my own thoughts. It might encourage action. I would need to think through what I used. Some of my directors are OK. I wouldn't want them to worry, or to try and be something else, when what they are seems to suit me and the company.

It would be nice if we could agree what to 'shoot' for. My people would want to become better if they had a 'route map'. At the moment we are committed and do our best, but we are not really sure what needs to be developed.

The list of quotations is long, but the issues they raise do need to be addressed by a board before it moves ahead. Concerns should be 'put on the table' and thoroughly discussed. Ultimate implementation may be smoother as a consequence of spending more time at an earlier stage flushing out and debating reservations, some of which may be well-founded in the context of a particular board.

Competences, expectations and actual practice

Many of the confusions of directors concerning directorial competence stem from the fact that many chairmen and CEOs are not clear about the contributions they expect from directors in the boardroom.[7] Selection may be upon the basis of perceived directorial qualities. However, once directors have been appointed to a board, the functional contribution of the executive director ranks equally with strategy formulation and the general direction of the company.[7]

Directors may be more willing to participate in training activities when competence requirements are related to the company's own development needs. A board should feel confident that what is to be defined and developed will be of practical value and of relevance to its own situation.

The qualities actually found in boardrooms do not always reflect the rhetoric of chairmen. One chairman who was interviewed expressed the view that: 'The dynamics of a board thrives on the creative interplay of diverse but complementary qualities and personalities. I would hate to spend money on developing "clone" or "identikit" directors, and driving all variety and balance out of the boardroom.'

This need for diversity, complementary qualities, and a variety of experiences was mentioned many times by interviewees. Yet, in practice, many boards appear to consist of people with very similar backgrounds, and drawn from a narrow element of society. The membership of the board of a 'representative' large company is predominantly composed of males in late middle age,[12] even though key stakeholders in the company, and with whom the board needs to achieve rapport and mutual understanding, may have very different characteristics.

Those concerned with director development should take care not to raise expectations that may not be fulfilled. At the same time, effort should be devoted to encouraging the board to confront 'incompatibilities' between stated requirements and actual practice, and practical steps should be taken to bridge gaps between rhetoric and reality.

Directors and knowledge

What knowledge is required by the company director? A survey undertaken with my colleague Alan Wakelam suggests that while there is little consensus among chairmen concerning the overall contribution directors ought to make, the main contribution actually expected of many executive directors is expertise, knowledge and experience of their own areas.[7]

It should not be forgotten that 'employee directors' generally have both managerial and directorial responsibilities. In this and the next chapter we are examining the competence requirements of the directorial role.

The duties, accountabilities and responsibilities of the board and the director need to be understood, along with matters such as the structure, composition and operation of boards, and the selection, appointment, remuneration and conduct of directors. Certain legal and financial knowledge is also of value. We will be examining areas of knowledge of particular relevance to the director in the next chapter.

In difficult trading conditions, there are particular matters that should be brought to the attention of board members. They need to know what to do when a company gets into financial difficulties.[13] While managers worry about the prospects of redundancy, their directorial colleagues may be more preoccupied with the risks of investigation and the prospect of legal action or disqualification.

Information and knowledge will not of themselves result in competent direction if a vision is not clear, goals are not shared, objectives are confused, and a strategy is inappropriate.[14] Information does not necessarily increase understanding.

What is needed is knowledge that is relevant to the type of company, its stage of development and its business.[15] Thus the knowledge required by a director of a large and established public company will not be the same as that needed by the owner-director of a small start-up enterprise. The dynamics of a board of owner-directors can be different from those found in the boardroom of a larger business where most of the directors are 'hired employees'.

Applying knowledge in the boardroom context

Acquiring relevant knowledge is but one aspect of being an effective director. A competent director needs not just knowledge, but the ability to use that knowledge in the boardroom context.

It is advantageous for directors to be well informed and this might be the product of a broad, rather than a specialist or technical, education. Apart from having a sound understanding of their own field, executive directors with functional responsibilities should:

- know how to obtain relevant knowledge and information about unfamiliar areas, and
- know how to apply their knowledge, as appropriate, to unfamiliar situations.

Specialists who are managers tend to apply their knowledge within particular fields, leaving the directors (as we shall see in Chapter 14) with the task of integrating the experts' views into the context of the company's needs.

The individual qualities and particular knowledge of a director are not as important as the way these come together in the context of the boardroom to add value to the discussions and decisions of the board. It is possible to be very knowledgeable, yet contribute little. An effective contribution often requires a mastery of the dynamics and processes of the board, which may be different from those found in other boardrooms.

Just because someone has been an effective member of another board, it does not follow that that person may not require some development. The various elements that come together to enable a person to make a significant contribution in one boardroom context may not be 'portable'.

Any knowledge, and other aspects of competence, that have been acquired need to be kept up to date and relevant to contemporary boardroom issues and concerns. John Harper, Head of Professional Development at the IOD, is of the opinion that: 'Too few directors . . . spend sufficient time in raising their awareness, updating their knowledge and improving their understanding on matters of concern to professional directors. It is not surprising, therefore, that many boards do an adequate, rather than an excellent job.'[5]

One regularly updated compendium of information and advice of value to the director is *The Directors Manual*.[16] This summarizes much of the knowledge needed to be a competent director.

Development implications

How might a ranking, grouping or categorization of directorial competences be used? It could contribute to the preparation of a development programme for the board as a whole, as well as one for each of its individual members.

- Discussing the rankings and groupings that emerge, and exploring the reasons for the inclusion or exclusion from a 'priority action list' of certain competences, can reveal clues concerning the situation or 'health' of the company in general, and the board in particular. As a result, there could be development activity which the board might wish to undertake as a team.
- Assessing the competences of individual directors against a priority list could enable competence gaps and mismatches to be identified. The ranking of deficiencies could depend upon the extent to which they hinder the achievement of corporate vision, goals, values or objectives. The results could be used as a basis for drawing up director competence development plans for each member of the board and the board as a team.

- The nature of the deficiencies that are identified will determine whether formal or informal learning would be more appropriate. Many directors naturally learn from each other, and there may be many opportunities to learn from both individual experience and the collective work of the board.[11,17]

An overview of requirements might enable more general needs to be addressed. For example, in order to be more objective and independent, a sense of balance and perspective may need to be developed. The members of a board might be perceived as 'too narrow'. A chairman could encourage a broader perspective by suggesting that all directors have a relevant learning experience. Depending upon the needs of the individual director, the possibilities might include:

- the acquisition of a foreign language, or the coordination of operations in a certain part of the world;
- the assumption of responsibility for a particular project or cross-functional process;
- taking on an external voluntary, or non-executive board, appointment.

The boardroom itself represents a potentially rich learning environment. The board as a team could review and assess particular decisions or developments to see what can be learned from what happened. Individual directors could adopt a similar approach towards situations they encounter.[11,17]

Exercise 2.3 could be used to match individual directors against a set of competence requirements such as those that might emerge from a review along the lines of Exercise 2.2. This enables competence gaps and deficiencies to be identified.

Exercise 2.3: Assessing the competence of the individual director

This exercise aims to assess the individual members of a board in relation to an agreed priority list of competences.

(Assess the current competences of the individual members of the board against the priority list produced as a result of Exercise 2.2.)

1 What are the major 'competence' strengths and weaknesses of the individual members of the board? Where an atmosphere of openness and trust exists, this part of the exercise could be undertaken by (a) the chairman, (b) the directors and (c) boardroom colleagues, and the results could be compared and discussed.
2 What are the key competence deficiencies of each director?
3 To what extent do these hinder the pursuit of corporate vision, goals, values or objectives?
4 Which deficiencies derive from a weakness in the structure or operation of the board? (For example, the lack of understanding of certain directors could reflect the way in which information is brought to the boardroom.)

(Prioritize the competence deficiencies.)

5 **What are the priority competence development needs of each director? (Rank in priority order the competence development needs of each director.)**
6 **Which of these should be addressed by development activities aimed at individual directors, the board as a whole, or both at individual members of the board and the boardroom team?**

It should be borne in mind that while it may be helpful for all directors to share a minimum core competence, not all members of the board need possess all the individual competences that have been identified as long as these are satisfactorily covered within the boardroom team. How directors and boards should be developed will be covered in Chapters 7 and 8 respectively.

Factors affecting directorial competences

When assessing the competence development needs of directors, consider the extent to which the following factors may need to be addressed.

- How portable are the qualities that need to be developed? (How might they relate to a move to another board within the group? Could a deficiency gap be filled by bringing in someone with the required qualities?)
- How do the competence requirements that have been developed relate to the expectations the chairman has of members of the board? (Have these expectations 'distorted' or inhibited the development of certain board members? Do these expectations conflict with the development priorities that have emerged?)
- What is the relationship between the competence requirements that have been identified and the vision, goals, values and objectives of the company? (Before taking action, check that they are consistent and supportive. Should the development priorities be amended, or do the vision, goals, values or objectives of the company need to be reviewed?)
- How do the development needs of individual directors relate to those of the board as a whole? (Assess whether particular initiatives should involve individual directors, or the board as a whole. What has been learned concerning how the structure or operation of the board might be changed in order to improve its effectiveness?)

Directors need to be robust and resilient, as well as sensitive and aware. A certain level of energy and commitment may be needed in the case of a board that has to bring about a fundamental change.

Finally, directors need not be perfect if they are self-aware. Many directors interviewed have admitted to deficiencies that might prove fatal to the career prospects of an ambitious manager. However, awareness of deficiencies allows them to be taken into account, while directorial colleagues can bring compensating strengths to the boardroom.

Developing Directors

Checklist

1 What are the advantages and disadvantages of attempts to define (a) core and (b) standard directorial competences?

2 Have the members of the board of your company (a) identified and (b) prioritized their key competence requirements?

3 Are the executive members of the board of your company able to distinguish between the competences applicable to their managerial responsibilities, and those that relate to their directorial role?

4 Are the priority competences consistent with the vision, values, goals and objectives of the company?

5 Have the individual members of the board been assessed against a prioritized list of core and group requirements?

6 What action is to be taken in respect of any gaps or deficiencies that have emerged?

7 Can the competence gaps be filled by director development only or by changing the composition of the board?

8 Is there other action, to complement director development, that should be taken?

9 Which directorial competences are best developed by formal activities, and which could be built as a result of informal development by such means as action learning?

10 How might the operation of the board be changed in the light of what has been learned about directorial competence?

Notes and references

1 W.J. McDougal, *Corporate Boards in Canada*, Research report, University of Western Ontario, 1968.

2 R.K. Mueller, *The Incomplete Board*, Lexington, 1981.

3 David Norburn and Franklin Schurz, 'The British boardroom: Time for a revolution?', in Bernard Taylor, *Strategic Planning: The Chief Executive and the Board*, Pergamon Press, 1988, pp. 43–51.

4 Jay Lorsch and Elizabeth MacIver, *Pawns or Potentates: The Reality of America's Corporate Boards*, Harvard Business School Press, 1989.

5 Colin Coulson-Thomas, *Professional Development of and for the Board*. A questionnaire and interview survey undertaken by Adaptation Ltd of company chairmen. A summary has been published by the IOD, February 1990.

6 Colin Coulson-Thomas, *The Role and Function of the Personnel Director*. An interim Adaptation Ltd survey carried out in conjunction with the Research Group of the Institute of Personnel Management, 1991.

7 Colin Coulson-Thomas and Alan Wakelam, *The Effective Board: Current Practice, Myths and Realities*. An IOD discussion document, 1991.

8 Colin Coulson-Thomas and Richard Brown, *Beyond Quality: Managing the Relationship with the Customer*, BIM, 1990.

9 J. Charkham, *Effective Boards: The Independent Element and the Role of the Non-executive Director*, Institute of Chartered Accountants in England and Wales, 1986.

10 Peter Morgan, *Why an Institute of Directors?* Lecture to the Cardiff Business Club, 3 February 1992, p. 12.

11 Colin Coulson-Thomas, *Creating Excellence in the Boardroom*, McGraw-Hill, 1993.

12 Heidrick & Struggles, Inc., *The Changing Board*, Heidrick & Struggles, 1987; Louis Boone and James Johnson, 'Profiles of the 801 men and one woman at

the top', *Business Horizons* (February 1980), 47–52; and Korn/Ferry, *Boards of Directors Study UK*, Korn/Ferry International, 1989 and 1992.

13 Institute of Directors, 'Guidelines to boardroom practice: Companies in financial difficulties', *Direct Line*, No. 94 (January 1991); and *Directors' Personal Liabilities*, Corporate Governance Series, No. 6, Director Publications, June 1992.

14 J.D. Aram and S.S. Cowen, *Information Requirements of Corporate Directors: The Role of the Board in the Process of Management*. Final report to the National Association of Accountants, 1983.

15 Abbas Alkhafaji, 'Effective boards of direction', *Industrial Management and Data Systems*, **90**, No. 4 (1990), 18–26.

16 Bernard Taylor and Bob Tricker (eds), *The Directors Manual*, Director Books, 1990.

17 Alan Mumford, Peter Honey and Graham Robinson, *Director's Development Guidebook: Making Experience Count*, Director Publications, 1990.

3 Directorial knowledge and skills

The competent and effective director is distinguished by a combination of relevant personal qualities and skills, particular knowledge and experience, and appropriate attitudes, values and perspective. It is the combination of these factors, and their application to the business of the board in each company context, that is important, not the acquisition of knowledge and skills *per se*.

The acquisition of the individual areas of knowledge and skill considered in this chapter will not of itself automatically lead to success in the boardroom. Much will depend upon the extent to which they are:

- accompanied by relevant experience, and appropriate personal attributes and qualities;
- related to the situation, circumstances and context of the individual company; and
- complemented and balanced by the experience, qualities, knowledge and skills of the other members of the boardroom team.

Some skills are of value to a certain extent, but can become counter-productive when possessed to an excessive degree. For example, a director should not believe in consensus and become a team player at the expense of detachment and objectivity. Dr Ingram Lenton, chairman of Compass Group plc, stresses the importance of 'independence of thought and the ability and willingness to think the unfashionable'.

In this chapter, we examine the legal and financial knowledge, and the personal and facilitating skills and competences, that are desirable in a director. We shall also consider the understanding of boardroom issues, and of management and business processes, that might be sought in an individual company director and collectively in a board.

When determining skill requirements it is necessary to maintain a directorial perspective. The exercises in this chapter could be used to identify and prioritize individual and group knowledge and skill requirements.

The relevance of knowledge and skills

In the previous chapter we introduced the knowledge required by directors, and this will now be explored in greater detail. An awareness of relevant knowledge and skills, and of where to go, or to whom to turn, for further information or advice is desirable in a director. In view of their number and variety, this chapter can do little more than outline the knowledge and skill areas that may need to be addressed.

The degree of knowledge or skill required by an individual director could depend on a number and combination of circumstances. For example, factors to take into account could include:

- the type of company, and the nature of its ownership, e.g. whether 'public' or 'private';
- the priority requirements of stakeholders, and particularly of customers;
- the vision, values, goals and objectives of the company, and its development or 'next steps' needs;
- the market or business context in which the company operates, e.g. high or low tech, or whether domestic or international;
- the particular role (e.g. chairman, 'functional' director, non-executive, etc.) of the individual directors;
- whether or not the membership of the board includes those with specialist knowledge—e.g. legal or financial—and the quality of external and affordable advice available to the board;
- each individual director's existing directorial and managerial knowledge and skill base.

Particular attention should be paid to the existence of particular areas of deficiency that have been identified, either in the individual director or in the board as a whole.

A more comprehensive listing of possible factors that might influence directorial skill requirements is given in Example 3.1.

It is the combination of factors that will determine what is desirable in an individual director. Thus a non-executive director of a public company may need to be more informed of, and concerned with, issues relating to 'corporate governance' than the owner and executive director of a private company.

Whatever the particular circumstances that apply, the director should at least:

- understand his or her accountabilities to stakeholders, legal duties and responsibilities, and particular boardroom role and responsibilities; and
- possess sufficient knowledge and skill to discharge these responsibilities satisfactorily.

The factors of Example 3.1 can affect the composition and operation of a board, and this will impact upon skill requirements. For example, boards of 'owner-manager' directors can vary in structure and style from those composed of 'hired employees'.[1]

Example 3.1 *Factors influencing skill requirements*

Company type
Domestic:
  Private
  Owner managed
Public
Foreign
Euro-company
Holding company
Subsidiary company
Joint venture

Company size
Small
Medium
Large
MNC

Company market
Local
Regional
National
International

Company role
Chairman
CEO
Non-executive director

Functional director
Owner-director
Newly appointed director

Business sector
Manufacturing/production
Leisure
Utilities
Financial services
Retail/distribution
Public administration and
  government
Construction/engineering
Educational body
Professional, scientific or
  consultancy
Transport/communications
Other services

Directional challenge
Demanding customers
Competitive pressures
Technological change
Arrangements and joint ventures
Internationalization
Corporate transformation, etc.

Exercise 3.1 illustrates how a list of factors, such as those in Example 3.1, could be used to identify general skill requirements.

Exercise 3.1: Identifying general skill requirements

The commitment of a director to acquiring additional knowledge, or a new skill, is likely to reflect how relevant and 'practical' these are perceived to be. The production of a long 'shopping list' of skills is likely to be counter-productive. In order to be selective:

1 Examine and review the factors influencing the directorial skill requirements set out in Example 3.1. As far as your board is concerned, which of these factors apply? Are any other factors relevant?
2 Draw up a checklist of the key factors that will influence the identification of the directorial skill requirements of the members of your board.

The appendix to this chapter illustrates how a list of factors, such as those in Example 3.1, could be used to identify key skill requirements for an individual director or board. In this particular case the skills are taken from Example 3.2.

In carrying out an assessment similar to that shown in Exercise 3.1, care should be taken to avoid wasting the time of busy directors on the production of a long 'wish list' of 'motherhood statements'. Instead, aim to focus on those items that are really essential. For example, when asked about the qualities that are desirable in non-executive directors, Sir Brian Wolfson, chairman of Wembly plc, replied simply that the key requirement is the ability and willingness 'to ask the questions in the boardroom no one else is prepared to ask'.

Legal knowledge   Let us turn now to the first area of knowledge that should be considered. Reference has already been made to the need for directors to understand their legal duties and responsibilities.

Some relevant areas of legal knowledge are listed in Example 3.2.

Example 3.2 *Legal knowledge*

(a) General
Introduction (e.g. sources of law)
Role of the board
Duties and responsibilities of individual directors
Liabilities of directors
Duties and responsibilities of the board
Corporate governance
Company law
Law of contract
Other relevant law (e.g. corporate taxation or EC requirements)
Legal disputes and processes

(b) Specific
Group structure (e.g. holding companies and subsidiaries)
'PLC' duties and responsibilities
City institutions and the stockmarket
Listing and public flotation
European and international requirements
Foreign directors

(c) Advice
Company secretarial function
Duties and responsibilities of professional advisers to the board
Legal processes and procedures

The knowledge requirements set out in Example 3.2 are split into three categories:

1 There is a general area that should be understood by all directors. In addition to a basic understanding of legal principles and procedures, the director should be aware of areas of the law that specifically relate to (a) the duties and responsibilities of directors and boards and (b)

the work of the board. The sources of relevant law could be national or regional (e.g. the EC).

2 There are specific areas that may be of relevance to some companies, but not to others. Thus directors of 'public' companies need to be aware of both statutory and Stock Exchange requirements. Directors of companies that begin to operate internationally may encounter unfamiliar actors, and additional considerations that did not apply to the domestic context.[2]

3 A director needs to be aware of the main sources of legal advice, and of the circumstances in which it is wise to obtain a professional opinion. A board also needs to ensure that the necessary processes and procedures are in place to enable all relevant legal factors that apply to the operations of the company in general—and the activities of the board in particular—to be taken into account.

The chairman should ensure that all new directors fully understand their accountabilities, duties and liabilities. Members of the board should be encouraged to approach the company secretary for advice on matters of concern. The company secretary should also update all directors on relevant legal developments as they occur, and monitor the extent to which the board is meeting its legal obligations and commitments.

Financial knowledge

Directors have legal duties and responsibilities that relate specifically to accounts and financial information. For example, companies are required to produce, report and file audited accounts that satisfy certain reporting requirements. Quoted companies must also comply with additional Stock Exchange requirements.

Accounting professionals are expected to conform to certain accounting standards when they prepare accounts. While members of the board should not expect to match the specialist expertise of those who draw up accounts, they might wish to question, or make a judgement on, the extent to which certain items should be treated in order to give a more favourable impression of performance.[3]

Directors should have a sufficient understanding of accounts and accounting to discharge their reporting accountabilities and responsibilities. In particular, they should be aware of how to conduct themselves during a period in which their company is experiencing financial difficulties.[4]

Example 3.3 lists aspects of financial and accounting knowledge of particular relevance to company directors. As with other, and similar, lists in this chapter, the aspects selected for inclusion in this example are designed to be suggestive rather than definitive.

Financial and accounting knowledge is a problem area for many directors. In several business functions it is possible to reach a relatively senior position without being able to 'read' a balance sheet or understand financial information.

Example 3.3 *Financial knowledge*

Financial reporting requirements
Reporting issues and procedures
Accounting standards
Appointment and qualification of auditors
Understanding accounts (e.g. accounting ratios)
Relationship between financial and management accounts
Financial discretion and processes
Financial control
Cash cycles and cash flow considerations
Evaluating opportunities
Assessing financing options
Investment appraisal and decision
Risk analysis and management
International exposure
Currency and the corporate treasury function
Budgeting and profit planning
Monitoring corporate performance
Raising finance

While not needing to understand all the intricacies of the process of preparing financial accounts, the director should have an awareness of the meaning and significance of financial information. This requires an understanding of financial and accounting ratios, an appreciation of the perspective of the analyst and investor, and sensitivity to financial danger signals.

On occasion, a board can be mesmerized by numbers. Financial knowledge can be used to conceal and confuse, and a director should be prepared to challenge and probe in order to clarify understanding. 'A director needs a sense of balance when using financial information, and an awareness of its significance and implications. Professional accountants may need to be reminded that their purpose is to serve the board and not confuse it, and to assist the business and not inhibit or distort it.'[5]

In the final analysis, customers determine value; and they are people, not statistics. The board should not become so obsessed with financial ratios that they lose touch with underlying reality.[6]

The directors of a company are in a fiduciary relationship with it, and will be expected by a court to be aware of their legal duties and responsibilities. Exercise 3.2 could be used to assess the extent to which the board is equipped to handle legal and financial matters.

Exercise 3.2: Legal and financial understanding

The following questions could be used as an element of a review of the extent to which the members of a board have, and make use of, an adequate legal and financial understanding:

1 Has the board defined and agreed the legal and financial understanding its members should have?
2 Are all directors aware of their legal and financial duties and responsibilities? (The directors could be asked to sign a declaration to this effect.)
3 Does the chairman ensure that all new directors are aware of their legal and financial duties and responsibilities?
4 Is the board properly served in respect of legal and financial advice, and does it make proper use of it?
5 Does, or should, a properly qualified company secretary attend all meetings of the board?
6 What are the arguments for or against the appointment of a 'director of legal services' to the board? (The question of functional directors is considered in Chapter 14.)
7 Does the board regularly examine the 'legal aspects' when it reviews its management processes, and how effective are the company's legal processes and procedures?
8 What are the arguments for or against the appointment of a 'director of finance' to the board? (The question of functional directors is considered in Chapter 14.)
9 Do all members of the board actively participate in financial discussions, and the review of accounting and financial information in the boardroom, or is the contribution to their consideration limited to those members with specialist expertise?
10 Does the board make excessive use of financial information during its deliberations? (Does it make use of other, i.e. non-financial, quantitative measures of output and performance?)
11 How appropriate and fair are (a) the company's financial measures of performance and (b) the financial criteria used in decision making?
12 What does the board learn from the company's 'annual audit'? (If an annual and independent audit were not a statutory requirement, would the board want one, and how much would it be prepared to pay?)
13 Is there a separate audit committee of the board? (Where the membership of the board includes them, are the non-executive directors members of the audit committee?)

In view of the importance of the legal and financial responsibilities of directors, Exercise 3.2 could be used to form the basis of an 'away-day' review.

Personal skills and competences

We have already identified a wide range of skills and competences that 'the competent director' should possess (Chapter 2). For those seeking additional clarification, the skills and competences that distinguish the director from the manager are considered in Chapter 13. Of particular interest to those concerned with developing directors is the question of how skill requirements might be structured into 'modules' or 'elements', so that they can be addressed by specific development activities.

An example of a breakdown of elements into modules that might be addressed by a directors' seminar or workshop is presented in Example 3.4 (The headings used in this example do not coincide precisely with the terminology employed elsewhere in this book, because each of the elements represents an actual or 'real world' development activity, or event, which has been specifically designed for the company director.)

Example 3.4 *Personal skills and competences*

(a) Strategic awareness
Strategic awareness
International awareness
Corporate environment issues
Issue monitoring and management
General business understanding
Identifying and understanding stakeholder interests
Business ethics

(b) Strategic processes
Determining the essence or purpose of a company
Formulating vision, goals, values, mission, and strategic objectives
Creating the adaptable, responsive and learning organization
Changing the corporate culture
Creating corporate policies
Government and external relations

(c) Business development
Marketing strategy focus, segmentation and differentiation
Business development:
    (i)   from small to medium-sized company
    (ii) from medium- to large-sized company
    (iii) from national to international company
European business strategy
Arrangements and joint ventures
Mergers and acquisitions

(d) Customer processes
Assessing and understanding customer requirements
Establishing and maintaining relationships with the customer
Delivering customer value and satisfaction
Establishing cross-functional 'customer' processes
Quality issues and total quality management

(e) People processes
Organization and motivation of people
Employee involvement
Empowerment
Human resources issues
Managing knowledge workers and professionals
Developing directors

(f) Management processes
Formulating and achieving objectives
Establishing, measuring and monitoring outputs
Policy deployment
Benchmarking
Re-engineering management and business processes
Simplifying management and business processes
Internationalization
Information management strategy

(g) Group skills
Visioning
Barrier analysis
Effective teamwork
Management of change
Decision making
Using external resources
Management of major projects
Management of R&D/Science & Technology

(h) Individual skills
Integrity and role model conduct
Self and time management
Learning and creativity
Leadership and power
Communication, personal and interpersonal skills
Negotiation and bargaining

The categorization of directorial skills and competences in Example 3.4 represents but one possible approach. Nevertheless, it enables certain points to be made.

- The importance of 'strategic awareness' and perspective, and of general business understanding. These are often too important to be addressed by a single development module or activity. Directors need to be able to structure their understanding of relevant issues, relate them to the situation and context of a company, and initiate appropriate responses. They also need to ensure they fully understand the requirements of their 'stakeholders'.
- Directors need to understand how to use 'strategic processes' for such boardroom activities as formulating the vision, goals, values or objec-

tives of a company. While the effective use of appropriate processes will not guarantee a satisfactory outcome, their ineffective use, or the use of inappropriate processes, can constrain and inhibit a board. A board should be prepared to work at perfecting its processes.

- A board should not lose sight of the need for 'business development'. Few companies can afford to 'tread water' in a competitive and changing marketplace. Stakeholders may assume a growing business, and a board should endeavour to meet and exceed their expectations. Too many director level programmes assume the board is 'presiding over a steady state'.

- An acceptance of 'customer focus', or statement of the importance of the customer as the 'source of all value', needs to be matched by 'customer processes' that enable a board to (a) understand what represents value to a customer and (b) ensure that this value is delivered in a way that results in satisfied customers. There are some directors and boards who regularly undergo some form of development activity, without ever seeking to understand the cross-functional processes, or 'pathways' through the organization that actually deliver value to customers.

- Directors and boards must do more than articulate the importance of harnessing the talents of people. 'People processes' are needed to involve and motivate people, and to energize and empower them. Directors need to understand these 'people processes' as they will certainly become involved with them. Sharing, involving, motivating and empowering must begin in the boardroom.

- 'Management processes' need to be understood by directors as many of them will start or end in the boardroom. Directors should be 'role models' in the use of appropriate processes (e.g. benchmarking). Significant contributions to customer satisfaction and cost savings can usually be achieved by a re-engineering of key management and business processes. Many companies are effectively competing on the quality and relevance of their management and business processes.

- The 'group skills' of a board will determine the extent to which it harnesses the potential that is latent in its members. Deficiencies should be addressed directly by group action and activities. It is important to understand that the effective management of major projects, or of 'R&D', does not 'just happen', but requires special skills. Undertaking development activity as a group can itself improve mutual understanding and teamwork in the boardroom.

- The 'individual skills' needed by directors are of significance not only to the directors concerned but, also to their boardroom colleagues. Directors need to understand that they, too, can learn and benefit from development activity undertaken by other board members. Some 'individual skills'—for example, self- and time management'— may have their managerial equivalents, but the director development emphasis should be upon requirements that derive from, or relate to, board membership. Particular attention should be given to skills concerned with establishing and sustaining relationships.

The directorial perspective

Certain skills that appear in Example 3.4 might be found within a list of management courses. However, it should be remembered that their use in a directorial context needs to reflect the distinct perspective of the director. For example, consider benchmarking[7] which appears as a 'management process':

- A manager is likely to be primarily concerned with what his or her equivalents in non-competing companies are doing in respect of a particular responsibility or activity. The responsibility or activity in question might well be confined to one function or business unit.
- A director ought to be more concerned with the actions that other companies might take. The director should give more attention to benchmarking thought and processes, and to understanding intentions, aspirations and dreams. These might have implications for various functions or business units, and perhaps for the company as a whole.

Attitudes and thoughts may not be easy to benchmark. However, their consequences can be profound, and directors need to be strategically aware. For example, let us consider attitudes towards the environment. Should these be of mild interest to the director or of fundamental concern?

The benchmarking of environmental attitudes could enable the board to initiate action 'today' that might enable it to avoid the loss of an approved supplier status 'tomorrow' as a result of a failure to satisfy the environmental aspects of future purchasing criteria introduced by customers.[8] Understanding the concerns of customers could enable a supplier to work with them in the drawing up of either corporate or supply chain environmental standards. A number of boards have established councils and panels to advise them on environmental and other matters.[9]

Boardroom issues

Another area of knowledge and skill requirements concerns what could be termed boardroom issues, i.e. various matters to do with (a) the role, composition, structure, and functioning of the board itself and (b) the appointment, remuneration, role, contribution and conduct of the individual director.

A selection of possible issues for consideration is given in Example 3.5. The items listed are those that have actually been addressed in specific development activities devised for company directors.

Boardroom issues such as those in Example 3.5 could be categorized into those which concern the board as a collective entity, and those which concern the relationship of the individual director to the board. In practice, such a distinction may not be easy to sustain. For example, the role of chairman is a matter that affects both the relationship of an individual with the board and the efficiency with which the board as a group collectively conducts its business. However categorized, boardroom issues should be of concern to all directors and should be considered by the board as a whole.

Example 3.5 *Boardroom issues*

(a) Concerning the board
Function of the board
Stakeholder relationships
Board structure (e.g. committees, group relationships, etc.)
Corporate governance (e.g. EC and alternative models)
Boardroom dynamics (e.g. teamwork, processes)
Board requirements (e.g. information for the boardroom)
Board effectiveness
Succession

(b) Concerning individual directors
Director appointments
Boardroom qualities
Assessment of directors
Remuneration of directors
Executive and functional directors
Non-executive directors
Roles of chairman and CEO/MD
Roles of specific directors
Effective boardroom practice

At this point, a board that has been addressing many of the questions raised so far may wish to use an approach along the lines of Exercise 3.3 to re-examine the directorial competence requirements that have been identified.

Exercise 3.3: Directorial skills and competences

In order to meet directorial skill requirements, it may be necessary to group or categorize them into 'modules' that can be addressed by specific development activities.

Exercise 3.1 concluded with the drawing up a checklist of the key factors that might influence the identification of the directorial skill requirements of the members of a particular board. The following steps could now be considered:

1 In the light of the sections on 'personal skills and competences' and 'boardroom issues' it may be necessary to refine the checklist of requirements.
2 Structure the requirements that have been identified and prioritized into 'modules' or 'elements' that might be addressed by specific development activities (e.g. a directors' seminar or workshop).
3 Ensure that a sensible and workable distinction has been made between 'group skills' to be addressed by group activity and 'individual skills' to be addressed by individual activity.
4 Prioritize and 'weight' the resulting modules in terms of their relative importance. (It is not just a matter of what comes first in terms of urgency. The amount of time and effort that ought to be devoted to tackling each

requirement should also be assessed. Consider: Is sufficient weight being given to customer issues, or to strategic, board and management processes?)

5 **Carry out a final critique, or review, by relating the list of possible development activities to the requirements for (a) 'developing the business' in line with the vision, goals, values and objectives of the company, and (b) achieving satisfactory and beneficial relationships with stakeholders.**

Issues and development needs

The relative significance of boardroom issues at any given time will vary between boards. However, certain issues appear to be of concern to a wide range of boards. For example, consider the relative importance given by the participants in a survey of directors undertaken by Adaptation Ltd for the IOD[10] to a small selection of 'boardroom' issues. The responses are summarized in Table 3.1 which ranks the issues in terms of 'very important' responses.

As shown in the table, 'teamwork' and 'succession' emerge as the 'top' issues in terms of 'very important' replies. Six out of ten respondents regarded them as 'very important'. Interviews with chairmen[10] suggest that:

- Many boards do not operate effectively as a team. A commitment to group development activity sometimes results in the realization that the need for improved teamwork may be greater than was first thought.
- 'Teamwork' as an issue is not just limited to the board. Effective teamwork is considered to be important at all levels within an organization. However, action to change attitudes and behaviour may need to start in the boardroom, and may not begin to carry conviction elsewhere until the board itself is seen to be behaving as a 'role-model'.
- Many chairmen, who find it difficult to identify potential candidates for boardroom appointments, acknowledge that their problems are exacerbated by a lack of agreement within the board concerning both the qualities that are sought, and how they might be developed.

A recent survey by a team from Cranfield suggests that almost 50 per cent of chairmen and chief executives are dissatisfied with the 'team skills' of their boards.[11]

The absence of disagreement in the boardroom need not be evidence of an effective team. While a shared purpose and values can be of considerable value, the chairman of the Professional Development Committee of the IOD warns of: 'the dangers of "Groupthink" when there is a collective effort to rationalize and to discount warning signs. Dissent is taken as disloyalty and there is a shared illusion of rightness and unanimity where silence is assumed as consent.'

In the survey presented in Table 3.1, 'teamwork' and 'succession' were followed by 'adaptability and flexibility' and 'continuing updating and development'. More than one in three of the participants thought 'continuing updating' to be 'very important'. The continuing updating and development of 'knowledge' ranks ahead of that of 'skills'.

Table 3.1 *Professional development needs: boardroom issues*

Issue	Ranking (%)*
Teamwork	61
Succession	59
Adaptability and flexibility	39
Continuing updating and development of knowledge	38
Continuing updating and development of skills	34
Europeanization: preparation for 1992	25
Remuneration	24
Preparation for appointment to the board	24
Internationalization: preparation for the globalization of business	15

*Ranking in terms of 'very important'.
Note: Some respondents considered more than one issue to be 'very important'.

The relatively low importance attached to 'internationalization: preparation for the globalization of business' and 'Europeanization: preparation for 1992' reflects the preponderance of small and medium-sized companies in the sample, many of which were perceived by their chairmen as serving local or regional, rather than European or international, customers. Among interviewees, internationalization was a particularly significant and pressing problem for the chairmen of larger companies, especially those with international ambitions or facing international competitive threats.

Facilitating skills and processes

Are there particular areas of directorial skill that are assuming a higher priority? In response to various challenges in the business environment (which we shall examine in Chapter 11) and the emerging requirements we identified in Chapter 2, the issues of (a) directorial competences related to the facilitation of learning, change and corporate transformation and (b) personal qualities such as flexibility and open-mindedness among directors, are expected to become increasingly important.

The ability to articulate and share a distinctive and compelling vision, both inside and outside the corporation, is assuming a special significance:

- More people within corporate organizations are needing to share and understand their company's vision, and assume personal and team responsibility for 'adding value' to customer requirements.
- Many customers, some suppliers, and business partners are also becoming effective 'participants' or 'colleagues' in the corporate enterprise. A common vision can help to hold a supply chain together.

In the case of the flexible and responsive 'network organization', a directorial overview is still needed. The role of the director may become more, rather than less, challenging. For example:

- Greater time, and considerable skill, may need to be devoted to establishing criteria for determining those matters that should be brought to the board.
- More attention may need to be devoted to the continuing review of relationships, roles and responsibilities, and management and business processes.

An organization that is making continuous and ongoing incremental adjustments to change has been compared with a log floating down a river:[12]

While the managerial team concerns itself with ensuring the log flows on to its eventual destination by avoiding entanglements with the bank and other obstacles, the board needs to keep an eye on the presence of waterfalls ahead and the need to explore alternative routes. From the viewpoint of the log a waterfall might be glimpsed when all else is under control and yet it is too late to react.

Communication skills

Reference has been made to the need for boards to communicate effectively in order to (a) build and sustain relationships with a range of stakeholders and supply chain partners, and (b) bring about change and corporate transformation. Directors require the ability to communicate internally and externally, and across both functional and organizational barriers.

The main barriers to both 'internal' and 'external' communication, as ranked by the participants in an Adaptation Ltd survey *Communicating for change*,[13] and in order of 'very significant' replies, are 'communication skills' and 'top management commitment'. Those at director level who were interviewed related the perceived lack of top management commitment to the failure of their boardroom colleagues to communicate.

What are the deficiencies in the communication skills of directors? Surely most directors have been on public-speaking and other communication skills courses? They probably have, but the failure of directors to communicate is sometimes the result of their training in communication techniques:[13]

- Communications from directors can be so polished as to be bland, so slick as not to reveal any hint of emotional commitment, and so confident as not to give any indication of a desire to share and involve.
- The technology, channels and occasions of communication may give little opportunity to enter into a dialogue, while superior technique may actually inhibit participation and discourage feedback.
- The approach directors have towards communication, the attitudes they betray towards others, and the inconsistencies between the words they use and their own conduct, that are evident during 'formal' or 'organized' communication, can reduce rather than enhance mutual trust and respect.

One senior manager summed up a general sense of frustration:

When did you last meet a director who is interested in you and your views, or who is interested in the company rather than him or herself? When did you last meet a director who *really and sincerely* believed and cared, and *really* showed commitment, as opposed to saying the right or expected thing? . . . If they are interested, and if they do care, they keep it well hidden.

Roger Graham, chairman of the BIS Group, believes it is particularly important that a director has 'an ability to communicate in a relevant way to the top team'.

A board needs to ensure that its members are properly equipped to communicate and share vision, goals, values and objectives, and to demonstrate the extent of the commitment of the boardroom team to their achievement. As far as addressing the communication skill requirements of directors is concerned, it should be borne in mind that:

- the lack of communication skills in the boardroom is often a matter of general attitudes, approach and perspective rather than specific techniques;
- there are plenty of programmes on communication techniques, but rather fewer that focus upon attitudes and approaches to communication from a directorial perspective;
- communications do not exist in a vacuum, and need to be complemented by other factors such as role model behaviour on the part of directors, supporting management and business processes, and a compatible reward and remuneration system.[6]

We shall return in later chapters to how directors and boards should behave in order to demonstrate commitment and bring about change.

The distinction between directorial and managerial skills

It is important that directorial skill requirements are addressed from the perspective of the director. In order to encourage a discussion of the distinction between directorial and managerial skill requirements, a board could be invited to consider how the communication skills needed by a director might differ from those required by a manager (e.g. with whom does the board need to communicate, why and by what means?).

Alternatively, if a more general focus upon directorial skills as a whole is preferred, directorial and project management skills could be compared (Exercise 3.4). Project management skills are distinct, in certain respects, from management skills generally.[14] They are also becoming increasingly important in the boardroom as:

- boards increasingly allocate specific responsibilities for the achievement of tangible and measurable 'outputs' or objectives; and
- more companies are disaggregating into distinct and accountable business units, groups and teams, becoming in effect 'portfolios of projects' to be managed by the board.

Exercise 3.4: Direction and project management

Invite the board to consider how the personal qualities, knowledge and skills required by a competent director differ from those that are desirable in a project manager. (If necessary, review the 'project management' competences listed in Table 8.1 of Chapter 8.)

The board could also be invited to consider:

1 the relevance of project management skills to the board's own role and specific accountabilities;
2 how project management skills might be relevant in terms of the board's desire to move from aspiration to achievement, i.e. 'make it happen';
3 whether (and, if so, the extent to which) the acquisition of project management skills might form a desirable and valuable element of an individual's preparation for a boardroom appointment.

Whether or not individual executive directors will require project management skills will depend upon the allocation of roles and responsibilities to the members of the boardroom team. In this chapter, we have seen that the relevance of directorial knowledge and skills will depend upon the nature, situation and context of a company. The knowledge and skill requirements of individual directors will reflect, and should complement, those of other members of the boardroom team.

Checklist

1 What are the key influences on the knowledge and skills required of the members of your company's board?
2 Has your company identified the knowledge and skills that should be possessed by the members of its board?
3 Do they understand their legal and financial duties and responsibilities?
4 How is the extent of this understanding tested and kept up to date?
5 Who advises and updates the board on legal, accounting and reporting requirements?
6 To what extent is the financial information received by the board a 'help' or a 'hinder'?
7 If an 'internal market' existed within the company, how much would other functions and business units be prepared to spend on the 'services' they receive from the 'accounts department' or its equivalent?
8 Does the board encourage internal surveys of line management attitudes towards service departments?
9 Do the knowledge and skills that have been identified match the requirements for success in the context of the business the company is in?
10 Are they appropriate to the particular circumstances of the company?

11 Is there a process by which the actual knowledge and skills of individual members of the board are compared with what they should be in order to identify development needs?

12 Are the knowledge and skills sought in individual directors matched to the needs of the board as a whole?

13 How effectively do the members of the board work together as a team?

14 Is the board committed to the regular review of the skills that are required in order that they may be kept up-to-date?

15 Are the skills of directors, in terms of determining what needs to be done, matched by the facilitating competences and communication skills needed to turn intention into reality?

Notes and references

1 Abbas Alkhafaji, 'Effective boards of direction', *Industrial Management and Data Systems*, **90**, No. 4 (1990), 18–26.

2 Colin Coulson-Thomas, *Creating the Global Company: Successful Internationalization*, McGraw-Hill, 1992.

3 Terry Smith, *Accounting for Growth*, Century Business, 1992.

4 Institute of Directors, 'Guidelines to Boardroom Practice, Companies in Financial Difficulties', *Direct Line*, No. 94 (January 1991); and *Directors' Personal Liabilities*, Corporate Governance Series, No. 6, Director Publications, June 1992.

5 Colin Coulson-Thomas, *Creating Excellence in the Boardroom*, McGraw-Hill, 1993.

6 Colin Coulson-Thomas, *Transforming the Company: Bridging the Gap between Management Myth and Corporate Reality*, Kogan Page, 1992.

7 Robert Camp, *Benchmarking: The Search for Industry Best Practices that Lead to Superior Performance*, Quality Press, 1989.

8 Colin Coulson-Thomas and Susan Coulson-Thomas, *Managing the Relationship with the Environment*. An Adaptation Ltd survey sponsored by Rank Xerox (UK) Ltd, 1990.

9 Peter Knight, 'Advice to turn a director green', *Financial Times* (22 January 1992); and Robert Mueller, *Directors and Officers Guide to Advisory Boards*, Quorum Books, 1990.

10 Colin Coulson-Thomas, *Professional Development of and for the Board*. A questionnaire and interview survey undertaken by Adaptation Ltd of company chairmen. A summary has been published by the IOD, February 1990.

11 Andrew Kakabadse, *The Wealth Creators: Top People, Top Teams and Executive Best Practice*, Kogan Page, 1991.

12 Colin Coulson-Thomas and Alan Wakelam, *The Effective Board: Current Practice, Myths and Realities*. An IOD discussion document, 1991.

13 Colin Coulson-Thomas and Susan Coulson-Thomas, *Communicating for Change*. An Adaptation Ltd survey for Granada Business Services, 1991.

14 Colin Coulson-Thomas, *The Role and Status of Project Management*. An Adaptation Ltd survey and report for the Association of Project Managers, 1990; and, 'Project management: A necessary skill?', *Industrial Management and Data Systems*, No. 6, (1990), 17–21.

Appendix: Determining directorial skill requirements presented in Examples 3.1 and 3.2

FACTORS (from Example 3.1)	Role of Board	Duties/ resp. of individual directors	Liabilities of directors	Duties/ resp. of the board	Corporate governance	Company law	Law of contract	Other relevant low	Legal disputes and processes	Group structure	PLC duties/ resp.	City institutions/the Stock Market	Cont.
Company Type: Domestic: Private Owner-managed													
Public													
Foreign													
Euro-company													
Holding company													
Subsidiary company													
Joint venture													

LEGAL KNOWLEDGE (from Example 3.2)

Company size: Small	Medium	Large	MNC	Company market: Local	Regional	National	International

4 The effective board

The key decisions are taken by the board collectively, rather than by individual directors; and a group of competent, even outstanding, directors will not necessarily constitute an effective board when they come together in the context of the boardroom. For example, the interpersonal chemistry may not work, or a board might be badly chaired.

In this chapter, we shift the focus of our attention from the competence of directors to the effectiveness of boards. The exercises are concerned with the assessment, establishment and maintenance of board effectiveness. Particular attention is paid to the responsibility of the board for implementing change, and those corporate processes that deliver customer satisfaction and achieve business objectives.

What is an effective board?

An effective board is one that discharges its collective duties, responsibilities and accountablities, provides direction and purpose, 'develops the business' and 'makes things happen'. According to Peter Morgan, director-general of the IOD, 'the greatest service a company can perform for any community is to survive and thrive', and the directors must 'encourage the innovation and initiatives which will ensure that the company survives and thrives'.[1]

The effective board is awake, alert, united and committed. It is able to articulate, communicate and share vision, values, goals and objectives, and motivate, enable and empower people to achieve them. The composition of a board—its tone and atmosphere, the openness of debate, the willingness to listen and learn, the rigour of its processes and many other factors—and the relevance of all of these to the situation, circumstances and development needs of the business, could all be *prima facie* evidence of an effective board.

Structure and effectiveness

Board effectiveness is the product of a combination of factors and circumstances. It can be fleeting, and should never be taken for granted. Board structure of itself might, or might not, be an indicator of effectiveness; it all depends upon directorial awareness, attitudes, commitment and perspective.

People can have different views on what represents an appropriate structure in a particular context. In the case of the public company, the separation of the role of board chairman from that of CEO, and the inclusion of non-executive or independent directors among the membership of the board, could be thought desirable. A division of responsibilities between chairman and CEO could allow the chairman to concentrate upon building relationships with external stakeholders, and to manage and maximize the strategic contribution of the board, while the CEO could provide executive leadership in the refinement and implementation of corporate objectives and strategy, and the communication, sharing and achievement of the vision, goals and values established by the board.

The *Financial Times* is of the view that: 'for big companies to combine the role of chairman and chief executive in one individual is almost always a mistake'.[2] Business leaders do not always agree on this point. For example, Peter Bonfield, chairman and chief executive of ICL, believes that it all depends upon the situation, circumstances and context, and the decision of whether or not to combine or separate the two roles should be taken on a 'horses for courses' basis.[3]

Non-executive directors can provide balance, additional and wider experience, independence and objectivity, and enable a company to establish audit and remuneration committees.[4] However, what happens in practice, i.e. how objective and robust these people are, is what really matters. For example, there are many practical problems facing the individual non-executive director with genuine concerns.[5]

Those advising a board should address the 'realities' of the particular, rather than 'mouth' the general, few people are interested in the wider population of boards. Most chairmen and CEOs seeking counsel have a pragmatic concern with a particular board, and how it might be made more effective.

Board practice and actual conduct

The development adviser and counsellor needs to look beyond structure, formal procedures, and the 'biogs' and 'role descriptions' of directors, and examine the dynamics and chemistry of the boardroom, and how the board actually transacts its business. Boards vary significantly in terms of composition and organization, and also in how they are used. For example:

- Some are active and creative, and drive initiatives through, while others review papers submitted by management.
- There are boards that take a succession of decisions, while others act more as a forum for discussion and debate.[6]
- A board could 'compartmentalize' issues and take discrete decisions, or it could adopt a holistic perspective and focus upon processes.
- One board may focus upon strategic issues, while another deals in trivia.
- A board could be 'open' with agreed criteria for putting items on the agenda, or its business could be 'fixed'.
- There are democratic boards that encourage contribution and debate,

and boards that are dominated by a small clique, if not a dominant personality.

- A board could be cohesive or fragmented, homogeneous or diverse, united or divided.
- A board can confront or avoid reality, welcome challenges or fear change and avoid confrontation, and deal with symptoms or 'root causes'.[7]
- Discussion in the boardroom could be based upon assumption, prejudice, heresay and self-interest, or upon analysis, fact and a shared sense of purpose.[7]

How a board is chaired, and the secretarial support it receives in terms of such matters as adequate notice of meetings and business and the timely distribution of relevant papers, can have a significant impact upon board effectiveness.

The core procedures and basic practices of a board should be written up, agreed by the board and circulated to all directors. The Institute of Chartered Secretaries and Administrators suggests they should be reviewed periodically, and compliance monitored by an audit committee of the board. [8]

Assessing board effectiveness

The chairman should bear the prime responsibility for ensuring that the members of the board work together effectively as a team in discharging their accountabilities and responsibilities as a board. The chairman needs to conduct the business of the board in such a way as to achieve this. As well as drawing upon the collective strength and wisdom of the boardroom team, the chairman should also tap the skills of the individual members when it is appropriate to do so in the interests of the board and its business.[9]

How effective is your board? Exercise 4.1 could be used to form an initial overview of areas that may need to be addressed by development activity.

Exercise 4.1: Indicators of board effectiveness

The following questions could be used to evaluate the prima facie effectiveness of a board:

1 Is the board properly and correctly constituted?
2 Does the board meet regularly, and conduct formal business?
3 Do the processes of the board focus upon those things that are really important for customers and other stakeholders?
4 Is sufficient time devoted to the consideration of matters of importance?
5 How competent are the individual members of the board, and how well do they work together as a team?
6 If a corporate management committee is thought to be necessary, are separate and formal meetings of the board also held? (For example, management committee meetings could be held weekly, and a board meeting once a month.)
7 Do members of the board behave as 'subordinates' of the chief executive officer?

8 Are the meetings of the board chaired by someone other than the chief executive officer?

9 Does the membership of the board include non-executive directors?

10 To what extent is the full potential of the board and its members being tapped?

11 How well has the board responded and contributed in crisis situations?

12 Are the expectations which the chairman has of the board, and of its members, such as to encourage it to become more effective?

13 Does the board learn from its own experience, and is it prepared to challenge fundamental assumptions?

14 Is the presentation of information in board papers conducive to understanding?

15 Does the board use appropriate review processes and techniques?

Some boards attempt to define and measure board 'outputs'. There are tangible items such as an annual report and accounts that can be examined, but an IOD survey[10] revealed that chairmen generally find it difficult to define outputs in respect of many areas of board responsibility and accountability, and hence they rely upon personal qualities in the case of individual directors, and impressionistic measures such as the atmosphere of the boardroom in the case of boards.

Simplistic measures can lead to an excessive focus upon particular aspects of the role of the board. Many of the accountabilities and responsibilities of the board are 'given', and the directors ignore them at their peril. Situations and circumstances also change. They may be in a continual state of flux. Hence, if formal criteria or measures are used to assess performance, they should match the requirements for success in the contemporary marketplace.[11]

Rubber stamp and challenging boards

The effective board is proactive, questioning, challenging and thrusting. It takes the initiative. Too many boards are reactive, and are not in control of events or the destinies of companies. They stumble forwards by means of incremental adjustments to various forces and pressures.

The effective board operates as a board, and not as a management committee composed of a CEO and executive subordinates. If it is necessary to hold management meetings, these should take place in addition to, and between, formal meetings of the board.

A board that is subservient to a powerful CEO, and does not complement the CEO, add value or cause him or her to reflect and reconsider, cannot be said to be effective. Evidence suggests that many CEOs play a leading role in identifying candidates for non-executive director appointments, and act as 'gatekeepers' of the information they receive.[6]

Roderick M. Hills, while chairman of the US Securities and Exchange Commission, found that: 'Information provided to boards of directors in too many cases is entirely the product of management, and no effort is made and no authority is given to outside directors to make an independent investigation.'[12]

Survey evidence suggests that many chairmen look for new directors who will 'fit in' and be loyal and supportive, and they avoid those who may 'challenge' or 'rock the boat'.[10] Some chairmen and CEOs pack their boards with 'cronies', while others, for example Sir Allen Sheppard, the chairman and CEO of Grand Metropolitan plc, appear to positively seek out challenging boardroom colleagues.[13]

In the case of public limited companies, there are occasions when 'strong' chairmen and chief executives have been removed by a combination of directors.[14] A group of non-executive directors who are able to work together can have a significant impact.[15] The appointment, assessment and, if necessary, removal of the CEO is regarded as one of the most important opportunities that non-executive directors have to make a major contribution.[16]

Since 1978 the New York Stock Exchange has required all listed companies to have an audit committee composed solely of independent directors. By 1992, around two-thirds of the top 250 UK listed companies had audit committees, and the 'Cadbury Committee' recommends that all listed companies should establish an audit committee and a remuneration committee.[17]

A board should be seen as it is, rather than as it ought to be. Exercise 4.2 could be used by a board that is willing to confront realities.

Exercise 4.2: The board in practice

What the board could, or should, be may be very different from what it is in practice. If the effectiveness of a board is to be genuinely improved, it needs to be seen as it is, 'warts and all'. The following questions could be used to make a realistic assessment of your company's board:

1 **Whose interests does the board really serve?**
2 **Does the board really focus on those 'vital few' activities that add most value for customers?**
3 **Are the cross-functional processes in place to allow it to do this?**
4 **Who really 'calls the shots' in the boardroom?**
5 **What important decisions are taken outside the boardroom?**
6 **How free and frank are boardroom discussions?**
7 **What are the undercurrents, the 'hidden agendas', the tensions, the rivalries, the incompatibilities, the clashes of personality, etc.?**
8 **How many of the directors are really encouraged or prepared to speak their minds?**
9 **What happens when the going gets tough?**
10 **Why were the last few directors appointed to the board?**
11 **Are the non-executive directors really independent?**

Having established a sense of realism in the boardroom, the directors could next be encouraged to undertake a formal evaluation of where they feel they are in relation to where they ought to be, in order to identify and prioritize development actions. This could be done along the lines of Exercise 2.1. The outputs of Exercises 2.1, 2.2 and 2.3 should be taken into account, insofar as they relate to the effectiveness of the board.

Helps and hinders

Reference has already been made to such factors as poor chairmanship, inadequate information, a dominant personality, and departmental rivalries that can 'hinder' the effectiveness of a board. There is insufficient space to be other than very selective in terms of other constraints upon performance.

A board needs to be open-minded, and both willing and able to learn. Success can breed complacency. A board should be a learning board. It should be willing to challenge and test basic assumptions, and appropriate review processes should be in place. The network organization could establish learning partnerships and processes, and become a learning network.[7]

It helps if a board has a holistic perspective, and avoids the lure of simplistic solutions. The perspective of the board should also extend beyond the company to embrace competitors, and the wider network of people and organizations that make up the value chain that delivers the value sought by customers.[18]

A board collectively has to understand the distinction between direction and management. We will examine this in Chapter 13.

Board effectiveness is often a question of achieving and maintaining a balance between extremes and contending pressures. For example, a degree of unity, a shared vision, and common goals and values may be essential if a board is to achieve fundamental change . At the same time, disagreement and diversity should not be driven out of the boardroom to the extent that 'groupthink' occurs.[19]

Martin Bartholomew, director, Mercury Communications Mobile Services, believes diversity is the key to the performance of teams: 'Some teams have clones, some arguing misfits. They should be constructively varied. . . . Teams that value a variety of personality type are better at finding and analysing opportunities or problems, developing practical solutions, developing themselves.'[20]

Barriers to the effective conduct of the business of the board

The members of a board should assume that there are likely to be some barriers to their effective operation, and they should take steps to identify and overcome them. To improve the conduct of business within the boardroom, the following should be done.

- Identify the main barriers to the conduct of business. (Encourage people to be open and forthcoming. Matters which may at first sight seem trivial to one director might assume greater significance when 'put on the table' and discussed by others, or viewed in the context of other concerns which emerge.)

- List the barriers, then group related items together (if possible) and rank them (or the groups) in order of concern or perceived importance.
- Analyse the barriers: what do they suggest or reveal? (Encourage board members to be open, honest and frank.)
- Understand the nature of the underlying problems. (Before rushing into action make sure the roots of each 'problem' have been reached, e.g. is the cause an individual or a board process?, does it emanate inside or outside of the boardroom?, etc.)
- Draw up a priority list of problems that need to be adressed.
- Set objectives, and identify the actions that need to be taken to tackle the priority problems. (Be bold. Many boards operate within self-imposed constraints.)
- Check that all proposed actions are 'constitutional' in terms of obligations to stakeholders and the legal framework, including the Articles and Memorandum of Association.
- Establish timescales and responsibilities (e.g. chairman, whole board, individual directors, company secretary, etc.) for action and 'next steps'.
- Monitor the implementation of the proposed actions, and the continuing efficacy with which the board conducts its business and reviews its effectiveness.

Many boards find it easier to address such matters as those listed when their review is facilitated by someone with experience of similar exercises. Such an 'independent' person ought to clear 'the ground rules' in advance, and the facilitator with integrity will seek to ensure that latent issues are 'brought to the surface'.

The board is also responsible for the performance of the management team. Hence, a similar approach should be taken in the assessment of managerial performance in relation to corporate vision, values, goals and objectives.[9]

Making it happen

The acid test is the extent to which the board is able to overcome barriers and obstacles, bridge gaps between words and deeds, transcend the gulf which so often occurs between expectations and performance, and turn aspiration into achievement.

According to Vernon Zelmer, managing director of Rank Xerox (UK) Ltd: 'The right strategy may look great on paper, and everything that is relevant and good may have gone into its formulation. At the moment of its agreement, the strategy is just intention. Out there—outside of the boardroom—nothing has happened yet.'

The effective board is purposeful, positive, probing, enterprising and energetic. It 'gives a lead'. It also undertakes, or subjects itself to, regular reviews along the lines of Exercise 4.3 to ensure that it maintains its effectiveness and capability to 'make it happen' in the face of continual challenge and change.

Exercise 4.3: Maintaining board effectiveness

The following are some questions to consider when reviewing the continuing effectiveness of a board:

1 How self-critical is the board, and how willing is it to learn from its own evaluation of its effectiveness?
2 How perceptive, open and frank are members of the board in raising issues, and how rigorous and persistent are they in seeking to reach 'root causes'?
3 Does the board systematically and consistently review management performance?
4 Does the board ensure that all people in the organization know specifically what their tasks are, the standard of performance that is expected of them, and how they will be measured?
5 How does the board ensure that people are equipped, empowered and motivated to act and achieve?
6 How does the board remain aware of the potential 'arenas of conflict' that can arise within the company?
7 How does the board ensure that its priorities remain appropriate in relation to the changing situation and context of the company?
8 Does the board devote sufficient time to sharing, listening and the maintenance of relationships?
9 Does the vision and focus of the board cover the supply chain, and how is it extended to embrace new supply chain relationships?
10 How much attention does the board give to the review and re-engineering of management and business processes?
11 Are there specific processes to ensure ongoing learning, adaptation and change?
12 Does the board always keep in mind, and periodically review, the purpose of the company and its vision, goals, values and objectives?

Too many boards are reactive, and not in control of events or the destinies of companies. They stumble forwards by means of incremental adjustments to various forces and pressures.

Management processes In order to steer a corporate 'log' to its 'eventual destination', or 'make it happen', a board needs to ensure that a company makes proper use of appropriate management processes. In a changing business environment, and in competitive markets, these need to be kept under review.

Interviews carried out during a survey[10] suggest that, in the past, too many boards have felt constrained by the history and organization of their company. There is a tendency to sit around the boardroom table and address the question: 'How do we keep the organization alive for another year?'

Many boards use an existing organization as a point of departure when discussing strategy, determining objectives and initiating new activities. Often these discussions are held, and decisions taken, without reference to any agreed corporate vision, goals or values.

For example, in the 'human resource' area, many companies impose a standard form of organization and a particular pattern of work. People are not employed to work in a certain way, but to add value for customers and achieve business objectives. They should be motivated and empowered to deliver certain outputs.

Rather than assume and perpetuate a particular structure, a board should consider whether a new approach is needed:

- This might involve managing on the basis of 'output' rather than 'input', making use of shared vision, goals and values, and consistent objectives rather than 'structure' to 'hold the organization together'.
- It could involve encouraging people to work in whatever way best enables them to harness their talents in the generation of value and satisfaction for customers .
- Use could be made of facilitating processes and supporting technology to ensure consistency and compatibility.
- An evolving form of organization, that could vary according to function and business unit, might emerge, depending upon which management processes and work patterns prove most relevant and productive.

Increasingly, corporate organizations are distinguished by their management processes rather than by their structures. In the new, more flexible, approach that has been suggested,[10] the question of the form of organization should be left open until the board has first established management processes for deciding what needs to be done, by whom and how their contribution might best be facilitated (Figure 4.1). The results of using management processes appropriate to the situation and context of the company can then determine the form of organization.

A board that initiates a 'new approach', and switches its focus from changing the organization structure to establishing, reviewing and re-engineering management (and business) processes, may find that the consequences impact upon its own role and operation.

- Very often, in the case of the 'old' approach (Figure 4.1), incompatibilities would arise between people, the resources that were demanded, and the 'organization'. Such incompatibility would manifest itself in complaints regarding the bureaucracy, and conflicts brought into the boardroom. The operation of the board was sometimes dominated by the reactive resolution of disputes.
- Under the 'new' approach (Figure 4.1), 'organization' is less of a constraint. There are processes that cut across traditional functional barriers, match available resources to roles and responsibilities, and empower. 'Organization' tends to match, and can be tailored to meet, the needs and interests of people. The role of the board is to facilitate, and also to anticipate proactively and avoid conflicts by using appropriate processes to ensure that (a) all people have output objectives, and (b) they are equipped and empowered to achieve them.

Most management processes will begin in the boardroom where objectives are set. They are likely to end in the boardroom when performance is

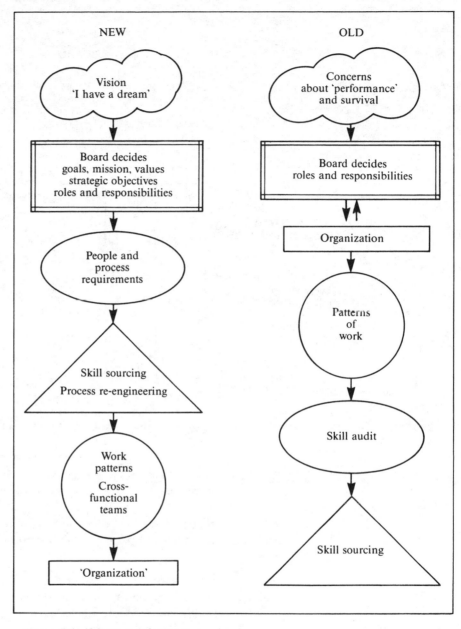

Figure 4.1   Structure and process

matched against expectation. Hence the board should assume responsibility for their effective operation.

Business processes   In addition to putting a higher priority upon the 'management processes' for the direction and management of a company, boards of 'benchmark' companies are devoting more time to reviewing the 'business processes' that harness relevant recources, and apply them to the generation of customer value and satisfaction .

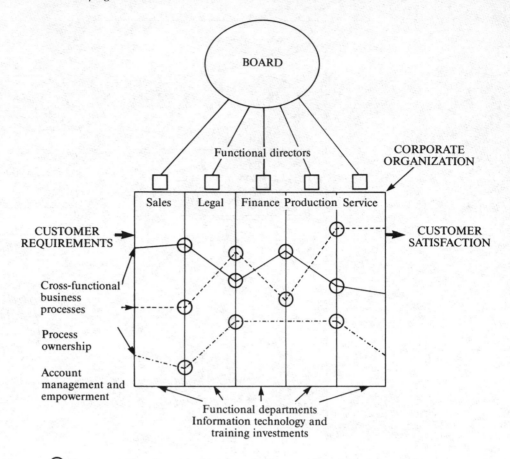

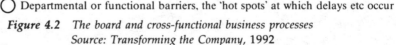

○ Departmental or functional barriers, the 'hot spots' at which delays etc occur

Figure 4.2   *The board and cross-functional business processes*
Source: Transforming the Company, 1992

Why does the board as a team need to get involved with business processes? Can they not be left to the 'functional' directors, and their departmental staffs?

We shall see in Chapter 11 that many corporate organizations are undergoing transformation to more flexible and customer-focused forms based upon multi-function and multi-location teamwork. However, many companies remain organized on a functional basis, as illustrated diagrammatically in (the highly simplified) Figure 4.2.

A central goal of the organization portrayed in Figure 4.2 is to: (a) to identify and understand customer requirements; (b) to establish relationships with customers; and (c) to use the resources of the various departments to deliver value or benefits that result in satisfied customers. Features of the 'functional' organization that should be of particular concern to the board are as follows[7]:

• Responding to the needs of a customer usually requires the involvement of a number of separate departments. For example, an order obtained by sales may need to pass through legal and financial checks, before being passed to production for manufacture, and then to service for installation. Such a path is, in effect, a cross-functional business process, but in some companies it is not even recognized as such, let alone documented.

- The business processes of Figure 4.2 are relatively straightforward. Many 'real-life' processes, even in companies that have reputations for being well managed, are extremely tortuous and can involve 'return visits' to some departments. Progress along certain parts of the path can be particularly slow when the activities in question are not high departmental priorities, and there will often be detours, perhaps involving much work, that generate little if any value for customers.
- Often the longest delays occur at the departmental or functional barriers, the 'handover' points where documentation passes from one part of the organization to another. Some paperwork might spend almost the whole of its organizational 'life' waiting at 'handover' points.
- The 'handover' between functions or departments may not be perceived as anyone's responsibility. It may be hidden. Management attention may be focused upon securing small incremental improvements in the visible activity within departments, while ignoring the much greater potential for improvement that lies in the relationship between departments.
- Functional departments can be relatively self-contained worlds with their own people, priorities and procedures. Some will be run by their own functional director. Even the technology and the systems may be 'departmental' and focused on functional activity. The information technology may not 'talk' to that in a neighbouring department.
- With the functional directors focused upon their own departmental responsibilities, there may be few business processes that are understood on a cross-functional basis, or supported by cross-functional document management systems.

In the circumstances described, which represents the reality of many companies, the board can play a critical role in ensuring that the directors focus collectively upon:

- identifying and analysing, or determining and establishing, the cross-functional business processes that make, or have the potential to make, the biggest contribution to customer satisfaction;
- ensuring that they are re-engineered to minimize waste and maximize the generation of value for customers, and are regularly reviewed; and
- supporting them by appropriate cross-functional document management systems.

When roles and responsibilities are allocated within the boardroom, a board should ensure that the effective operation of every key management and business process is the specific responsibility of a particular director.

The executive members of tomorrow's board could well be 'process owners' rather than 'functional heads'. Such directors are more likely to have a cross-functional perspective, and to view the company as a whole, rather than from a departmental perspective.

Whatever the calibre of the individual members of the board, it is the management processes of the company that will determine the extent to which their potential is harnessed, and their vision, goals, values and objectives are shared and acted upon by the management team. Similarly, whatever the commitment of the board to 'putting the customer first', the company's business processes will determine the extent to which its energy and resources are translated into the generation of value for customers.

The key processes of a company could be assessed by means of Exercise 4.4.

Exercise 4.4: Management and business processes

In order to assess a company's management and business processes, a board might wish to consider the following questions:

1 What are the company's key management and business processes?
2 How many of them are, or should be, cross-functional?
3 Are they fully documented, and are they understood by members of the board and by the employees of the company? (Customers, suppliers and business partners may also need to understand certain processes.)
4 Are all management and business processes supported by appropriate cross-functional document management systems?
5 What should the role of the board be in respect of management and business processes?
6 Are there clear roles and responsibilities in respect of each key process?
7 Should a specific member of the board assume responsibility for each key process?
8 Do the processes focus on those things that are really important from a customer point of view? (Too many processes serve the interests of the 'organization' rather than those of the external customer.)
9 Are customer requirements regularly researched or surveyed, and is what represents value to them periodically reassessed?
10 What steps are taken to uncover and rationalize 'hidden' activities?

The operation of all processes should be regularly reviewed, in relation to changing customer requirements and the elimination of activities that do not add value for customers, and re-engineered as appropriate. The various barriers at 'handover' points should be identified. Throughout an exercise such as Exercise 4.4 a cross-functional perspective should be maintained, and where it is lacking a review of management and business processes could encourage its development.

Corporate transformation skills

A substantial proportion of larger companies are undergoing some form of cultural or organizational transformation. This can require special directorial skills, as well as a management team that is equipped and empowered to bring about the desired changes.

As far as management skills are concerned, a BIM survey[20] has examined the requirements for the management of the flatter and more responsive organizations that are sought. 'The ability to communicate' emerged as the principal quality when these were ranked in order of 'very important' replies.

But what of directorial qualities and priorities? To achieve a successful transformation, a board needs to confront reality, avoid simplistic solutions, maintain a holistic perspective, and assemble a combination of change elements that can overcome the obstacles and barriers in the particular corporate context.[7]

Some further clues are suggested by a survey undertaken by Adaptation Ltd, and sponsored by Granada Business Services, which was concerned with 'communicating for change'.[21] The priority change requirements, when these are ranked in order of 'very important' replies, are emphasized in Table 4.1.

Table 4.1 *Change requirements*

Source: Communicating for Change, 1991.

Requirement	Ranking (%)*
Clear vision and strategy	86
Top management commitment	86
Sharing the vision	71
Employee involvement and commitment	65
Communicating the purpose of change	65
An effective communications network	54
Communicating the expected results of change	44
Understanding the contributions required to the achievement of change	42
Communicating the timing of change	38
Linking a company's systems strategy with its management of change	38
Project management of change	27
Ongoing management education and development programmes	23
One-off management education and development programmes	8

* Ranking in order of 'very important'.

The two priority change requirements, 'clear vision and strategy' and 'top management commitment' both concern the board and are interrelated. The determination and sharing of a clear vision and strategy should be a key priority of a board. Interviews carried out in the course of the 'communicating for change' survey[21] revealed the following observations.

- Few companies that are seeking to change have a clear, shared and understood vision and strategy. A representative 'management' view was: 'Our vision is a pious declaration, a wish list. It bears little relation to my world, and does not guide me in terms of what to do.'
- In many companies, the vision is not regarded as agreed and shared by the board as a team. One interviewee observed: 'There is not a united boardroom team behind it.'
- The commitment of the boards of many companies to the visions and missions they have articulated is regarded as suspect. As one interviewee stated: 'They say one thing and do another. Why should I respond when the board is not really committed to it?'
- Many boards that declare themselves to be committed are finding it difficult to communicate this commitment. One chief executive officer exclaimed: 'I do all the usual things like giving speeches and appearing on videos, but nothing happens. What do I need to do to show that we mean business?'

The next three 'change requirements'—'sharing the vision', 'employee involvement and commitment' and 'communicating the purpose of change'—emphasize that articulating and agreeing a vision and a change strategy in the boardroom are not enough.

Every respondent in the 'communicating for change' survey[21] considered 'clear vision and strategy', 'top management commitment', 'sharing the vision', 'employee involvement and commitment' and 'communicating the purpose of change', to be either 'very important' or 'important' in the management of change. The vision and the strategy of the board must be communicated and shared, and employees need to be involved and empowered. They should understand the purpose of change, and what they have to do to help bring it about.

Because of the urgency of the transformation challenge in many companies, director development may need to focus upon it. We shall examine the evaluation of performance in Chapter 9, and shall return to the role of the board in relation to corporate transformation in Chapter 10.

Checklist

1 Does the board of your company operate effectively as a team, and discharge its various accountabilities and responsibilities?
2 How regularly and systematically does the board assess its own effectiveness?
3 Are 'output' measures used, and what other indicators of effectiveness could be used?
4 Does the board operate as a board or as a corporate management committee?
5 Do individual members of the board feel a sense of 'challenge', and do they share a common challenge?
6 Does the board listen and learn?
7 Does the board probe and endeavour to uncover what is hidden?

8 Has an assessment been made of the factors that help or hinder the effectiveness of the board?

9 How much 'politics' is going on within the boardroom?

10 Does the board act as a role model in terms of its own conduct?

11 Are its actions consistent with its rhetoric?

12 Are the priorities of the board appropriate to the vision, values, goals and objectives of the company?

13 Has the board focused upon and reviewed the processes that identify and deliver the value that is sought by customers?

14 If so, have the results lead to an examination of whether additional, or different cross-functional, processes might be required?

15 Does the board have an adequate understanding of management and business processes, and what needs to (and might) be done to increase this understanding?

16 Is the board equipped to bring about a fundamental transformation of the company?

17 Has the board articulated, agreed, communicated and shared a distinctive and compelling vision, and are its actions and conduct consistent with it, and supportive of it?

Notes and references

1 Peter Morgan, *Why an Institute of Directors?*, Lecture to the Cardiff Business Club, 3 February 1992, pp. 11 and 12.

2 'The lessons of Mr Horton's exit', *Financial Times*, Editorial (29 June 1992), 12.

3 Peter Bonfield, *Corporate Governance and Managing Change: Fad or Common Sense?* Keynote address at 1992 IOD Diploma Reunion, 10 July 1992.

4 Institutional Shareholders Committee (ISC), *Role and Duties of Directors: A Statement of Best Practice*, ISC, 1991.

5 Jerry Shively, 'Confessions of a non-executive', *Financial Times* (15 July 1991), 11; and Norma Cohen, 'Getting directors on board', *Financial Times* (6 April 1992), 12.

6 Jay Lorsch and Elizabeth MacIver, *Pawns or Potentates: The Reality of America's Corporate Boards*, Harvard Business School Press, 1989.

7 Colin Coulson-Thomas, *Transforming the Company: Bridging the Gap between Management Myth and Corporate Reality*, Kogan Page, 1992.

8 *Good Boardroom Practice: A Code for Directors and Company Secretaries*, The Institute of Chartered Secretaries and Administrators, February 1991.

9 Colin Coulson-Thomas, *Creating Excellence in the Boardroom*, McGraw-Hill, 1993.

10 Colin Coulson-Thomas and Alan Wakelam, *The Effective Board: Current Practice, Myths and Realities.* An IOD discussion document, 1991.

11 A.M. Pettigrew and R. Whipp, *Managing Change for Competitive Success*, Blackwell, 1991.

12 Roderick M. Hills, 'Ethical perspectives on business and society', in Yerachmiel Kugel and Gladys W. Gruenberg (eds), *Ethical Perspectives on Business and Society*, Lexington Books, 1977, p. 38.

13 Carol Kennedy and Stuart Rock, 'The man who bet the management', *Director* (August 1992), 32–35.

14 See, for example, Robert Peston, Paul Betts and Roland Rudd, 'Bloody battle in the boardroom', *Financial Times* (27 September 1991) and John Plender, 'Tougher at the top', *Financial Times* (28 and 29 September 1991), 7.

15 Christopher Lorenz, 'Knives are out in the boardroom', *Financial Times*, (1 May 1992), 11.

16 M.S. Weisbach, 'Outside directors and CEO turnover', *Journal of Financial Economics*, **20** (1988), 431–60.

17 Committee on the Financial Aspects of Corporate Governance (chairman: Sir Adrian Cadbury), Draft report issued for public comment, Committee on the Financial Aspects of Corporate Governance, 27 May 1992.

18 Michael Porter, *Competitive Strategy: Techniques for Analysing Industries and Competitors*, Free Press, 1980; and *Competitive Advantage*, Free Press, 1985.

19 I.L. Janis, *Victims of Groupthink*, Houghton-Mifflin, 1972.

20 Colin Coulson-Thomas and Trudy Coe, *The Flat Organisation: Philosophy and Practice*, BIM, 1991.

21 Colin Coulson-Thomas and Susan Coulson-Thomas, *Communicating for Change*. An Adaptation Ltd survey for Granada Business Services, Adaptation, 1991.

PART TWO

Developing directors and boards

5 The route to the boardroom

An appointment to the board is often seen as an extension of a management career. However, there are distinct directorial qualities which an effective manager may or may not possess (see Chapters 2, 3 and 13). Sir John Harvey-Jones points out that: 'It does not always follow that the best executive manager will become the best director, and, indeed, I have sometimes wondered whether we should stream and select directors quite differently to the way we stream and select chief executives.'[1]

A career as a company director should be regarded as distinct from a managerial career. It should be perceived as a separate arena of activity, rather than as something that follows on inexorably, at an appropriate moment, from satisfactory performance in a succession of managerial roles.

Managerial experience of itself, or 'picking things up as one goes along', will not necessarily equip an individual for the boardroom. As Brian Rowbotham, chairman of London Newspaper Group Ltd, points out: 'the career paths of most executives do not provide corporate experience. Regrettably, long service alone is not the training which will equip an executive to direct a company.'

At the same time, there will be those whose managerial roles do not allow them to express the directorial qualities they possess. The membership of a board can be a question of 'accident' rather than 'design'.

How do people become directors? Why are some chosen and not others? This chapter examines routes to the boardroom, the criteria used to select directors, and their implications for director development. The exercises will explore these issues, and examine how routes to the boardroom can be made more open and how selection criteria can be made more explicit.

Owner and family company directors

The route taken to a boardroom can have significant development implications. For example, let us consider the case of the owner-director. Most companies are small businesses (see Chapter 12), and a significant proportion of these are 'owner-managed'.

Those who are owner-directors, or directors of family companies, can represent a particular development challenge:

- Because they may not have been required to satisfy 'normal' selection criteria, involving objective assessment by those who are impartial, individual owner-directors may have significant and evident deficiencies.
- Because of the power of their positions, owner-directors may be surrounded by others who are reluctant to 'raise', or draw attention to, their deficiencies.
- As a result of not having to compete or compare themselves with others within the company, many owner-directors may not even be aware of their own deficiencies.
- Even if they are aware of their deficiencies, owner-directors may chose to ignore them 'for the time being'.
- In the case of owner-directors, 'turning a blind eye', or not addressing their deficiencies, will probably not result in the loss of a seat on the board.

While they pose a development challenge, owner-directors also represent a considerable development opportunity. Consider the following quotations from owner-director interviewees:

The business is my baby, my child. I am totally committed to it. I want it to go on and on after I retire.

The development of the business is constrained by us [the directors]. It will grow to the extent that our capability grows. Develop us and you develop the business.

If a small business fails it's generally the fault of the directors. Maybe it's a case of right idea, but wrong board. Developing the board is the best way of helping the smaller business.

Governments shouldn't have small business development programmes. They should have director development programmes.

As people, owner-directors are generally practical, and concerned to obtain 'value for money'. The cost of director development may be more significant in relation to the bottom line than would be the case with a larger company; hence the desire for activities that can be shown to benefit the 'development of the business' as well as the directors.

Given the necessary commitment, the development of the owner-directors of the smaller company can have a very tangible impact upon business performance. Owner managed and family companies present particular problems to those concerned with director development.[2] But directors of other types of company, and those operating in certain sectors and countries, can also require special consideration and treatment.

Understanding the route to the boardroom

Director development should take account of, and build upon, what has gone before, i.e. previous learning experiences. This requires an understanding of the various routes that have brought existing and potential directors into, or close to, the boardroom.

There are many routes to the boardroom, and they can vary by country, company type and business sector. Some people form their own companies, or join the boards of family companies. Employed managers are promoted to boards and professional advisers are invited to join them. Certain stakeholders may seek to be 'represented' on the board.

There are those who 'package' a board, perhaps to reassure or to 'create the right appearance'. 'Looking right' may be more important as a selection criterion than 'doing right'.

The routes to the boardroom can also vary by function and type of director. Thus the backgrounds and experience of non-executive directors might lie in very different organizations and business sectors.[3] Whatever route has been taken, the distinction between direction and management needs to be borne in mind when assessing the relevance of what has gone before.

Bob Garratt, a recent chairman of AMED, believes: 'There is a huge difference between managing and directing. Wise companies are beginning to recognize this, and are finding that good managers do not necessarily make good directors. This challenges the current notion of a manager's career progression.'[4]

What appears 'impressive' in a résumé of managerial achievements may not be of relevance to the key qualities that distinguish the director. For example, to obtain an overview perspective, it may be more desirable to obtain experience of a number of functions than to excel at one. Thus, in the case of board responsibility for IT, Roger Graham, chairman of the BIS Group, advocates 'experience in other functions such as marketing, personnel or finance at a senior level, attendance at courses to ensure a wide strategic view of the business, as well as leadership training'.

What are the implications of routes to the boardroom for the development needs of directors and boards? Exercise 5.1 could be used to discuss and understand the routes to the boardroom within a particular company. It should not be assumed that these are consciously considered.

Exercise 5.1: Routes to the boardroom

Members of a board should be encouraged to think through the implications of their own routes to the boardroom for their individual and collective director development needs. Questions along the following lines could be used to initiate a discussion:

1 How should a directorial career relate to a managerial career?
2 What route did each director take to the boardroom?
3 How well 'trodden', generally understood, documented, etc., was each route?
4 In each case, how much was either judgement or 'planning', or simply luck and chance 'accidents'? (In response, raise the issue: Was each of the paths to the boardroom actually a route?)

5 Who determined the routes that were taken? (For example: (a) the individual; (b) line managers; (c) the board; (d) the company's personnel department; etc.)

6 Who should have determined the routes that were taken?

7 What factors influenced (a) the nature of the routes that were taken, and (b) each individual's decision to take a particular route?

8 What director selection criteria were either (a) implicit or (b) explicit in the routes that were taken?

9 How has each route benefited (a) the individual, (b) the board, and (c) the company?

10 What were the main 'helps' or 'hinders' that were experienced 'on the way'?

11 How significant for progress along each route was (a) mentoring, 'sponsorship', favouritism or other type of 'informal' help, or (b) formal development activity?

12 What are the advantages or disadvantages of each route (e.g. did it take too long?); and how might each route that was followed have been improved?

13 What are the risks or dangers of each route? (NB: advantages or disadvantages, and risks or dangers, could be approached from the perspective of (a) the individual, (b) the board or (c) the company.)

14 How did others (e.g. colleagues) react to each of the routes that were taken? (For example, were the routes perceived as fair?)

15 If they were able to start again, what route to the boardroom would each director attempt to take?

The key issues to address in the light of the responses to the questions of Exercise 5.1 are: What are the 'directorial development requirement' consequences of the routes that the directors have taken to the boardroom for (a) the individual directors and (b) the board as a team?

At the conclusion of a review such as Exercise 5.1, a board could be invited to consider whether, in the context of the particular situation and circumstances of the company, there ought to be a 'normal' route (or routes) to the boardroom. In many companies, a standard path to a directorship may be neither possible nor desirable if a board is to be balanced.

Changes in a 'normal' route (assuming that one is thought possible) may need to be made to accommodate the requirements of particular boardroom roles (e.g. chairman, non-executive director, particular functional director, etc.).

Directorial qualities and the relevance of director development

The qualities sought in new directors can have a significant impact upon the director development requirement. What are these qualities?

In a survey undertaken for the IOD, 'strategic awareness', 'objectivity' and 'communication skills', closely followed by a willingness to assume 'individual responsibility' and 'customer focus' were ranked at the head of a list of qualities sought in new directors.[5] An open-ended question concerning the 'other qualities' that are sought in company directors produced a long list that is dominated by personal qualities and characteristics.

Strategic awareness, an overview perspective, business acumen and personal qualities also emerge at the head of a list of directorial qualities ranked by senior personnel professionals in another survey.[6]

A further study[7] has suggested that the qualities sought by some chairmen tend to relate to the present circumstances of their companies, rather than to their future growth. There is little evidence of an active search for revolutionaries—i.e. those who 'thrive on chaos' and are determined to challenge and turn every aspect of corporate organization upside down, as suggested by Tom Peters.[8] Without a sense of balance and a holistic perspective, such an approach could be disastrous.

There is also evidence that the boards of many companies focus excessively upon short-term operational performance,[9] and do not always display the longer term perspective that company chairmen believe distinguishes direction from management.[5] Development activity should not become so esoteric as to overlook the essence of what direction is all about. The essentials should not be assumed.

One of the 'essentials' is being receptive, and willing to challenge and change. Open-mindedness and a commitment to learning are important requirements in directors. Colin St Johnston, director of PRO NED, has suggested that:

The willingness to learn is the key requirement . . . no-one seeks to become a non-executive director for the money. Candidates for non-executive director appointments are interested in finding new learning situations, an opportunity to see inside the culture of another company.'[10]

Many boards have not drawn up, discussed, or agreed, the qualities they are looking for when assessing suitable candidates for a potential boardroom appointment. In order to make use of formal selection criteria and plan relevant development activities, it is first necessary to define the directorial qualities that are being sought, otherwise the selection criteria employed may not reflect them.

A review within the framework of Exercise 5.2 could be used for this purpose.

Exercise 5.2: Directorial qualities

A board might wish to consider the following questions in order to ensure that selection and development activities reflect the qualities it is seeking in its members:

1 Has the board established and agreed a list of directorial qualities it considers desirable in its members? (Such a list can be relevant to the determination of the development needs of existing board members, as well as to the assessment of potential directors.)
2 Who established the list of directorial qualities (e.g. chairman?; personnel director?; board as a whole?; etc.) and who is responsible for ensuring that they match the changing situation and context of the company?

3 How do the qualities that have been chosen relate to those sought by other boards (possibly a 'benchmark' board with which views on directors and boards are exchanged), or by boards in general?

4 Do the qualities that have been identified reflect (a) the basis of the distinction between direction and management (Chapter 13), (b) what is required of an effective director (Chapter 2) and (c) the competences a director should possess (Chapters 2 and 3)?

5 Are there omissions or inconsistencies in the qualities that have been identified? (For example, do they meet the development needs of the business?)

6 Are the directorial qualities that have been identified actually used? (For example, are they embedded in formal selection criteria, or are they used to determine the development needs of existing board members?)

7 Does the company have a director development capability or process for addressing specific deficiencies that emerge when potential board candidates and existing board members are matched against the agreed list of desirable qualities?

Director development may not offer a 'total solution' to the deficiencies that emerge from a review in the style of Exercise 5.2. For example, new directors could be appointed to fill skill and experience gaps on the board. The Chartered Institute of Management Accountants has identified a range of areas in which non-executive directors could 'balance' the board of smaller companies.[11]

Some skill and experience requirements may be temporary, in which case the use of advisers, counsellors and consultants might be preferable to development activity or director recruitment. John Thompson, CEO of CSC Europe, has said of consultants: 'when they have done the job you can take them out and shoot them, which is their great advantage over getting new directors.'[12]

The selection of directors

What role does development activity play in the selection of directors? Past development activity appears to be of little significance. According to an IOD survey of chairmen,[7] personal qualities demonstrated by an individual's 'track record' emerge as being the most significant criteria for selection to a board.

It is not necessary to put individuals on the board if you wish to obtain the benefit of their advice. In appointments to the board, 'Steve' Shirley, founder director of F I Group plc, believes: 'Background discipline is immaterial. You can buy in corporate advice on anything from tax to computers.'

Formal qualifications are of little or no significance. In the IOD 'chairman' survey,[7] not a single respondent mentioned the possession of academic or professional qualifications as a criterion for selecting members of a board. Nor was the possession of a working knowledge of, or fluency in, a foreign language mentioned by any of the respondents as a selection criterion.

The possession of language skills *per se* does not necessarily indicate an international perspective.[13] A company that is seeking to build a capability for successful international operation might wish to internationalize its main board, and appoint local nationals to the boards of its national operating companies. Recruiting a local board of directors has been identified as one of the keys to the effective penetration of the Japanese market.[14]

Director selection and company type

A significant proportion of directors are not selected. In one survey of directors of smaller companies, over a third of the respondents were 'founder members'.[15] In effect, by incorporating a company, founder directors select themselves.

Most appointments of directors of larger companies are to an existing board, and hence new directors are required to complement the qualities of other members of the boardroom team and contribute to an ongoing situation. Fitting in and 'team spirit' are valued, and people who make deliberate attempts to appear bright, challenging and full of ideas may diminish rather than enhance the prospects of a boardroom appointment.

In many companies, and especially smaller companies, there is little evidence of succession planning as far as directorial appointments are concerned, and formal selection criteria are rarely established. Hence, it is not easy to plan development activities to build the attributes that are sought.

Appointments are often made of those who 'seem right', 'look the right stuff', 'suit the mood', or 'fit in'. Being able to command the respect of existing members of the boardroom team is an important requirement.

How does one develop the qualities that determine whether or not an individual will be regarded as likely to 'fit in'? This can be a difficult question to answer, and a troubling one when those considering it may feel that the last person the board ought really to consider is someone the chairman believes would 'fit in'.

The survey of 'chairmen'[7] concluded that: 'the ability to listen, think, reflect and assess are attributes which can, to some extent, be nurtured and developed'; and 'latent qualities can . . . be brought to the surface and self awareness increased'; but 'qualities such as loyalty, style, etc., can defy training and development, except on a very superficial level'.

Exercise 5.3 could be used to identify and review the formal or informal selection criteria that are used in the case of a particular board.

Exercise 5.3: Selection criteria

Not all companies use formal selection criteria when evaluating suitable candidates for a potential boardroom appointment. When selection criteria are used they may not reflect the qualities that are being sought. A board might wish to consider the following questions:

1 Does the company use formal and agreed criteria when selecting board members?
2 Who drew up the selection criteria (e.g. chairman?; personnel director?; board as a whole?; etc.) and who is responsible for ensuring that they match the changing situation and context of the company?
3 Do the selection criteria that have been established reflect the qualities that are sought in (a) potential board candidates and (b) existing board members?
4 How do the selection criteria that have been established relate to those used by other boards (possibly a 'benchmark' board with which views on directors and boards are exchanged), or by boards in general?
5 Are there omissions, gaps, inconsistencies etc., in the selection criteria? (For example, do they reflect (a) the ethical dimension or (b) the international or development needs of the company?)
6 How significant are 'personal qualities' among the selection criteria that have been established; and how susceptible are such 'personal qualities' to relevant—i.e. rigorous, objective, fair, etc.—assessment? (Focus on directorial rather than managerial qualities.)
7 What evidence would satisfy each element of the selection criteria that have been established, and is such evidence likely to be available?
8 Are formal directorial selection criteria actually used, and, if so, how effective are they? (For example, are the terms used too general?)
9 Does the use of the selection criteria that have been established reflect the group needs of the boardroom team?
10 Would existing members of the board meet the requirements of the selection criteria if they were subjected to them today?

The key issue at the conclusion of an exercise such as Exercise 5.3 is whether a company has, or should create, a director development capability or process for addressing specific deficiencies that emerge when potential board candidates and existing board members are matched against the agreed selection criteria.

The professional dimension

On occasion, one encounters senior professionals who believe they should have a seat on the board 'as of right' by virtue of heading a functional department or professional group. We saw in the last chapter that an effective board is made up of those who can see beyond a professional viewpoint and develop a holistic perspective.

Many directors articulate the distinction between direction and management in terms of the difference between formulating and implementing strategy. The past professional backgrounds of functional directors in a specialist area like IT may not have prepared them for a directorial role.

- According to Jane Tozer, managing director of Softwright Systems, 'IT directors differ from IT managers. The IT director's role is to identify the overall company objective and to formulate IT strategies to enable the company to achieve this. The role of the IT manager is to fulfil the IT strategy formulated by the director.'
- Professor John Larmouth, director of the IT Institute at Salford University concurs: 'At the management level we are concerned primarily with efficient and effective operation of information systems, but at the board level we need the understanding and vision to set strategies to drive the IT support for the business in new directions.'

Geoffrey Holland, managing director of Intra Systems, believes that: 'The application of IT has become so pervasive within organizations that all future directors must have a sound appreciation of the opportunities available for the application of IT at the strategic level for business advantage.'

Professionals in other areas share similar views. For example, senior personnel professionals do not believe that the head of the personnel function should have a seat on the board unless the individual concerned has the personal attributes and qualities expected of a director.[16] All directors need to ensure that the people of an organization are equipped, empowered and motivated to do what is expected of them.

Selection: the development considerations

In order to derive development requirements from director selection criteria, certain questions need to be asked:

- Which of the criteria that have been established relate to personal qualities?
- Do the criteria that have been established reflect the need to balance and complement the various qualities of the existing directors?
- Do the criteria embrace both: (a) the qualities needed to achieve a successful induction into, or transition to, the boardroom; and (b) the qualities required subsequently to make a distinctive contribution to the work of the board?
- Which of these qualities could be enhanced by means of formal or informal development activity?
- What advice or guidance should be given in respect of the other qualities?
- What is done to acquaint new directors with (a) the prevailing views, attitudes, perceptions and prejudices of current members of the board; and (b) the vision, goals, values and objectives they share?
- Do the selection criteria that have been established favour certain groups within the company rather than others?
- How many people within the company are aware of the criteria for director selection?
- What groups that might contain individuals with directorial qualities would appear to be excluded? (For example, junior managers, women candidates, non-nationals, members of minority groups, etc.)

- How balanced is the board? (Is the composition of the board con-strained by the difficulty of identifying people with certain characteristics who also have directorial qualities?)
- To what extent could organized development activity be used to widen the pool of people from whom directors might be drawn?

The board could be invited to examine the criteria that have been estab-lished for selecting directors and address the above issues. This section could therefore be used as an additional exercise.

Subsequent director development activity

Once appointed to the board, a director will require some form of induction into the culture and ways of the board. While 'settling in', there will be matters to absorb, personalities to adjust to, and assump-tions to reflect upon. The new director might wish to become more familiar with the perceptions, priorities and practices of the board, and its approaches and attitudes, before 'jumping in with both feet'. It may take a few meetings before a director 'feels at home', and a year or more before an individual feels confident enough to make a full contribution.

Directors have varying development needs at different stages in their careers. A newly appointed director will have different requirements from a more experienced director who has been given an opportunity to take his or her first non-executive director appointment upon another board.

Peter Morgan, director general of the IOD, has pointed out that:

In the course of a career a director can be an employee director, a public direc-tor and an owner director at different career points. The role can also change: executive, chief executive, chairman, non-executive or independent. One of the features of the training offered by the IOD is that it prepares the member for the initial board appointment and can then prepare him or her for each subsequent transition.[17]

Different requirements may need to be addressed in stages. Figure 5.1 illustrates how a directorial career can evolve, and how the development need can change over time. An aware and competent director perceives development activities that can help to hone directorial skills as a continuing commitment.

Director development within a particular company should:

- be consistent with, and supportive of, the directorial qualities that are sought, and the criteria that are established to select directors;
- identify and tap as wide a pool of potential directorial talent as possible, in order to produce a flow of people who are eligible to be considered for a boardroom appointment.

Irrespective of the development activity undertaken, it may not, by itself, be decisive in the securing of a boardroom position. Directorial qualities have to be demonstrated and recognized as well as developed.

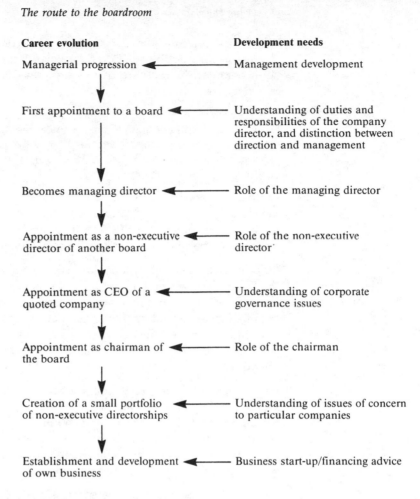

Career evolution

Development needs

Managerial progression ◄———— Management development

First appointment to a board ◄———— Understanding of duties and responsibilities of the company director, and distinction between direction and management

Becomes managing director ◄———— Role of the managing director

Appointment as a non-executive ◄———— Role of the non-executive director of another board director

Appointment as CEO of a ◄———— Understanding of corporate quoted company governance issues

Appointment as chairman of ◄———— Role of the chairman the board

Creation of a small portfolio ◄———— Understanding of issues of concern of non-executive directorships to particular companies

Establishment and development ◄———— Business start-up/financing advice of own business

Figure 5.1   The directorial career

In many companies, whether or not a particular person becomes a director appears to be largely a matter of individual choice on the part of the chairman or chief executive.[16]

Opening access to the boardroom

In many companies, recruitment to the board appears to be largely limited either to those who hold senior management positions within the corporate organization or, in the case of non-executive directors, to those who are aleady directors of a large or public company.[7]

People who satisfy these criteria could well have followed a similar career path as the chairman, and may have experienced similar approaches to management education and development. As a result, they may have certain attitudes in common, and the relatively 'narrow background' from which directors of public companies appear to be drawn can give rise to the accusation that an 'inner circle' exists when new appointments are made.[18]

With few exceptions, the directors of larger companies are male of middle or late middle age. Robin Gowlland, for many years a director of Egon Zehnder International, has noted that CEOs are being appointed at a younger age:

This is a reflection of the pace of modern business life. Chief and senior executives are expected to jump on a plane at the drop of a hat and proceed to meetings anywhere in the world. Clearly executives have to be in better physical shape to undertake such high pressure work and international travel.[10]

The current situation is far from satisfactory. PRO NED has uncovered some dissatisfaction with the contribution being made by non-executive directors.[19] Because of the emphasis upon 'track record', it can be difficult for women to break into the boardroom.[20] How might the pool from which potential directors are drawn be widened?

More managers are being encouraged to be aware of developments in the business environment and to build longer term relationships with customers.[7] Through participation in cross-functional, inter-organizational and international project groups and teams, they are developing a more holistic perspective. Many share vision and values to such an extent that it is 'top management commitment' that they question.

People below senior management level should not be 'written off' in the search for directorial talent. Status is less important than capability. A key question is: How many people should be exposed to various training and development activities designed to develop directorial competences? Directorial succession can be facilitated through having a pool of people with directorial qualities outside of the boardroom.

How might a company ensure that there is a boardroom agenda in every trainee's briefcase? A review along the lines of Exercise 5.4 could be undertaken to determine the extent to which potential directorial talent is likely to find its way into the boardroom.

Exercise 5.4: Access to the boardroom

Questions within the following framework could be used to assess the extent to which various routes to the boardroom are open, understood, and encouraged:

1 **What are the major characteristics of the existing members of the board?**
2 **How balanced and 'representative' (vis-à-vis stakeholders such as customers, the community, employees, etc.; the problems, activities, etc., of the company) is the board in terms of the characteristics of its members?**
3 **What other characteristics, qualities, experiences, etc., would improve the balance of the board, and should these be actively sought? (Could desired qualities, experiences, etc., be obtained by developing the existing members of the board?)**
4 **For those likely to have the required characteristics, what 'helps' or 'hinders'**

would encourage or inhibit their identification by, application to, selection by, or appointment to the board?

5 Do the qualities that are sought in directors, or the selection criteria that are used, discriminate against those with certain characteristics?

6 What prejudices, myths and stereotypes colour the perceptions of members of the board concerning the directorial qualities and characteristics that are sought? (Are the desired characteristics consistent with the qualities that are sought?)

7 How might the desired characteristics be encouraged or built, or the 'hinders' overcome by appropriate development activity?

8 How often does the board review (a) its existing membership and (b) the criteria for board membership?

9 What happens, or should happen, when directors 'come up for re-appointment'? (e.g. review of performance and development needs)? (Are the shareholders a 'rubber stamp'?)

An assessment of how open access to the boardroom is for those from certain groups who might possess directorial qualities or potential could reveal that there are categories of people who may require special help. Women appear to be seriously under-represented in the boardroom,[21] and a special development programme for potential women directors could be introduced. Scott Bader has introduced a training programme aimed specifically at the employee director.[22]

The adequacy of the director selection process

The process by which people become directors should be of some concern to those with director development responsibilities, as it may largely determine the pool of people to be developed. It may be possible to widen access to development opportunities, and open up new routes to the boardroom. This requires a broad and holistic approach to the director development role, which might embrace, for example, creating opportunities for promising directorial talent to obtain experience on divisional boards, or on the board of a smaller company.

Further questions to ask when assessing the adequacy of a director selection process include:

- What advice or guidance, if any, does the board give concerning how an individual might become a 'director person'? (Is there an individual or 'source' to whom people in the company may turn for advice?)
- Does the advice or guidance that is given reflect the lessons for aspiring directors that are to be drawn from (a) the qualities that are sought in directors and (b) the criteria that are used to select them?
- What motivation, other than personal ambition, is there for anyone in the company to seek directorial status or to acquire directorial qualities? (What incentives are there?)
- Are directorial development activities limited to current and potential directors? (If so, what other groups among the employees might benefit from certain directorial qualities?)
- Does the company participate in various initiatives (e.g. such as the

exchange of senior executives, or of subsidiary company directors, with their equivalents in other groups) in order to widen the pool from which future main board directors might be selected?

Many responses are possible, depending upon the outcomes to the above questions. For example, a group of companies could set up a director development consortium. They could share the costs of director development activities, and provide development opportunities for each other's 'high fliers'.

Checklist

1 What routes did each of the directors of your company take to the boardroom?
2 What route would each director like (or prefer) to have taken?
3 What route to the boardroom (or a boardroom) would each director recommend his or her son or daughter (or a representative young manager) to take?
4 How satisfactory are the routes to the boardroom in the context of the nature, situation and circumstances of the company and its development needs?
5 Is the board made up of clones, or a healthy mixture of those who are recognizably 'individuals'?
6 Has the board identified and agreed the qualities it is looking for in its members?
7 Are these reflected in formal selection criteria, and are the latter used when new appointments are made to the board?
8 Do the questions that are used in interviews and assessments relate to directorial criteria, and are they posed in such a way as not to discriminate between candidates?
9 Is a development framework in place that can help candidates to meet the selection criteria that have been established?
10 What, if anything, is done to bring the criteria for director selection to the attention of various groups outside of the boardroom?
11 Does the selection process that is used encourage or discourage the availability of candidates?
12 What new routes to the boardroom might be opened up?
13 Is the re-appointment of directors automatic?
14 Does the company actually encourage employees to acquire directorial qualities?
15 Overall, how adequate is the process that is used to select new board members, and how might it be improved?
16 What contribution should director development make to the building of a more balanced board?

Notes and references

1 Sir John Harvey-Jones, *Making it Happen: Reflections on Leadership*, 3rd impression, Fontana/Collins, 1989, p. 186.
2 Stuart Rock, *Family Firms*, Director Books, 1991.
3 Ken Lindon-Travers, *Non-executive Directors: A Guide to their Role, Responsibilities and Appointment*, Director Books, 1990.

4 Bob Garratt, 'The good manager is not necessarily a good director', Letter to the Editor, *Financial Times* (8 April 1992).

5 Colin Coulson-Thomas, *Professional Development of and for the Board*. A questionnaire and interview survey undertaken by Adaptation Ltd of company chairmen. A summary has been published by the IOD, February 1990.

6 Colin Coulson-Thomas, *The Role and Function of the Personnel Director*. An interim Adaptation Ltd survey carried out in conjunction with the Research Group of the Institute of Personnel Management, 1991.

7 Colin Coulson-Thomas and Alan Wakelam, *The Effective Board: Current Practice, Myths and Realities*. An IOD discussion document, 1991.

8 Tom Peters, *Thriving on Chaos: Handbook for a Management Revolution*, Alfred A. Knopf, 1987.

9 J.H. Horovitz, 'Strategic control: A new task for top management', *International Studies of Management and Organisation* III, No. 4 (1979), 96–112.

10 Colin Coulson-Thomas, *Too Old at 40?*, BIM, 1989.

11 Diane Summers, 'A brief to beef up the boardroom', *Financial Times* (25 August 1992), 8.

12 Chris Partridge, 'How to direct on three Ps', *The Daily Telegraph*, Appointments (18 July 1991), A1.

13 Colin Coulson-Thomas, *Creating the Global Company: Successful Internationalization*, McGraw-Hill, 1992.

14 Edward W. Desmond, 'Byting Japan', *Time*, (17 August 1992), 40–41.

15 Alan Wakelam, *The Training and Development of Company Directors*. A report on a questionnaire survey undertaken by the Centre for Management Studies, University of Exeter for the Training Agency, December 1989.

16 Colin Coulson-Thomas, 'What the personnel director can bring to the boardroom table', *Personnel Management*, (October 1991), 36–39.

17 Peter Morgan, *Why an Institute of Directors?* Lecture to the Cardiff Business Club, 3 February 1992, p. 7.

18 Helen Kay, 'Inner City circle holds the key to top boardrooms', *The Sunday Times*, Business section (14 June 1992), 3:8.

19 PRO NED, *Research into the Role of the Non-executive Director*, PRO NED, July 1992.

20 Elspeth Howe and Susan McRae, *Women on the Board*, Policy Studies Institute, 1991.

21 Viki Holton and Jan Rabbetts, *Powder in the Boardroom*, Report of a survey of women on the boards of top UK companies. Ashridge Research Group, Ashridge Management College, 1989.

22 Worker Director Training at Scott Bader, *Industrial Relations Review and Report*, No. 478 (21 December 1990), 11–14.

6 How directors are prepared

How directors have been, and in many cases still are, prepared for the boardroom suggests that one should not expect directors to be competent, or boards to be effective. Formal preparation for the boardroom is almost non-existent:[1,2]

- Survey evidence has revealed that over nine out of ten respondents have received no preparation for the board, or have been prepared by such informal means as 'experience'.[1,3]
- There is limited association of 'training' with preparation for the boardroom. Only 8 per cent of respondents in one survey cited 'training' in the context of preparation for the board.[1]
- Professional qualifications are not perceived as relevant to directorial requirements. Less than a quarter of respondents referred to the possession of professional or management qualifications in the context of preparation for the board.[1]
- The few who claim to have received some formal preparation invariably cite one or more management or professional courses, rather than an activity specifically concerned with company direction.[1,2]

The situation does not improve after an appointment to a board. Over two-thirds of respondents in a survey of directors[3] received no formal help after their appointment.

This chapter focuses upon how directors are prepared, and prepare themselves, for directorial roles. We shall also examine how they stay up to date, and the directorial view of various sources of advice and support. The exercises in this chapter are largely concerned with helping boards to identify (a) any gaps and deficiencies in their past development, and (b) to whom they can turn for director development advice and services.

Should we be concerned?

On the whole, aspiring corporate leaders are left to their own devices. Warren Bennis believes that 'more leaders have been made by accident, circumstance, sheer grit, or will than have been made by all the leadership courses put together'.[4]

The effectiveness of many directors is largely a tribute to their own initiative, patience and determination, rather than a reflection of the efforts and concerns of others. Few groups in society are so badly served in terms of training resource and expertise.

Not surprisingly, this situation is the cause of some concern. Many chairmen are not satisfied with the contributions of their boards. Three out of four respondents to one survey believe the effectiveness of their board could be improved.[5]

Many boards that 'just managed to cope' in less demanding times are finding it difficult to implement fundamental changes. Few corporate transformation or quality programmes appear to be having a significant impact upon attitudes or behaviour, and very often the board itself is the source of many of the problems involved in turning aspiration into achievement.[6]

Improving this position is not easy when many directors are reluctant to acknowledge their development needs and are often suspicious of the relevance and value of much that is offered by those claiming to have director development expertise. The reliance upon such informal approaches as observation, discussion with colleagues, background reading, and asking relevant questions[5] is a reflection of how difficult it can be for the trainer without main board experience to persuade a director with a track record of success that what is on offer could enhance directorial effectiveness.

Examining the mix of formal and informal activity

Prior to initiating development activity, the previous experience that members of the board have had of both formal and informal development should be assessed. This could be done by posing questions along the lines of those in Exercise 6.1.

Exercise 6.1: Formal and informal preparation

How does the experience of members of the board compare with that of directors in general? In order to move forward one needs to understand the current situation. The following questions could be asked:

1 What formal preparation (if any) did you undertake for the role of company director?
2 How valuable was it? (For example, did it address the distinction between direction and management?)
3 What informal preparation (if any) did you undertake for the role of company director?
4 Again, how valuable was it? (For example, did it address the distinction between direction and management?)
5 Why did you resort to informal preparation? (For example, preference, lack of alternatives, etc.?)
6 Which (if any) form of preparation was the more valuable, the formal or the informal? (Why?)
7 What were the sources (if any) of (a) formal preparation and (b) informal preparation, and how authoritative were they?

8 Did the formal and/or informal preparation (if any) that was received address (a) your needs as an individual director or (b) your requirements in relation to the board as a team?

9 How might the preparation (if any) that you received or undertook have been improved, or made more relevant?

10 What development needs or requirements were not addressed by the preparation (if any) that you received or undertook?

11 Since becoming a director, what formal and/or informal preparation (if any) have you come across that might have been (more) relevant?

12 If you could 'start again', what formal and/or informal preparation (if any) would you undertake? (What advice would you give to a young directorial aspirant?)

In the case of a company facing fundamental challenges, or experiencing a gap between aspiration and achievement, an asessment should be made of whether the formal and/or informal preparation (if any) that has been received was in any way concerned with making it happen (e.g. turning the 'words' or rhetoric of vision, goals, values and objectives into tangible achievement).

The responses to questions such as those in Exercise 6.1 could be very revealing of the attitudes of members of the board towards director development. It should not be assumed that formal development is necessarily better, or indeed worse, than informal development. In reality, a mix of formal and informal development may be required.[7]

There is much that directors, both individually and collectively, can do to learn from their experience.[7,8] Whether formal or informal development is relevant, will depend upon the development requirement and the learning styles and preferences of those concerned.

Nigel Stapleton, finance director of Reed International, believes that director development is sound in principle but: 'making it a condition of election to the board is carrying it to absolute excess. . . . No formal course is a real substitute for what a company secretary should be doing on a one-to-one basis for a new director—in terms of taking him [or her] through the . . . Companies Acts and so on.'[9]

Identifying the obstacles and barriers to director development

A latent requirement for director development appears to exist. It has already been mentioned that three out of four respondents believe the effectiveness of their board could be improved.[5] The potential contribution of training is also acknowledged. Over a fifth of respondents in one survey[5] mentioned training as a means of improving board effectiveness. A further fifth mentioned requirements that could be addressed by courses such as those run by the IOD.

As yet, however, awareness of the need for director development rarely results in action. There are many reasons for this.[7]

- The function of the board, the distinction between direction and management, and the qualities sought in a director are often not understood, or are inadequately thought through. Development needs, and motivations or reasons for seeking help can greatly vary,[10] and will change over time.

• Questions are raised about the credibility of many of the director development services that are on offer, and many sceptics remain to be convinced that the services they have encountered would significantly change directorial attitudes, awareness and perspective.

• In view of the practical problems and timescales involved in many companies that face the need to bring about a fundamental transformation, the composition of the board is altered and new blood is recruited, as an alternative to investing in director development in the hope that existing members can be 'changed' or 'grown'.[11]

• Use can also be made of external consultants and facilitators to supplement and enhance the capabilities of the board where the nature of skill requirements could itself change during the course of a corporate transformation programme.[12]

If development requirements are to be met, a board needs to commit itself to a programme of practical 'next steps' with identified accountabilities and clear output objectives. An assessment along the lines of Exercise 6.2 could be undertaken to identify the barriers to effective action in the case of a particular board.

Exercise 6.2: Barriers to development action

The following questions could be used to assess the extent of 'barriers to action', and the commitment of the directors to overcoming them:

1 To what extent is the requirement for director development latent or hidden? (Is the true nature of the problem really understood?)

2 Are development needs explicit and acknowledged? (In general or specific terms?)

3 Have the acknowledged development needs been prioritized and agreed by the board as a whole? (Was this regarded as a matter of importance, or 'dealt with in passing'?)

4 Have the implications of development needs been thought through? (Is the debate stalled or moving forward?)

5 What are the likely implementation barriers that lie between development need and development action? (The experience of 'benchmark' companies could be compared.)

6 Has a list of 'helps' and 'hinders' been drawn up?

7 What has been done to move from rhetoric to action (e.g. specific objectives, roles and responsibilities, 'next steps', etc.)?

8 Have the identified 'barriers' and 'hinders' been used to rationalize a lack of action? (Is director development really a priority of the board?)

Even effective boards need to consider their development. Arrogance and complacency should not be allowed to become barriers. According to John Harper of the Institute of Directors: 'Becoming a director is not the end of a career path or an end to a process of learning and improvement. Rather it is an area of activity in which people can progress from novicehood to excellence, just as they can in management, and other professional activities.'

Preparation for implementation

There are boards that concentrate upon crafting strategy or 'corporate governance', while neglecting their responsibilities for the achievement of their goals and objectives. In the case of a board, with an agreed and shared vision, goals, values and objectives, that is operating in a demanding and competitive marketplace, and/or is seeking to bring about significant change, the emphasis may be upon implementation. The members of such a board should pay particular attention to the extent to which they have they been prepared (by formal or informal means) to:

- 'make it happen', implement, turn rhetoric into reality, etc.;
- work with others in bringing about significant change (including determining and encouraging 'helps', and identifying and overcoming 'hinders' or barriers to change);
- communicate and share vision, goals, values and objectives, and monitor their achievement;
- establish and allocate roles and responsibilities;
- identify, establish and support management and business processes for achieving objectives and delivering value to customers;
- undertake activities such as empowering, enabling, cascading, resourcing, etc., to ensure that all those concerned understand what they need to do and are equipped and motivated to do it.

A board that is committed to the achievement of corporate transformation needs to be sure that it is equipped with the attitudes, perspective, approaches and techniques to bring it about.[6] According to Adrian Davies: 'the board must not (only) establish and sell a challenging strategy, but also deploy its resources and skill over the time needed to achieve that strategy.'[13]

The initiation of a corporate transformation or 'change' programme could represent an opportunity to introduce director development. The members of a board may be less reluctant to acknowledge deficiencies, when these relate to circumstances and challenges they have not previously encountered.

Directors and boards need to be equipped to implement strategy as well as to determine it. (In the case of some boards, this statement may need to be discussed.) Exercise 6.3 could be used as a sequel to Exercise 6.1, or combined with it in an 'away day' discussion.

Exercise 6.3: Preparation for implementation

With a specific focus upon the implementation of vision, goals, values and objectives, the board could be invited to re-address certain questions of Exercise 6.1. For example:

1 Did the formal and/or informal preparation (if any) that was received address (a) your 'implementation' needs as an individual director or (b) your requirements in relation to the board as a team?
2 How might the preparation (if any) that you received or undertook have been improved, or made more relevant?
3 What 'implementation' skills needs or requirements were not addressed by the preparation (if any) that you received or undertook?
4 Since becoming a director, what formal and/or informal preparation (if any) have you come across that might have been (more) relevant to (a) your 'implementation' needs as an individual director or (b) your requirements in relation to the board as a team?

Objectives derived from the vision should be achievable and measurable. The board should do whatever is necessary and practical by way of sharing, empowering, enabling, motivating, monitoring, facilitating, supporting, etc., to ensure that objectives are accomplished. In all these areas the board should consciously seek to 'add value', and should challenge the extent to which it has contributed.

Keeping directorial skills and awareness up to date

Once appointed, how do directors ensure that their qualities and skills remain relevant to the situations and contexts of their boards? The participants in a survey of directors undertaken by Alan Wakelam[3] were asked how they remain up to date with changes in the business environment and developments relating to their directorial roles.

The most common means of staying up to date was discussion with colleagues, which was cited by eight out of ten respondents (Table 6.1). This finding is consistent with the results of a survey undertaken by Adaptation Ltd in conjunction with the Research Group of the Institute of Personnel Management (IPM)[2] in which 'discussion with colleagues' was ranked as the most valuable source of information:

- Two-thirds of the respondents consider 'discussion with colleagues' to be 'very valuable'; while all but two respondents consider it to be either 'very valuable' or 'valuable'.
- A half of the participants who are board directors seek the advice of boardroom colleagues, while the other half turn to 'network' colleagues such as specialist or professional advisers, peer colleagues in other companies, or the IOD.

The 'IPM' survey[2] also throws some light on the colleagues that are consulted. The managing director, rather than the chairman, was the most

Table 6.1 *Ways in which directors keep up to date*

Method	%
Discussion with colleagues	80
Professional journals	77
Courses/seminars/workshops	71
Newspapers	62
Books/journals	33
Television	22
Radio	14

Source: The Training and Development of Company Directors, 1989.

frequently cited 'source of advice on directors and boards' for board directors.

Following 'discussion with colleagues', the next ranked ways in which directors keep up to date suggest that 'it is not clear that all respondents distinguished between direction and management issues in their replies':[3]

• Almost eight out of ten respondents read professional journals, one-third of the respondents cited 'books/journals', and over six out of ten referred to newspapers as a means of remaining up to date.
• Only about one in five respondents cited television, and about one in seven radio, as a means of remaining up to date. The print media would appear to be a more significant source of business information than the broadcast media.
• Seven out of ten respondents cited 'courses/seminars/workshops' as a means of keeping up to date. Although there is a relative lack of courses dealing specifically with direction, many directors appear to make some effort to keep their management skills current.

John Harper, head of professional development at the IOD, believes that: 'All professional directors should spend time off the job to help sharpen their skills, acquire new knowledge and update their thinking.'[1]

Active and passive updating

Directors often appear to be passive recipients of information, rather than active seekers of updating opportunities and materials. Many have not significantly changed their priority sources of updating information since becoming directors. Many European executives, it appears from one survey, would mourn the loss of the *National Geographic* more than the *Financial Times* if both ceased publication.[14]

The chairman has a special responsibility for the competence of directors and the effectiveness of a board,[15] and should ensure that all members of the board demonstrate a positive commitment to remaining up to date with prevailing circumstances and requirements. Their past experience, and that of those who advise them, might not be relevant to their particular situation or current roles as directors.

A chairman should also evaluate the extent to which updating activity results in a sharpened awareness and perspective. We shall see in Chapter 12 that directors need to look to the future when determining vision, establishing values and goals, planning, setting objectives and formulating policies. While the past can be a guide, decisions concerning the future require access to contemporary thought, and the judgement to distinguish what is likely to be of lasting significance from the ephemeral and transient.

Once appointed, directors need to ensure that their qualities and skills remain relevant to the situations and contexts of their boards. Exercise 6.4 could be used for this purpose.

Exercise 6.4: Staying up to date

Members of the board could be asked how they remain up to date with (a) changes in the business environment and (b) developments relating to their directorial roles. The results could then be compared with survey findings regarding 'directors in general' (see Table 6.1). The following questions could then be asked:

1 How effective are these means of staying up to date?
2 How relevant are the inputs that are obtained to the specific requirements of individuals in their directorial roles? (Information sources could be given a points ranking.)
3 To what extent are executive board members distinguishing between their roles as directors and managers respectively?
4 How committed are members of the board to remaining up to date?
5 Which colleagues are being consulted most often?
6 To what 'directors networks' do members of the board belong? (Should all directors be encouraged to belong to one such network?)
7 Does the pattern of consultation suggest the need for formal updating processes? (For example, issue monitoring, updates on changes affecting the legal duties and responsibilities of directors, etc.)
8 What role does, or should, the company secretary play in ensuring that the board is fully informed of developments relating to its function, accountabilities and responsibilities?
9 What helps or hinders the directors in their attempts to remain up to date?
10 What information, or updating service, would the directors like to receive, and how might this be provided?
11 Does the chairman actively assume responsibility for ensuring that the directors stay up to date?
12 Do the chairman and the chief executive act as role models in terms of their own commitment to remaining up to date?

There is no substitute for thought and a challenging attitude on the part of directors themselves. Specialist expertise is not as significant for directors as one might expect:[5]

- Many of the issues on boardroom agendas are relatively new. They may be unfamiliar to the world at large, and there may be little that is known or written about them.
- By the time 'the books are published' and particular issues are understood, they may no longer be of concern to the board. Events may have moved on. Some boardroom decisions have to be taken against tight deadlines and a high degree of uncertainty.

There are times when the situation or occasion will require directors to be self-reliant as the pressure of events may preclude lengthy consultation. In such cases, past investments of time by the chairman in building a confident, secure and balanced boardroom team can 'pay dividends'.

When advice is sought, it is often those with a similar perspective—and who understand the pressures and other circumstances in which board decisions are taken—to whom directors turn. Hence the value of a directors' network that can provide flexible access to those who may add value to, and offer a perspective on, contemporary understanding.

Sources of director development advice

Let us now consider sources of advice concerning the development of competent directors and effective boards. Sir John Harvey-Jones has commented that:

it is surprising how little guidance is available to people who become directors. . . . You try getting advice, guidance, a course, or a specialist book on the skills of being a good director of a company, and you will find almost nothing except a great deal of mystique. . . . Not only is there little external guidance about the changes required of you, but all too often no one inside the company guides you either.[16]

So, to whom do directors turn? Survey evidence suggests that chairmen are not resorting to many of the traditional sources of management education when seeking director development advice.[1,3,5] Why is this?

It is important that directors should distinguish between the various sources of advice in terms of the extent to which these focus upon the distinct development needs of directors, and understand how these needs differ from those of managers. As one interviewee stated:

Many consultants and some business schools attempt to 'retread' management courses for directors. They are often taught by people who have never been near a boardroom. It doesn't work. Directors have different expectations, a different awareness and a different viewpoint. They want to meet other directors, and to share boardroom experience.

The sources of advice on management development issues have been examined in an Adaptation Ltd survey sponsored by Surrey European Management School.[17] The sources cited most often by the respondents are internal human resource, personnel or training specialists, followed by external consultants and advisers (Table 6.2). Some respondents mentioned more than one source of advice.

Table 6.2 *Sources of authoritative advice and information on management development issues*

Source	No. of organizations
Internal HR/personnel/training specialists	41
External consultants/advisers	25
Business school	16
Professional and national/international associations	8
Other educational institutions	6
Various/others	5

Source: Human Resource Development for International Operation, 1990.

A different picture emerges when one turns to advice on director rather than management development. For example, in a survey undertaken by Adaptation Ltd for the IOD:[1]

- The IOD itself, and company lawyers and accountants, were the most frequently cited sources of authoritative advice and information on matters concerning 'professional development of and for the board'.
- The IOD also came first among 'external' sources of advice and help, and ranked ahead of management consultants and professional advisers. Business schools in this context were not mentioned by any of the respondents.

Those who were interviewed referred to the perceived 'objectivity' of both professional associations and professional firms of lawyers and accountants. It was felt that (a) a company's professional advisers would be in possession of background information and understanding that might help them to give more relevant advice, and (b) they could be expected to observe confidentiality.

The corporate HRD professional and advice on directors and boards

While the advice of 'internal' or corporate human resource development (HRD) professionals may be respected and sought in the area of management education and development, it does not appear to have an equivalent standing in the area of director development. Chairmen who were interviewed do not doubt the integrity and commitment of their company's HRD professionals, but doubt their boardroom experience and awareness. This impression is supported by survey findings:

- The 'IOD' survey[1] suggests that internal HRD specialists are not regarded as an authoritative source of advice on matters to do with directors and boards. As one chairman put it: 'They are not directors themselves. They are not in a position to evaluate how we perform, and they do not have a director's perspective concerning how we should perform. I worry that they will assess us as managers rather than as directors.'
- The results of the interim survey of personnel directors undertaken by Adaptation Ltd in conjunction with the Research Group of the

IPM[2] suggests that: 'internal expertise in the area of management development may not be relevant to the needs of those at board level'. In-company trainers are ranked as 'not very relevant' or 'irrelevant' as a source of development services by some six out of ten respondents.

There is recognition among personnel professionals that more effort needs to be devoted to improving directorial competence and board effectiveness. According to Ian Higgins of Nacanco:

When we recruit for the boardroom we tend to assume that the individual appointed is fully equipped for the job. It is perhaps taken for granted that highly motivated people will fill any gaps in their knowledge without need for prompting. . . . [This is] at best challengeable and at worst dangerous.[18]

Henry Fairweather, group services director of Scottish and Newcastle Breweries plc, believes that 'the personnel director, perhaps more than anyone else other than the chairman or chief executive, should see it as part of his role to assist the board to work as a cohesive team'.[18]

Director development services

The participants in both the 'IOD' survey[1] and the 'IPM' survey[2] were also asked to rank the relevance of various sources of director development services. One interviewee stated: 'Advice on what to do is one thing, help in doing it is another.'

The relevance that the 'IOD' survey respondents attached to the 'development of the competences of individual directors' services offered by various sources are summarized in Table 6.3. This presents the rankings if one adds together the 'very relevant' and 'relevant' replies.

From the table it can be seen that, in terms of the perceived relevance of their services for the development of the competences of individual directors, 'functional professional associations', and the IOD itself, rank ahead of 'specialist consultants' and 'postgraduate business schools'. The IOD offers a range of courses, workshops, conferences and publications which are also available to non-members.

Table 6.3 *Professional development services (individuals)*

Service	Ranking (%)*
Functional professional associations	70
Institute of Directors	63
Specialist consultants	60
In-company trainers	57
Postgraduate business schools	52
Open/distance learning	41
Management consultants	39
'Consortium' participation	38
Individual academics	33

* Ranking in terms of 'very relevant' and 'relevant'.

Note: Some respondents considered more than one service to be of relevance.

It should be remembered, when interpreting these findings, that the initial questionnaire was sent to those members of the IOD who were chairmen of the boards of their companies. These individuals might be expected to have a greater awareness of the IOD's own programmes than chairmen in general. However, the sample of companies covered by the 'IOD' survey[1] is thought to be representative of the distribution of company size in the UK.

The responses of the personnel director participants in the 'IPM' survey[2] are broadly similar to those of the chairmen returning the 'IOD' survey questionnaire.[1] For example, professional associations are given the highest ranking among various sources of services relating to the development of competent personnel directors. Approaching two-thirds of respondents rank them as 'very relevant'.

However, there are also some areas of difference. For example, participants in the 'IPM' survey[2] rank business schools more highly, and management consultancies less highly, than participants in the 'IOD' survey.[1]

Developing directors can be a relatively high-risk activity. In the case of management development: 'The *de facto* position is that most major multinationals recruit from, and make use of the services of, a number of business schools.'[4] Warren Bennis has warned that sending high fliers to business schools and on management courses can result in 'identikit people swamped in work'.[4]

Interview discussions suggest that CEOs are becoming more aware of the need for diversity. There is some resistance to the risks involved in putting 'all of one's eggs in one basket'. For a development need at main board level, there may be but one opportunity to address the problem.

Board development services

The relevance that the respondents to the 'IOD' survey respondents attached to the 'development of whole board's competences' services offered by various sources are summarized in Table 6.4. This again presents the rankings if one adds together the 'very relevant' and 'relevant' replies.

The table shows that 'specialist consultants' rank ahead of 'functional professional associations' when concern shifts from the requirements of individual directors to developing the competences of the board as a whole. There are consultancies, such as Adaptation Ltd, that specialize almost entirely in the area of boardroom issues and development.

The most relevant source of services relating to the board as a whole was thought to be the IOD, which ranked ahead of 'specialist consultants', and significantly ahead of 'postgraduate business schools'. Those interviewed found it difficult to identify specific IOD services relating to board rather than individual director development. However, they considered that the IOD had the capability and contacts to provide the services required.

Table 6.4 *Professional development services (whole board)*

Service	Ranking (%)*
Institute of directors	58
Specialist consultants	56
Functional professional associations	50
In-company trainers	40
Management consultants	39
Postgraduate business schools	36
'Consortium' participation	36
Open/distance learning	29
Individual academics	28

* Ranking in terms of 'very relevant' and 'relevant'

Note: Some respondents considered more than one service to be of relevance.

Development preferences

Professional bodies, such as the IOD, emerge as a clear 'first choice' in the field of director training,[1,5] while certain consultancies are acknowledged to have a special role in relation to developing the board as a team.[1] How strong are these preferences? Do they reflect availability or capability?

In the survey undertaken by Alan Wakelam:[3]

- Strong preferences were not evident. Over half of the respondents did not have a preference between courses, seminars or workshops run by the public sector, private consultancy or training firms, or professional bodies such as the IOD.
- Of those who did express a preference, more than two-and-a-half times as many opted for professional bodies rather than private firms, and three times as many preferred professional bodies as opposed to universities, polytechnics and colleges.
- Universities, polytechnics and colleges ranked last in terms of preferences. Interviews suggest these are 'not perceived as having any real expertise in "company direction" '.[5] While there were many management programmes 'on the market', relatively few of them appeared to focus on the distinct competences required by company directors.

The participants in Alan Wakelam's study were also asked for their views on the courses, seminars and workshops that had actually been used during the previous three years. Their responses suggest that the pattern of course provision does not necessarily reflect consumer preferences. For example:

- Over four out of ten of the respondents had attended private sector courses, compared with three out of ten who had attended courses organized by professional bodies.
- However, of those who had been on a private sector course only one in six expressed a preference for the private sector in respect of future

courses. More than twice as many expressed a preference for a course provided by a professional institute.

In reality, few professional bodies are equipped to offer director development services. However, they are described as 'independent', while in comparison, many consultancy firms are portrayed as having a vested interest in 'pushing' particular approaches. While able to deliver a 'packaged service', such firms, because of their organization and the specialist skills of their staff, find it difficult to adopt a holistic approach to the requirements of particular boards.

Perceptions of course providers

What perceptions do directors have of the major categories of provider of director development services? Some answers to this question are suggested by the surveys we have cited in this chapter.

The most diverse set of perceptions relate to consultancies. Those interviewed expressed a wide range of emotions from delight to disgust. While the services of a few suppliers appear to be highly regarded, the offerings of many consultancies are viewed with considerable suspicion:

- Alan Wakelam's survey[3] suggests that courses offered by management consultancies are not regarded as being as objective as those offered by professional and public bodies. Certain consultancies appear to regard those who attend their courses as a 'captive market', and attempt to sell them other services.
- In the case of the participants in the 'IPM' survey,[2] consultancies are ranked as 'not very relevant' or 'irrelevant' as a source of development services by over six out of ten respondents. The survey concluded that: 'Major consultancies have little if any credibility in the area of developing directors.'

The relative positioning of certain suppliers of development services is expressed diagrammatically in Figure 6.1.[5]

We saw in Chapter 3 that directors require both relevant knowledge and specific skills. It will be seen from Figure 6.1 that the perceptions and expectations of chairmen vary according to whether an educational or a professional institution is under discussion. Interviews with chairmen suggest:

- Each category of institution is considered more or less relevant, according to what is sought. For example, a business school might be considered more relevant in the case of a requirement for a 'board briefing session' on the impact that a development in the business environment might have on a company as a whole, while a course offered by a professional body might be perceived as more relevant to the needs of an individual director concerned with how his or her function might contribute to a response.
- Within each category, individual institutions are perceived to be of widely differing quality. When deciding which institutions to use, considerable emphasis is put upon the 'relevance' of a particular course

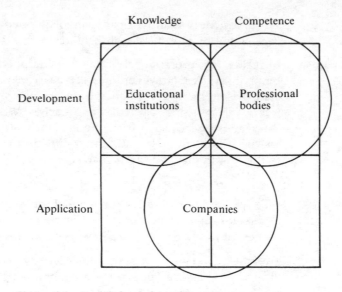

Figure 6.1   *Knowledge and competence*

or service, the credentials of the individuals behind it, and pragmatic considerations such as 'availability'. More than one interviewee used the phrase 'horses for courses'.

A board needs to ensure that it takes every opportunity to learn from relevant advice and expertise. At the same time, it needs to avoid inputs from sources of development advice and services that take no account of the distinction between direction and management or of the significant distinguishing features of the company's particular situation and context. Questions similar to those in Exercise 6.5 could be used to assess the existing sources of development advice and services that are used by a particular board.

Exercise 6.5: Sources of development advice and services

The following questions could be used to explore the relevance and value of different sources of development advice and services:

1 **To whom do you turn for (a) advice and (b) services relating to the development of individual directors?**
2 **To whom do you turn for (a) advice and (b) services relating to the development of the board as a whole?**

    (Use could be made of a 'questionnaire' sheet to collect 'ranking' information from each director.)

3 **How relevant and useful are these sources of advice and services? (For example: Do they focus upon the distinct development needs of directors?)**
4 **Why are these sources used? (Availability, lack of alternatives, outcome of positive search, etc.?)**

5 To what extent are each of the sources independent, objective and authoritative?

6 Do the services take into account the situation and circumstances of the company?

7 Who decides whether and how they should be used? (The individual director, the chairman, etc.?)

8 Does the use of director development advice and services occur within the context of an overall director development strategy and process?

9 What criteria are used to (a) select suppliers of services and (b) assess the relevance and quality of what is subsequently provided?

10 What is done to learn from the experiences of (a) other directors (e.g. directors' networks) and (b) other boards (e.g. benchmarking)?

11 Does the chairman ensure that the boardroom is an effective learning environment? (Are the members of the board encouraged to be open, and to share?)

Just raising such questions as those in Exercise 6.5 may alert directors to the existence of a wider range of possibilities. Because of the time it can take for a counsellor or adviser to build up a relationship with a particular board, and to understand its personalities and dynamics, some chairmen are reluctant to seek new sources of development input. Others adopt a different approach, and believe that over a period of time a board needs to be exposed to a variety of viewpoints, including those that challenge its assumptions—particularly as situations and circumstances change.

Educational and professional institutions

Let us look separately at director perceptions of educational institutions and professional associations. Some educational institutions are concerned with the development of competences and the application of knowledge. However, their primary focus is thought to be the development of knowledge (Figure 6.1).

Within the educational system, several business schools offer programmes that are aimed specifically at company directors. Programmes concerned with 'the company as a whole', such as long-term strategy and planning, appear to be preferred to those dealing with a particular functional specialism.[2] Personnel directors appear to be more willing than directors in general to consider business schools as a relevant source of director development services.[2]

Certain professional associations are active in the development of knowledge within their field. However, their main role is thought to be the development and assessment of competence and the monitoring of its application in the workplace. Individual associations tend to offer 'director level' services that are related to their functional area, for example, the Marketing Directors' Workshop of the Chartered Institute of Marketing.

The IOD is a professional association that was set up specifically to promote professionalism in direction. It offers an extensive range of courses, workshops, seminars and conferences for directors. Individual directors can undertake a programme of course modules leading to the IOD's Diploma in Company Direction.

All the institutions mentioned on Figure 6.1 could play a part in the development of a functional director. A comprehensive development programme could result in the collaboration of business schools, companies and professional associations. The network of relationships with particular business schools developed by the IOD is an example of such a collaboration.

Reasons for undertaking director development

There is little evidence of either individual directors or boards undertaking director development activities as a result of a systematic evaluation of performance against requirements in order to determine development needs. Few chairmen appear to give much thought to those development activities that might benefit particular members of their board, or the board as a whole. Participation in director development is more likely to be the result of a 'whim' or 'fancy' on the part of an individual director.

The most commonly cited reasons for participating in the IOD's director development programme are the opportunity 'to fill a particular knowledge gap' and 'a chance to meet other directors'.[3] Other 'attractions' of participating include 'the opportunity to examine a particular problem', and a chance to 'think about problems away from the office'.[3]

'Functional' professionals appear to be seeking to 'broaden' rather than 'deepen' when undertaking 'director development':[2]

- Their requirement is generally for directorial development activity that complements past professional development in a particular field, rather than functional programmes that extend and enrich expertise within the same specialist area.
- We have already seen in Chapter 5 that professional qualifications are not significant *per se* among the criteria used to select new appointees to the board.

On the whole, activities that develop overall strategic and business awareness are sought, rather than those whose purpose is to communicate professional or technical information. The development of strategic awareness is regarded as a core 'distinguisher' of what being a director is all about (discussed later in Chapter 13).

Awareness-building initiatives can be supplemented by whatever is necessary to meet the needs of a particular director. This may result in exposure to 'unfamiliar' knowledge and skills. For example, a board member with a marketing background might wish to increase his or her understanding of the meaning of financial information and company accounts.

The board as a learning environment

Employers—particularly large companies—are perceived as having an expanding role in the application and refinement of both knowledge and competence (Figure 6.1).[5] The larger professional practices and 'benchmark' companies are also contributing significantly to their development.

In the area of directorial knowledge and skills, the board should assume responsibility for its own development. Within the boardroom, the chairman has a special responsibility for ensuring that the directors are competent and that the board operates effectively. Competence and effectiveness will reflect their accountabilities and responsibilities, and the particular challenges and opportunities they face.

The boardroom itself represents the primary learning environment for most directors:

- The boardroom is 'where it happens'. Effective learning occurs when working and learning are integrated. A chairman should ensure that the culture and dynamics of the board are conducive to learning.
- The context of the boardroom, the nature of the individual company and of the business and market environment, can be a major influence upon director development needs. Within the boardroom, the director is aware of these factors.
- Each board comprises a combination of people that suits the situation and circumstances of the company. The subtleties and distinct culture of a particular boardroom may take some time to absorb. This process of absorption best occurs in the boardroom.
- A director is appointed to sit upon a specific board. The point was made in Chapter 2 that the competence of an individual director needs to be assessed in relation to a particular board. A director who makes a significant contribution to the work of one board may struggle to add value in another boardroom.
- A director is a member of a team. The qualities that individual directors need to develop and display are often those that relate to, and complement, the qualities of colleagues. It may not be easy to determine or assess them in the absence of fellow directors.

The process of learning to be a better director should continue throughout a directorial career.[7,8] The changing nature of the development requirement will reflect the evolving directorial challenge that faces a board. Detaching learning from the boardroom may give it the appearance of being a periodic requirement, rather than a continuous one.

In the next two chapters we shall consider how the boardroom might be used as a learning environment.

Checklist

1 What formal or informal preparation did the members of your company's board receive prior to their directorial appointments?
2 What practical steps have actually been taken to implement or undertake director development activities?
3 Have barriers to director development been identified, and have steps been taken to overcome them?
4 How much commitment is there in the boardroom to moving ahead and tackling the barriers that have been identified?
5 What do the directors do to keep up to date?

6 Are they passive recipients of background information, or do they actively seek out specific updating or development inputs?

7 How relevant and valuable are the director development services used by the board and its members?

8 Why are the services being provided? How did the 'relationship' begin?

9 Is the board a competent purchaser of director development services?

10 Is there a systematic evaluation of 'need', followed by a careful matching of 'service' options to particular requirements?

11 Is the culture of the board, and are its dynamics, conducive to learning?

12 Do the directors actively learn from each other, and from their experiences?

Notes and references

1 Colin Coulson-Thomas, *Professional Development of and for the Board*. A questionnaire and interview survey undertaken by Adaptation Ltd of company chairmen. A summary has been published by the IOD, February 1990.

2 Colin Coulson-Thomas, *The Role and Function of the Personnel Director*. An interim Adaptation Ltd survey carried out in conjunction with the Research Group of the Institute of Personnel Management, 1991.

3 Alan Wakelam, *The Training and Development of Company Directors*. A report on a questionnaire survey undertaken by the Centre for Management Studies, University of Exeter for the Training Agency, December 1989.

4 Anne Ferguson, 'The leading light shows vision and personality', *The Independent on Sunday*, (18 February 1990), 29.

5 Colin Coulson-Thomas and Alan Wakelam, *The Effective Board: Current Practice, Myths and Realities*. An IOD discussion document, 1991.

6 Colin Coulson-Thomas, *Transforming the Company: Bridging the Gap between Management Myth and Corporate Reality.*, Kogan Page, 1992.

7 Colin Coulson-Thomas, *Creating Excellence in the Boardroom*, McGraw-Hill, 1993.

8 Alan Mumford, Graham Robinson and Don Stradling, *Developing Directors, The Learning Process*, Manpower Services Commission, 1987; and Alan Mumford, Peter Honey and Graham Robinson, *Director's Development Guidebook: Making Experience Count*, Director Publications, 1990.

9 Jane Simms and Heather Farmbrough, 'Unfit for power or on course for achievement?', *Financial Director* (September 1992), 57–60.

10 Charles Batchelor, 'The boardroom beckons', *Financial Times* (3 March 1992); and *Boardroom Agenda*, No. 2 (May 1992), 16–17.

11 Michael Tushman, William Newman and David Nadler, 'Executive leadership and organisational evolution, managing incremental and discontinuous change', in R. Kilmann and T.J. Covey (eds), *Corporate Transformation*, Jossey-Bass, 1988, pp. 102–30.

12 Michael Beer and Elsie Walton, 'Developing the competitive organisation, interventions and strategies', *American Psychologist*, **45**, No. 2, (February 1990), 154–61.

13 Adrian Davies, *Strategic Leadership*, Woodhead-Faulkner, 1991.

14 MJP Carat International, *International Media in Perspective*, MJP Carat International, 1992; Gary Mead, 'TV looms larger for British execs', *Financial Times* (25 August 1992), 2.

15 Sir Adrian Cadbury, *Company Chairman*, Director Books, 1990.

16 Sir John Harvey-Jones, *Making it Happen: Reflections on Leadership*, 3rd impression, Fontana Paperbacks, March 1989, pp. 185–6.

17 Colin Coulson-Thomas, *Human Resource Development for International Operation*. A survey sponsored by Surrey European Management School, Adaptation Ltd, 1990.

18 Colin Coulson-Thomas, 'What the personnel director can bring to the boardroom table', *Personnel Management* (October 1991), 36–9.

7 How directors should be prepared

We have examined (a) the qualities that are desirable in directors and those that are actually sought (for the accountabilities, duties and responsibilities of directors, see Chapter 12), and (b) how directors are, or in most cases are not, prepared for their boardroom roles. So how should directors be prepared? Can they be prepared? Do they need to prepare themselves?

It is very difficult to generalize about how directors and boards should be developed. Boards and companies vary enormously in their nature, situation and context, and development requirements need to reflect the composition and circumstances of each individual board (to be discussed in Chapters 12 and 14). However, in relation to the particular context, the chairman[1] has certain responsibilities.

- The chairman should ensure that all new directors are properly prepared for the boardroom. At least, they need to be made aware of their accountabilities, duties and responsibilities.
- The chairman should ensure that the directorial skills of all directors remain current, and relevant to changes in the situation and circumstances of the company. The board and its individual members should 'develop the business' and 'develop with the business'.

The exercises and questions raised in this chapter are concerned with 'taking the temperature', assessing and mapping the development needs of both 'new' and existing directors, and exploring the potential for informal and formal learning, and the support of 'learning directors'.

Obstacles to director development

Those about to embark on a director development quest should not be under any illusions. There are many practical obstacles to director development, and these must be acknowledged and addressed. Understanding the barriers and the 'hinders' is best done at the outset, if a practical programme is to emerge.

The preparation of individuals for the boardroom is an activity that is not free of controversy. Director development is not always assumed to be a 'good thing'. Activities, such as 'top team development', that neither reflect the distinction between direction and management nor focus on the distinct requirements of the directors of a particular board, might do more harm than good. Much will depend upon who is being developed, by whom, and for what.

Executive directors, such as personnel directors who have functional responsibilities and are secure in their specialist knowledge, sometimes resist attempts to 'broaden' them. Henry Fairweather, group services director of Scottish and Newcastle Breweries plc, believes that 'the personnel director, like any other board director, has to think of himself or herself first as a director of the company and only secondly as a functional specialist'.[2] According to Nick Cowan, who has served on the boards of both TSB England and Wales and Unigate plc: 'The personnel director should be a businessman first and a personnel practitioner second.'[2]

It is particularly important that the role of the director is understood. According to David O'Brien, chief executive of the National and Provincial Building Society: 'It is difficult to build competencies for a role which is not understood. The director role is different from that of a manager, and if its particular competency requirements were understood people would be able to chose whether or not to occupy director roles.'

We saw in the last chapter that many directors are very reluctant to acknowledge or address their development needs. A position on a board can be a source of great personal satisfaction, the culmination of a lifetime of endeavour, an acknowledgement that one has 'arrived'. Addressing the development needs of directors and boards requires sensitivity and tact.

Directors can be resentful of, and may become annoyed with, people who suggest they are not entirely competent. When the inference emanates from those who are not directors, and especially when it comes from 'specialists' or 'trainers', annoyance sometimes turns to anger. As one interviewee put it: 'If I said that within the company, I would be "out the door".'

Directors who do recognize the need for development may come from diverse backgrounds, and may have differing reasons for seeking help.[3] Organizations offering formal programmes tend to focus upon the role of the board and the duties and responsibilities of the director. The distinction between direction and management might also be covered. Further and tailored development requires the continuing commitment of the individual director.

Scepticism and caution

Given the obstacles to director development, the support of the chairman and the chief executive is clearly desirable, but it should not be assumed. Many chairmen appear to adopt the view that directors are 'born, not made'.

As a first step, the attitudes of the chairman and members of the board towards director development should be thoroughly understood. An examination of a selection of comments concerning the attributes required by the competent director illustrates the nature of the 'director development challenge':

People either have personal qualities such as wisdom, judgement, tact and diplomacy or they do not.

How can a person be aware of the business environment when his or her past focus has been almost entirely 'internal'?

People in head office staff functions never go near customers. They have little if any awareness of what constitutes value to customers.

Some people have vision and others do not. You can't make a silk purse out of a sow's ear.

A life largely spent in one function in similar organizations is hardly likely to result in a balanced perspective.

Entrepreneurs are born with business acumen. If managers had it they would now be 'out there' running businesses.

Knowledge of the legal duties and financial accountabilities of directors is arid and hypothetical when it doesn't apply to you. It's boring and puts people off.

How can you get any feeling of board conduct and practice if you have never sat in a boardroom?

Skills in such areas as decision making, strategy formulation and teamwork in the boardroom are the result of practice. They cannot be taught.

If the experience needed in the boardroom was widespread in the company, a director appointment might not be so pressing.

How can you teach ethical awareness?

Some people just lack sensitivity to the attitudes and values of others.

Really good managers are scarce, and should be employed to 'deliver the business' rather than 'worry about strategy'.

As a manager you are given a job to do, you don't have to arbitrate between the interests of stakeholders.

These comments have all been made by those who challenge either the desirability, or feasibility, of director development. However, even sceptical board members may not deny the existence of a development 'problem' or 'challenge'. Many of those who are wary or cautious are not happy with their own preparation for the boardroom, or with the effectiveness of their boards.

The sceptics remain to be convinced that the services they have encountered would significantly change directorial attitudes, awareness and perspective. As one chairman stated:

I would like to be persuaded that something existed along the lines of management development which I could buy. But, heaven knows, changing managerial attitudes and behaviour is bad enough. How much more difficult it is in the boardroom, especially when those supplying services do not even attempt to understand the attitudes and personalities involved. The options that are safe tend to be bland and cosmetic.

Champions in the boardroom

Director development needs its champions in the boardroom, and if they are to become catalysts they may themselves have to be encouraged. There are many who are 'interested', but too few who are sufficiently enthusiastic and committed to persuade board colleagues to act.

Even those who favour director development tend to be cautious, especially when activities cannot be linked to a particular corporate initiative such as 'quality'. Let us now consider some other views that have been put by those who are generally supportive of steps to improve director competence or board effectiveness:

What personal qualities do people display in their family, social and recreational lives? Personal qualities can be indentified.

Customers are people, not statistics and trends. The awareness of employees does not come from our board papers but from the fact that they consume and use the company's products.

The boardroom can be rarefied and remote. The manager is in daily touch with employees and customers, and knows how they feel and 'sees it as it is'.

The manager knows that vision and strategy can be just 'words on paper'.

Perspective comes from living through frequent changes of strategy and keeping your sanity.

It looks good in the strategic plan, but managers have their feet on the ground and have to make it work.

When colleagues are made redundant, accountability 'comes home to roost'.

Negotiating with customers and suppliers sharpens your negotiating skills, and it is the managers rather than the directors who form the quality improvement teams.

Many managers sit on committees and councils outside their work, and others could be invited to sit on the board of a non-competing company.

The directors would benefit from spending a day with a member of the salesforce.

Staff can be involved in the drawing up and communication of a corporate code of conduct.

Working in cross-functional and international teams makes people aware that others may have different attitudes and values.

In comparison with colleagues, a good manager might make an even better executive director.

In a matrix organization full of project groups, and with everyone overworked, you survive by juggling priorities and steering a course between many competing claims upon your time.

This varied selection of views is taken from interviews with chairmen who are 'receptive' to development activity at board level. They acknowledge that directors are people, and as such they have both positive and negative attributes. Frequent comparisons are made with the experiences of managers, and managerial roles, in order to 'illustrate' a particular directorial requirement.

Some of those interviewed also believe that if deficiencies can be understood, in the context of the boardroom, it ought to be possible to address them. According to one chairman: 'The cautions and concerns will remain until you take positive steps to tackle them.'

There is some overlap of views between 'supporters' of director development and the 'cynics'. The supporters tend to put more stress upon deficiencies within the boardroom, and the existence of directorial potential outside it.

Assessing views and attitudes

Before embarking on a director development programme, it is advisable to assess and discuss relevant directorial views, attitudes and prejudices. These are likely to have a significant influence upon the extent of director commitment to, and involvement in, development activities. A series of questions, such as those in Exercise 7.1, could be used to bring them into the open in order to increase the extent of self-awareness in the boardroom.

Exercise 7.1 Taking the temperature

In order to judge how receptive a board might be to director development, directors could be invited to discuss either (a) one or more of the comments quoted in the section on 'scepticism and caution' or (b) a more general comment such as 'directors are born rather than made'. The purpose of such a discussion is to address the following types of questions:

1 How receptive is the board to the concept of director development?
2 What are the main concerns and reservations, and how might these be tackled?
3 How ready is the board to undertake development activities?
4 How self-aware is the board (e.g. honest, objective, etc.) concerning its development needs?
5 What priority does director development have?
6 Are there particular assumptions that need to be changed, prejudices that need to be tackled, and misunderstandings that need to be corrected?
7 Do attitudes need to be changed prior to introducing director development, or could they be modified while undertaking it?
8 Who are likely to be the champions of director development?
9 Are there particular directors who are cautious or sceptical, and if so, how might their concerns be addressed? (Where are the sensitivities?)
10 What are the main 'helps' and 'hinders' in terms of directorial attitudes?
11 How might the barriers be overcome? (Remember the difficulty of changing deeply ingrained attitudes.)

Where director development is not occurring, a key first step is to identify the best person to initiate director development activity: chairman, chief executive, 'champion', etc. In the case of reluctance or scepticism, the launch of a development programme could be timed to coincide with a particular event or set of circumstances. The development in question could relate specifically to the board (e.g. an anticipated or expected review of, and change in, the composition of the board), or to the company as a whole (e.g. corporate transformation or the introduction of total quality).

Inducting the new director

I have suggested in a companion book to this volume that the appointment of new directors to the board can represent an opportunity to initiate director development activity: 'The preparation of new directors for the boardroom may not be perceived by the existing directors to be as 'threatening' as directly confronting their deficiencies.'[4]

Even an experienced director will need to be inducted into the practices, ways and ethos of a particular board to which he or she has been appointed. Understanding the features, mores and subtleties that distinguish one boardroom from another is the mark of the sensitive and astute director. The process of adjustment, and the assimilation of stakeholder concerns and corporate issues, activities, priorities and capabilities can take some time.

The chairman should acquaint a newly appointed director with the routine of the board, opportunities for informal contacts between meetings, practice regarding the acquisition and presentation of information, how the boardroom agenda is drawn up and managed, and the role of the company secretary. A new board member should be provided with written copies of any agreed board procedures and processes, and be encouraged to ask questions, as existing directors may take certain familiar practices for granted.

Information of particular value to a new director might include:

- Details of the role and responsibilities of each director, together with a 'thumbnail sketch' of their particular qualities, and how their attributes complement those of other members of the boardroom team.
- Any formal criteria that are used to select directors, the nature of the qualities, conduct and contributions expected of them, and how individual directors are assessed.
- In the case of a subsidiary or public sector board, any strategic direction that has been provided by the group board or appropriate government minister, and details of the group or public accountability framework, respectively.
- A summary of the legal duties and responsibilities of directors, and their accountabilities to the various stakeholders in the business.
- In the case of a quoted company, details of Stock Exchange requirements; while those who have not previously served upon the board of a public company might benefit from an introduction to the world of investor relations, financial reporting arrangements and issues, and responsibilities and practice in relation to 'price-sensitive information'.
- Copies of relevant policy guidelines or corporate codes covering such matters as disclosure of interests, 'price-sensitive information', corporate hospitality, how to handle offers of gifts, etc.

- Details of past, recent, and any likely future developments relating to the board; and the key people and activities, and core capabilities and processes of the company.
- How members of the board relate formally and informally to each other, the chief executive and the chairman; and how they are briefed and supported in their role as directors.

When discussing roles and responsibilities, particular attention should be paid to the respective roles of chairman and chief executive,[5] and the remits of any committees of the board. A briefing from the company secretary on the more technical aspects of board procedures, and legal duties and responsibilities, is also advisable.

All directors should know to whom they should turn—for example, to the company secretary or the chairman—when they require information or counselling, or when they wish to raise issues.

We saw in Chapter 3 that certain aspects of legal and financial knowledge are of particular importance. A director will need sufficient knowledge in these areas to discharge his or her fiduciary, financial and reporting responsibilities.

Directors who are new to a company (for example, a non-executive director) may require a more extensive briefing on plans, policies, products, services, processes, values and culture of the company. Company expectations, attitudes and confidence can be significantly 'conditioned' by corporate history and the collective experience of the directors and the employees.

Assessing induction arrangements

The new director needs to be prepared for a directorial role and integrated into an existing boardroom team. The following questions could be posed to check the adequacy of existing induction arrangements, and to assess an induction programme:

- Are all 'new' directors properly prepared for their directorial accountabilities, legal duties and responsibilities, and their boardroom roles and responsibilities?
- Does the induction of new directors include their integration into the boardroom team?
- Are 'new' directors made aware of the vision, goals, values and objectives of the company?
- Who is responsible for the induction programme, and is it periodically reviewed and kept up to date?
- Does someone assess the impact of 'new' directors upon the existing members of the board?
- Are 'new' directors encouraged to ask questions, and do they have access to all the information they need? (What is their view of the induction process?)
- Does the induction process allow the other directors to learn from the initial impressions of a 'new' director?
- How might the induction programme affect the attitudes, conduct or

commitment of a 'new' director? (Are there 'negatives' that need to be addressed?)

- How easy is it for a 'new' director to be accepted as an integrated and trusted member of the boardroom team? (What are the main 'helps' and 'hinders'?)

These and other questions could in some cases be addressed by the board itself. Having assessed the current situation, the next step is to determine what needs to be done, either by a particular person (e.g. chairman, chief executive or company secretary), or by the board as a whole, to improve the induction process.

The induction and development needs of non-executive directors should not be overlooked. A survey of non-executive directors has shown that while 'companies rightly want non-executive directors to participate actively in board decision-making, . . . many of them have not been picked or trained to provide the added value of independence. Some have not even been told what is expected of them.'[6]

Mapping development needs

During a boardroom induction process, particular attention should be paid to the integration of individuals into a boardroom team as 'excellence in the boardroom is the product of relationships, the chemistry of interaction, the dynamics of the group or team.'[5]

In the case of some boards, the rate at which the membership of the board 'turns over' is such that it could be many years before a 'critical mass' of directors receive the benefit of a formal induction programme. Hence, certain deficiencies may need to be addressed by other forms of development activity.

The previous chapters of this book have contained a number of exercises for (a) determining and prioritizing skill deficiencies and (b) assessing development requirements. It is usually helpful to obtain an overview of the key directorial attribute deficiencies, before these are matched with appropriate development activities.

To ensure that all the knowledge and skill requirements of Chapter 3 are addressed, use could be made of a checklist, such as that shown in Table 7.1. This allows the importance of each area of knowledge or skill to be assessed.

Table 7.1 is not intended to be a model that should be applied to all boards. Those compiling a checklist may need to be selective if directors are to focus on the areas of greatest significance for the individual company. When such checklists are drawn up, the facilitating and transformation skills that may be needed in the boardroom are sometimes overlooked.

Individual and group needs

A separate checklist, similar to Table 7.1, could be used for each director, to assess the importance of further development in relevant knowledge or skill areas. The individual results could then be summarized to reveal the pattern of development needs for the board as a whole. By way of

Developing Directors

Table 7.1 *The relative importance of knowledge or skill requirements*

Area of knowledge or competence	Very important	Important	Not very important	Un-important
Legal knowledge:				
Role of the board	1	2	3	1
Duties and responsibilities, etc.	3	3	1	
Financial knowledge:				
Financial reporting requirements, etc.				
Knowledge of boardroom practice				
Decision making in the boardroom, etc.				
Personal skills and competences:				
Strategic awareness				
Negotiating skills, etc.				
Boardroom issues:				
Stakeholder relationships				
Board structure, etc.				
Facilitating skills and processes:				
Management processes				
Business processes, etc.				
Corporate transformation skills:				
Empowering, involving, etc.				
Others (please specify):				

an example, two lines of Table 7.1 have been filled in for a particular board with seven members:

- The role of the board appears fairly well understood. A group of experienced directors are both familiar and comfortable with the board's main functions. However, one director appears to be under some misunderstanding as to the purpose of the board. In this instance, the chairman had a lengthy discussion over dinner with the director concerned.
- The legal duties and responsibilities of directors appear less well understood. In this case, a recent change in the law concerning the potential liabilities of directors was thought to be of especial significance, because of the nature of the company's business. The requirement for 'updating' was met by a board briefing session arranged by the company secretary.

When using a development needs 'map' along the lines of Table 7.1, it should be borne in mind that certain directors may require individualized programmes, while there may be particular boardroom roles such as chairman, CEO or non-executive director that deserve, or demand, special attention.

Remembering the The development requirements of the business should also be
'needs of the business' addressed. Priority should be given to the knowledge and skill needs
that are most appropriate to the nature, situation, circumstances,
ambitions and priorities of the company.

Effectiveness in the boardroom is not sought for its own sake, but in
order to better serve the company and satisfy its stakeholders. The
board should have the capacity to 'grow' to match the capability of the
company, and the challenges and opportunities it faces, if it is to be a
'facilitator' rather than a constraint.

The business and market environment in which the company operates
should not be overlooked, as external changes can have a profound
impact on a company.[7] A board needs to monitor and respond to
significant developments in the external environment (see Chapter 11).

Using a checklist or questionnaire in the style of Table 7.1, the relative
importance of each director's need for development in the various areas
of knowledge and skill identified in Chapter 3 could be assessed. This
could be done by the directors themselves, or by the chairman. In the
case of a board that has a culture of openness and trust, the directors
could be encouraged to discuss each others requirements. Exercise 7.2
lists some questions that could then be asked.

Exercise 7.2: The mapping of development needs

**Following the use of a development needs 'map' in the style of Table 7.1, and
considering the overall picture for the board as a whole:**

1 **What can be learned from the overall pattern of needs? (For example, is the
board composed of subgroups with very different development needs?)**
2 **How effective, overall, is the board? (Is there a fundamental problem to be
addressed?)**
3 **Are there particular boardroom roles for which specific preparation is
required (e.g. chairman or non-executive director)?**
4 **Does the pattern of responses suggest that either formal or informal development is likely to be the main priority?**
5 **Should the self-assessments of individual directors be compared with those
of the chairman or boardroom colleagues? (What does this reveal about the
self-awareness or perceptiveness of certain individuals?)**
6 **Are the requirements (to meet deficiencies) for development that emerge the
source of operational problems in the boardroom, or the result of them?**
7 **Have the needs of the business been addressed? (Have the situation and circumstances of the company, and relationships with stakeholders, been taken
into account?)**
8 **What is the scale of the development challenge? (Is a major programme
needed, or are there just gaps to fill?)**

It is important, when doing this type of exercise, to identify and agree
the key priorities. The 'vital few' development needs that really must be

tackled should be underlined, and appropriate actions and activities identified.

The overall map of development requirements might reveal a general 'problem' that cannot be tackled by development initiatives alone. For example, the issue could really be one of membership and composition of the board. When in doubt, a useful question to ask of any proposed activity is: Would you do it if it were your company?

Addressing development requirements

Having identified development needs, the next step is to find some means of addressing them. Is formal or informal activity relevant? Should a response be aimed at individual directors, or at the board as a whole? Developing the individual director is the main concern of this chapter, while developing the board as a team will be considered in the next chapter.

Various checklists could be used to assist and record particular categorizations. An example, based upon a table that has already been considered (Table 7.1), is shown as Table 7.2. Again this is for the purposes of illustration, and is not intended as a model. Another form might include further columns covering the various formal and informal development options available.

How the effectiveness of 'functional' directors might be improved is suggested by a study of senior personnel professionals.[8] One respondent summed up the views of many directors by suggesting that the effectiveness of the board could be improved if there was 'less concentration on day-to-day issues, however vital, and more on strategic issues'. Another widespread requirement is for 'more time to reflect'.

Typical views on how the preparation of executive directors could be improved include: 'a line role prior to appointment', and experience in 'different types of organization' or in 'multi-functional project teams'. These options for 'broadening' are not made available to the specialists who join many companies.

It would appear that many directors have a requirement for coaching, counselling and mentoring. Discussion groups, workshops and networks, and opportunities for 'learning by doing' or working with other board members are all cited by directors themselves as preferred development options.[8]

Potential directors

In Chapter 5 we saw that many companies do not find it easy to identify potential directors, and 'boardroom succession' is an issue that concerns many chairmen. Certain director development activities, including the assessment of direction competences and qualities, could also be relevant, and of value, to a wider pool of people from whom 'tomorrow's directors' might be selected.

Although directors do have distinct requirements, it may be possible for some activities to be undertaken by existing members of the board and

Table 7.2 *Meeting the development need*

Area of knowledge or competence	Formal course	Informal learning	Individual programme	Board exercise
Legal knowledge: Role of the board	----------	----------	----------	----------
Duties and responsibilities, etc.	----------	----------	----------	----------
Financial knowledge: Financial reporting requirements, etc.	----------	----------	----------	----------
Knowledge of boardroom practice	----------	----------	----------	----------
Decision making in the boardroom, etc.	----------	----------	----------	----------
Personal skills and competences: Strategic awareness	----------	----------	----------	----------
Negotiating skills, etc.	----------	----------	----------	----------
Boardroom issues: Stakeholder relationships	----------	----------	----------	----------
Board structure, etc.	----------	----------	----------	----------
Facilitating skills and processes: Management processes	----------	----------	----------	----------
Business processes, etc.	----------	----------	----------	----------
Corporate transformation skills: Empowering, involving, etc.	----------	----------	----------	----------
Others (please specify):				
----------------------------	----------	----------	----------	----------
----------------------------	----------	----------	----------	----------

by those identified as potential future members of the board. For example, there should be a shared board and senior management commitment to the vision, goals, values or objectives of a company.

Senior managers and directors may need to work closely together. Common activities can help to build a unity of purpose, and nurture the relationships needed to introduce total quality successfully, or to 'internationalize' attitudes and perspectives. They may also provide precious opportunities for those with potential to learn from the relatively small number of people in the company with outstanding leadership qualities.[9]

Where a board establishes and nurtures mutual trust and understanding, the number of occasions on which the relationship between the directors and management has to survive shocks can be much reduced. According to Sir Allen Sheppard, the chairman and CEO of Grand Metropolitan plc: 'It's important that we don't expect our management to surprise us with a problem, and we similarly shouldn't be in the business of surprising them.'[10]

At the same time, relationships should not become too close, as directors can find themselves so engrossed in the details of implementation that they lose their sense of objectivity and detachment.[11] A sense of balance should be maintained.

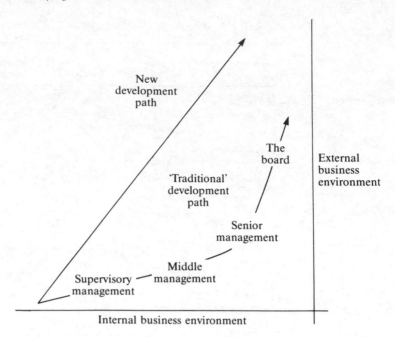

Figure 7.1   *Corporate development activity*

In many companies, while a wide range of managers are now focusing upon building relationships with customers and require 'external awareness', consideration of the external business environment is confined to senior management programmes. A new development path[1] that paid equal attention to internal and external requirements (Figure 7.1) would help to enlarge the 'external awareness' of a wider range of people, and strengthen the foundations upon which director development could be built.

New paths to the boardroom

Organizations are transitioning from bureaucratic to flatter and more flexible network forms.[12] While, as we saw in Chapter 5, the 'traditional' route to the boardroom may have been via a functional ladder up a corporate hierarchy, the route to the boardroom in the emerging 'network organization' is more likely to consist of a movement around the network in order to gain some understanding of its various members and processes (Figure 7.2).[1]

In such circumstances, vision, values and goals may have to be shared with other members of the value chain, in order to hold the network together. Without this 'cement', it could fragment. A board may need to ensure that any vision, values and goals it articulates are compatible with those of key members of the network.

A wider range of people will need qualities such as empathy, awareness, tolerance, etc., in order to build and sustain relationships with customers and other members of the network. They will also need an understanding

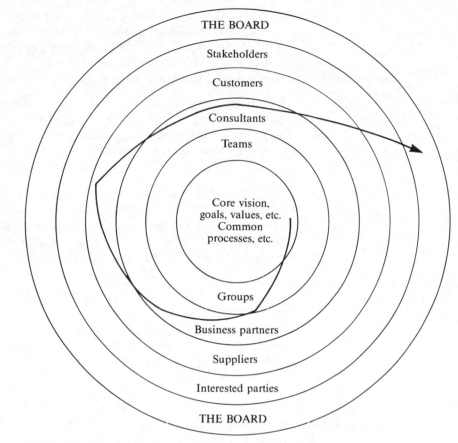

Figure 7.2 *The network organization: the route to the boardroom*

of the key cross-functional and inter-organizational processes that identify and deliver the value that is sought by customers.

Director development can focus upon incremental requirements—for example, refining the qualities just mentioned in terms of relationships with particular stakeholders. Of itself, however, it is unlikely to be sufficient. Warren Bennis is of the opinion that training courses do not make business leaders.[13] He advocates the provision of a succession of opportunities to grow and develop by learning through experience, and regards transfers and service on taskforces and special projects concerned with strategic issues as especially beneficial.

Informal learning and the learning board

We saw in the last chapter that many directors express a preference for informal over formal learning.[14] While informal learning can be particularly effective when it is conscious and actively encouraged,[15] in many companies it is unconscious and accidental.

Some directors have had unfortunate experiences of learning in the past, and may need to be encouraged to actively participate in learning activities. The chairman or CEO should become a learning role model. All directors should (a) aim to learn from their experiences, (b) regularly review what they have learned, (c) share what they have learned with fellow directors and (d) actively seek out new learning opportunities and 'learning triggers'.

A daily or weekly review of what has been learned can help consolidate insights that might otherwise be forgotten. Learning should become a way of life, and the meetings of the board should be considered as a prime and rich learning opportunity. Significant decisions and discussions could be reviewed in order to assess what has been learned from them.

The board could make a conscious attempt to create a learning organization.[16] 'Benchmarking', or the organized learning from others with similar problems in non-competing companies, could be used to encourage all employees to be open and receptive. A review or learning element could be built into certain, or all, main board and management processes.

Working together with external facilitators on a strategic business project can help to focus the board as a team upon issues of broader concern than individual irritants and day-to-day pressures. Looking back after such an experience, one director commented on the board's previous approach: 'The problems of the day were all-consuming. We were hands on managers rather than directors.'[17]

Learning opportunities Sir John Harvey-Jones considers joining the board of another company as a non-executive director to be a significant and challenging experience: 'There is little doubt in my personal experience that the task of becoming a non-executive director of another company is the biggest learning experience of all for the professional businessman.'[18]

Opportunities for informal learning are not confined to the boardroom, and further examples are given in Example 7.1.

What represents a useful 'learning opportunity' will depend upon an individual's development needs. Some directors find that as a result of a search for learning opportunities they discover that they have been learning intuitively for many years. This realization can motivate them to become more proactive and disciplined in their approach to informal learning.

We do not all learn in the same way. Each director should be encouraged to understand his or her own learning potential and preferences, and to adopt a personal approach to informal learning that builds upon natural strengths.[4]

Some directors may need to be persuaded of the rich variety of potential learning environments that exist. Exercise 7.3 could be used to bring the range of opportunities to their attention.

Example 7.1 *Opportunities for informal learning*

- Board and management meetings
- Living through major corporate developments
- Visits to corporate locations
- Travel and external visits
- Corporate and social events
- Contacts with customers, suppliers and business partners
- Public appointments
- Non-executive directorships
- Professional activities
- Recreational activities
- The family and friends

Exercise 7.3: Informal learning

Members of the board could be asked to draw up a list of opportunities for informal learning along the lines of Example 7.1. The following questions could then be addressed:

1 When did you first become aware of the value of informal learning?
2 Are you encouraged to learn? (What difference does it make? Who notices or cares?)
3 Which of the opportunities for informal learning do you grasp, and why?
4 Which do you regard as your 'priority learning opportunities' and why? (Why do you use some approaches more often than others?)
5 Which opportunities for informal learning offer the most potential in relation to your current boardroom role and particular responsibilities? (Then: How might you better tap this potential?)
6 Do you share with fellow directors what you have learned? (How open are you with fellow directors?)
7 Who do you learn with or from? (Do you network? Are there certain people you use as sounding boards?)
8 Who could you learn from (e.g. the chairman, the non-executive directors)?
9 How effective are you at learning from (a) subordinates and (b) customers?
10 Do you regularly review what you have learned? (Do you record what you have learned?)
11 What, if anything, do you know about (a) your own learning potential and (b) your learning preferences? (What does this suggest about the approach to informal learning that you should adopt?)
12 How proactive are you? (Do you set out consciously to create environments in which to learn?)
13 What new opportunities for learning could you create (e.g. volunteering for a certain role or task)?

The responses of the individual directors to the questions of Exercise 7.3 could reveal a great deal about the board's overall approach to learning. In the light of this and other information obtained, the following are among the questions that should be considered.

- Does the board regularly review what it has learned?
- Who on the board comes closest to being an informal learning 'role model' and why?
- Is the board itself a learning 'role model'?
- What (or who) 'helps' or 'hinders' informal learning in the boardroom? (Consider time, encouragement, presentation of information to assist understanding, etc.)
- Is learning built into the main board and management processes?
- Are there techniques such as 'benchmarking' that could be used to encourage learning throughout the organization?
- Do the culture and values of the company encourage active learning?

The responses to the above questions could suggest that one or more individuals should be encouraged to act as champions and catalysts of informal learning. The CEO may not emerge as the 'role model'. Many CEOs do not find it easy either to be open with colleagues, or to create informal learning opportunities within their own companies.

When CEOs raise issues, people often jump to conclusions, and sensitive matters may need to be treated with some caution. The CEO might benefit from a network of external contacts with people who are willing to act as 'sounding boards'.

Directors' networks   Confident directors build networks of people with shared interests and complementary skills, to whom they can turn for perception and perspective. It is possible to judge some people by the calibre and 'spread' of their 'network'.

To a certain extent, one can judge directors by the company they keep. Some have a penchant for associating with those who have already retired, and the cosy, comfortable and undemanding world of the golf club bar. Others are seeking opportunities to gain fresh insights into new worlds of experience and what may lie beyond the 'cutting edge'. The latter approach may be more desirable in a turbulent business environment. Figure 7.3 identifies some of those with whom a director could network, and from whom a director could learn.

Many executive directors have access to various sources of professional advice on matters relating to their management responsibilities. Fewer directors acknowledge the value of, or necessity for, a 'direction', as opposed to a 'management', input which is accessible on a continuing basis. To effectively contact and involve advisers and other directors as required, one needs some form of directors' 'network'.

All, or some, of the directors could constitute a corporate 'directors' net work'. This could create opportunities for interaction and learning apart

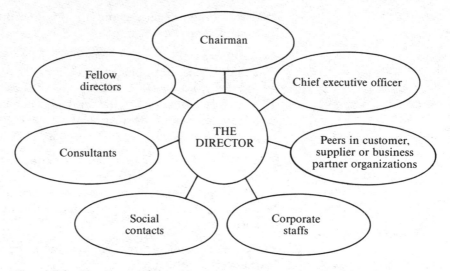

Figure 7.3 The director's network

from the formal meetings of the board. This can overcome some of the barriers of 'functionalism' and 'departmentalism', and could help to build a board team.

Information technology provides many options for directors who wish to be in contact with each other and to share information and views on an ad hoc basis.[4] However, in many companies, there is a reluctance to use technologies such as audio or visual conferencing to allow the board to operate in new ways.

The very existence of a 'directors' network' can make it difficult for a chairman or CEO to implement a 'divide and rule' policy. At the same time, there is a danger that the use of a network by some directors could encourage the formation of a boardroom clique or cabal. The non-executive director who becomes drawn too closely into a 'network' might lose his or her objectivity and independence. The risk of losing a critical perspective may need to be balanced against the benefits of greater involvement.

Directors, preferences and the technology of learning

We examined the learning and updating preferences of directors in Chapter 6. Although there is some awareness of the value of integrating learning and working,[19] directors tend to be conservative and express a preference for traditional courses over new approaches to learning that might, *prima facie*, appear more suited to their needs.[1] The limited availability of directors, and the challenge of coordinating the diaries of the various members of the boardroom team, can create practical constraints upon the use of traditional approaches to learning.

Many directors express a preference for learning in groups. Informal interaction and workshop situations appear to be preferred to the private study of printed materials, and rank significantly ahead of the use of audio and video tape material.[8]

Directors are often not convinced that many of the issues and matters that concern them can be 'packaged' in such a way as to be delivered by the printed word, or some other means of audio or visual communication.[1] They are also conscious of the particular needs of their own boards, and have a preference for development activities that, whatever their primary or ostensible purpose, can also 'build the team'.

Some boards make use of a development adviser or counsellor who understands the distinction between direction and management, has a directorial perspective, is aware of boardroom issues, and can facilitate board discussions. Such an individual tends to be a coach rather than a consultant.

While few directors are sufficiently convinced of the value of distance learning to adopt it, an infrastructure that could be used appears to be in place in many companies. The problem is a shortage of those who can facilitate the learning of directors, rather than of supporting technology. Directors of small and medium-sized companies (SMEs), in particular, could represent a 'market' for distance learning 'solutions':

- In a survey undertaken by Exeter University,[14] just over half of the respondents expressed an interest in a combination of distance learning materials on company direction and tutorial support. Almost 50 per cent of the directors owned a PC, while over six out of ten claimed to have the use of a PC at their workplace.
- In an Adaptation Ltd survey for the IOD,[20] four out of ten respondents thought open/distance learning services to be 'relevant' or 'very relevant' for the development of individual directors. However, the response fell to three out of ten when related to the development of the board as a whole.

Although directors of major corporations may prefer 'company specific' programmes, members of the boards of SMEs sometimes take a different view. In the Adaptation Ltd survey for the IOD, an open course for directors was preferred, by a ratio of two to one, to courses that were tailored to the needs of individual companies. It was felt that open courses allowed participants to discover, or uncover, how other boards were tackling some of the same practical problems that the interviewees were facing.

The learning director   A director who ceases to challenge, probe, question and learn can become a liability in the boardroom. Some questions that could be used to assess the commitment of each member of the board to active learning are listed in Exercise 7.4

Exercise 7.4: The learning director

The following questions could be asked to assess each director's commitment to active learning:

1 **Does the director actively participate in learning activities (a) inside and (b) outside the boardroom? (Is the participation reluctant? Does the director try to 'rush through' reviews?)**
2 **Has the director initiated or suggested any (a) formal and (b) informal learning initiatives and activities?**
3 **Does the director 'network' and sound out the views and opinions of others prior to, or between, board meetings?**
4 **With whom does the director associate and why? (What can one learn about the director's openness to new people and ideas, tolerance of diversity, etc.?)**
5 **Does the director listen to the views of others during board discussions? (Does the director modify his or her views in the light of such discussion? How good is the director at understanding and summing up the contributions of others?)**

At the conclusion of Exercise 7.4 (as was the case with Exercise 7.3) there are some further questions that should be asked to assess the extent to which corporate and board culture and practice either inhibits learning or is conducive to it. For example:

- What is inhibiting a greater commitment to learning? (Are the barriers within the individuals, or do they result from the board or company context?)
- Is director development likely to be enough? (For example, does the composition of the board, or the way in which it conducts its business, need to be changed?)
- Is there an internal directors' network that allows all directors to be 'brought together' (e.g. conference call) as required between 'physical' meetings, and could this be used as a learning network?
- Is an infrastructure in place that could support distance learning if the directors were convinced of its potential value? (What are the barriers to its use, and how might they be overcome?)

Formal learning and mode of study

In Chapter 6 we examined the attitudes of directors towards formal learning, and concluded that formal programmes need to be selected with care to ensure that they focus on the special needs of directors. The formal training that relatively few directors have undertaken appears to consist largely of management courses, rather than activities specifically concerned with the development of direction skills.[1,20] If formal training is to be provided concerning direction, what modes of study are likely to be most relevant?

Many of the qualities that are sought in directors (see Chapters 2 and 5) fall into the category of awareness, attitude, perspective, etc., rather than particular knowledge or technical skill. This is also true of 'international-ization',[21] and some clues as to preferred modes of study for directors may be obtained by examining what is being done to equip the senior management teams of major companies with an international awareness and perspective.

Human resource development (HRD) for international operation has been examined in a survey undertaken by Adaptation Ltd for the Surrey European Management School.[19] The companies covered by this survey are 'international', e.g. MNCs (multi-national corporations), rather than SMEs. When relating the findings to director development, certain combinations of the most highly ranked elements suggest themselves. For example:

- The most relevant 'modes of study' are thought to be 'tailored company specific programmes', with a 'project component' and 'in company delivery'. A directors' 'development session' along these lines could precede and support a board roles and responsibilities exercise.
- 'Issue-based', 'modular' and 'open' programmes are also thought to be relevant. A chairman might wish to attend a periodic 'chairman's workshop' to 'compare notes' with other chairmen on matters of common interest.
- A 'period of study in another EC country', a 'study visit abroad' and 'block release' are not thought to be very relevant. Most directors will not have time to undertake these types of activity, although board meetings of an international company could be rotated between the continents and linked to briefings on local operations and regional issues.[21]

Full-time study is ranked last in order of relevance when the 'very relevant' and 'relevant' replies are combined.[19] Few executive directors are likely to have the time to undertake full-time study for anything other than a relatively short period of time.

A degree of caution needs to be attached to these findings of the 'internationalization' study, bearing in mind the distinction between direction and management (see Chapter 13). They are of most relevance in understanding the development preferences of those who may well form the pool from which future MNC directors might be drawn.

Another 'clue' to be derived from the 'internationalization' survey is that national differences of perspective exist, and may need to be taken into account. For example:

- Compared with the replies from UK companies, the European and international respondents put a higher 'relevance rating' upon 'issue-based' programmes and a 'period of study in another EC country'. The directors of a Dutch subsidiary may be more receptive than their UK counterparts to the notion of a directors' workshop in Germany.
- Less relevance was attached to 'distance learning', 'block release', 'portability of credits/qualifications within UK' and 'mutual recognition of

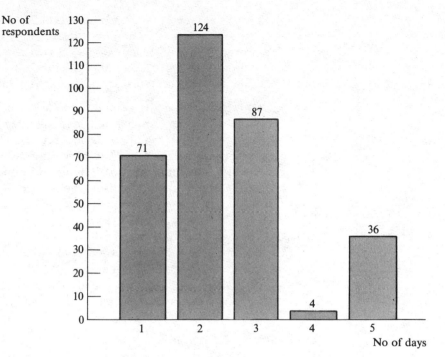

No of
respondents

No of days

Figure 7.4 *Preferences for length of courses*

qualifications' within the EC, than was the case with respondents from UK companies. The interest shown in a director's audio visual package could vary across different national operating companies.

Director courses Are there any particular factors that should be borne in mind when designing director level courses? The 'clues' of the 'internationalization' survey[19] are supported by the survey undertaken by Alan Wakelam of Exeter University:[14]

- Learning away from the boardroom and corporate context, and in a specialized educational institution is not the preferred option. Less than four out of ten participants expressed a preference for a residential course.
- A modular approach is preferred, with two days being the most popular length of course. About a third of chairmen and managing directors, and a third of all respondents, expressed such a preference (Figure 7.4). Over a fifth expressed a preference for three-day courses, while just under a fifth preferred one-day courses.

Compared with managers, directors are often more willing to participate in their own development. There is some evidence to suggest that directors seek some form of active participation in the formal courses they attend:

- An IOD study[1] concluded that: 'Few directors appear to be "shrinking violets". An active, rather than a passive, personality seems to be the more common among directors.'

- In an earlier survey,[14] while respondents were in the main satisfied with the formal programmes in company direction they had undertaken, case studies and workshops were the two elements that attracted the largest number of comments in response to a question about which activities should have had more time devoted to them.

Directors are often reluctant, for a variety of reasons, to raise certain issues with management colleagues. Contact with fellow directors on external courses can allow discussion of such sensitive matters. Exchanging ideas with other directors from non-competing companies can also allow notions, possibilities and points of view to be floated, and permit arguments to be tested, before exposing them to one's own board.

Sources of training

The sources of advice, and of director and board development services, that are used most often were considered in Chapter 6. The point was made that the use of certain services reflects their availability, and may not indicate 'satisfaction'. While there is no shortage of people seeking to relieve companies of their training budgets, there has for many years been a deficiency of those who specialize in, and can 'add value' to, director development.

In the field of management education and development, many companies 'play safe' and buy development services from leading business schools and international firms of management consultants. As one interviewee stated: 'If it goes wrong, you don't get so much flack if you have bought from a "name".' Does the same argument apply to director development?

Some boards do seek to avoid risks by buying from 'familiar sources', but the support they receive may be less relevant as a result.

- The larger organization is often more inclined to 'package' a standard product. In contrast, the individual board development adviser may not be under pressure to do other than consider each brief to be unique.
- Even the large organization may lack experience in the particular area in which director development is sought. Rather than 'disappoint' a regular client, a management course might be adapted for director use.
- The greater resources of the larger firm may not be so relevant when the training task shifts from 'thousands' of managers to a group that 'sits around a table'. The development support that has to be provided may involve no more than one or two people, but these should be of the highest quality.
- The development needs of directors rarely require the services of the experts and technical specialists that are maintained by the larger firms. The quality of a director development service generally depends upon the direct 'face to face' support that is provided in the learning environment.

A concern of many companies is that some consultants and business schools appear to be parasites rather than contributors. The consultancy firm can quickly 'repackage' and popularize a novel tool or approach that a particular board has used to secure competitive advantage. The prime consideration when selecting a source of director development services should be the personal qualities and experience of the person who will actually be working with the boardroom team.

Another area examined in Chapter 6 was the preferences of directors for various sources of training, and their perceptions of them. Participants in two surveys cited in this chapter,[1,20] expressed a preference for programmes and courses from a professional body over those provided by the private sector. Although not regarded as highly as the professional sector, public bodies, universities, polytechnics and colleges were on the whole perceived as 'independent and objective'.

Barriers to training

Reference has already been made to such 'barriers' as the reluctance of many directors to undertake development activities, and the shortage of those with relevant development experience. Are there problems which relate particularly to certain categories of company?

Survey evidence[1,20] does not suggest that directors of companies of a certain type or size are more or less committed to 'direction' than members of the boards of other companies. The size of the survey samples does not allow conclusions to be drawn with any degree of confidence concerning whether the absolute need for training varies between different categories of company.

However, there is some evidence that the cost of director development may represent a more significant barrier for the smaller company:[1,20]

- Smaller firms may have far fewer managers per director than is the case with larger companies. Therefore, if it is necessary to develop both managers and directors, expenditure on director and board development ought to represent a higher proportion of the training budget of the smaller firms.
- Given that the size of company boards does not appear to increase in direct proportion to turnover or the number of people employed,[1] expenditure on developing boardroom competences should claim a higher proportion of the total operating costs of the smaller firms.

Organizations offering specific courses for directors have tended not to vary their charges according to such factors as the size of a company. Daily rates reflect accommodation, support services, staffing, marketing and overhead costs, and these do not necessarily change according to whether those on a particular course are owner-directors of small family businesses, or executive directors of multi-national companies.

The cost of building the direction skills of a team of directors, and of developing an effective board, can represent a significantly greater financial challenge in the case of the smaller company. Many chairmen do not find it easy to quantify how much they should spend on director and board development.[1] We shall see in Chapter 9 that few chairmen measure effectiveness in the boardroom, let alone assess how much it has been, or could be, enhanced by development activity.

For many directors, particularly those of larger companies, the availability of time and of experienced development advisers, rather than cost or the lack of a budget, are the main barriers to formal training once its relevance has been accepted. Hence, a clear preference has emerged for short rather than long courses, and modular courses that could be taken in 'chunks' over a period of time.[1]

Updating

Director development needs to be a continuous process as the situation and circumstances of a company evolve—not to mention changes in the composition of the board. When assessing the various options for updating directors, there are a number of basic considerations that should be borne in mind:

- In the case of courses and other learning opportunities designed to improve, build upon, or refine knowledge, are they specifically designed for directors or for managers?
- Similarly, in the case of conferences and seminars designed to improve awareness of new developments, to what extent do these address issues from a boardroom perspective?
- Do activities such as workshops that are designed to improve directorial skills provide sufficient opportunities for the participants to interact with other directors?
- In the same way, do activities designed to share experience provide sufficient opportunities for interaction and discussions; and do the discussions go beyond generalizations concerning the need for action and tackle 'implementation issues'?

A director needs to be aware of, be sensitive to, and understand changes in the business environment that influence the business prospects of a company. The reading of newspapers, and listening to reports on social, economic and political developments in the broadcast media should not be passive but 'questioning': e.g. How will this affect the company?

Reference has been made earlier in this chapter to the value of informal learning, and of a 'directors' network'. A director should also actively seek out 'updating environments'. For example:

- Joining relevant institutions, societies and associations, and attending seminars and conferences—particularly those 'on the boundary of' the main focus of a company—can be of considerable value. Rather than seek the security of confirming what is already known, the director should positively search for opportunities to establish new angles or acquire fresh insights.

- The director should also learn from stakeholders and the various 'interests' in the company, particularly the customers, employees, and suppliers. On occasion, directors are so concerned with communicating the 'board message' to these groups that they forget to learn from them.
- A good director listens to internal company advisers and, externally, to those who consume the products and services of competitors, or who represent them at trade exhibitions. When meeting analysts or journalists with questions about the company, the director should endeavour to find out what they think about it, and what image they have of it.

Formal programmes

If formal director development programmes are to be used they should (a) reflect the needs and preferences of the board and its members and (b) take account of the availability of the 'customers', i.e. the directors. The following questions could be asked to help ensure that any programmes that are provided meet these requirements:

- What is the purpose of the activity? (For example: What knowledge or skill deficiencies need to be addressed? How urgent is the requirement?)
- Is a change of attitude, perspective or awareness sought? (This might require a number of related activities over a period of time.)
- What is known about the availability of the likely participants? (For example: Are certain directors planning business trips? What will directors' diaries allow?)
- What is known about the learning preferences and styles of those concerned?
- How might director development be integrated into the board's programme of work and meetings? (For example, could development modules be linked to particular agenda items, or known future tasks or events?)
- Could learning be incidental to, or derived from, a certain activity? (For example, rather than tell the board about mission statements, let them craft one—helped by an experienced facilitator.)
- What past experiences have members of the board had of formal programmes? (Do these 'help' or 'hinder' certain options?)
- Also, what are their expectations? (Is there a degree of cynicism and caution to be overcome?)
- What would represent a 'positive' outcome? (Are there specific out puts that could be generated?)
- Are there special factors that need to be addressed? (For example, do the perspectives and preferences of the directors vary between the boards of different national subsidiaries or 'operating companies'?)
- How can the desire of directors for active involvement and participation be met? (For example, how could a situation be created that would enable them to learn from themselves?)
- What value could the company's traditional sources of development services add at the level of the board? (Should the services of an individual with director and board development experience be sought?)
- Are there particular problems which relate to the nature (e.g. size, or

subsidiary rather than holding company), situation or circumstances of the company? (How might these affect needs and preferences?)

- How can director development be made a continuous process? (What updating requirements are likely to follow 'delivery' of the formal activity?)
- Is formal development something apart from, or is it integrated into, an active and general commitment to learning on the part of the board and its members? (If not, how might the experience of a formal development activity be used as a catalyst in (a) the creation of a learning board and (b) the encouragement of learning directors?)

In this chapter we have encountered a number of obstacles to director development, including the scepticism and caution of directors themselves. Director development can benefit from champions in the boardroom. Designing a 'workable' programme is a question of 'the art of the possible', and making the best use for learning purposes of every available opportunity.

Checklist

1 What is the attitude of the board of your company towards director development?
2 What are the roots or causes of boardroom views about director development, i.e. prejudice, myth or a bad experience?
3 How committed is the board to learning? Is there a sense of urgency or complacency?
4 What 'example' does the board set for the rest of the organization?
5 Can potential allies and opponents be identified?
6 Does your company have a formal director induction programme?
7 Are 'new' directors encouraged to 'fit in' or to be objective and critical?
8 How could the induction process at board level be improved?
9 Does your board have an overall picture of the development needs of its members?
10 Are the development needs that have been identified a 'symptom' or a 'cause'?
11 If it were your company, what would you do?
12 Do members of the board of your company ever ask the question: What have we learned?
13 Are the directors encouraged to seek new challenges that might force them to re-assess and question?
14 Do the company's management development activities encourage informal learning?
15 Do the directors actively learn on their own initiative?
16 Does corporate and board culture and practice inhibit or encourage learning?

Notes and references

1 Colin Coulson-Thomas and Alan Wakelam, *The Effective Board: Current Practice, Myths and Realities*. An IOD discussion document, 1991.
2 Colin Coulson-Thomas, 'What the personnel director can bring to the boardroom table', *Personnel Management* (October 1991), 36–9.
3 Charles Batchelor, 'The boardroom beckons', *Financial Times* (3 March 1992); and *Boardroom Agenda*, No. 2 (May 1992), 16–17.
4 Colin Coulson-Thomas, *Creating Excellence in the Boardroom*, McGraw-Hill, 1993.
5 Adrian Cadbury, *Company Chairman*, Director Books, 1990; and George Copeman, *The Managing Director*, 2nd edn, Business Books, 1982.
6 John Redwood MP, *Corporate Governance*, DTI Press Notice P/91/172, 27 March 1991, speaking at launch of a survey report, *Non-Executives in the Boardroom*, PA Consulting Group and Sundridge Park Management Centre, 1991.
7 P.R. Lawrence and J.W. Lorsch, *Organisation and Environment*, Irwin, 1967.
8 Colin Coulson-Thomas, *The Role and Development of the Personnel Director*, Issue Paper, Institute of Personnel Management, 1993.
9 W. Bennis and B. Nanus, *Leaders*, Harper & Row, 1985.
10 Carol Kennedy and Stuart Rock, 'The man who bet the management', *Director* (August 1992), 32–5.
11 Ada Demb and F-Friedrich Neubauer, *The Corporate Board: Confronting the Paradoxes*, Oxford University Press, 1992.
12 T. Burns and G.M. Stalker, *The Management of Innovation*, Tavistock, 1961; P.R. Lawrence and D. Dyer, *Renewing American Industry*, Free Press, 1983; Colin Coulson-Thomas and Richard Brown, *The Responsive Organisation*, BIM, 1989; and *Beyond Quality: Managing the Relationship with the Customer*, BIM, 1990.
13 Warren Bennis, *On Becoming a Leader*, Hutchinson Business Books, 1990.
14 Alan Wakelam, *The Training and Development of Company Directors*. A report on a questionnaire survey undertaken by the Centre for Management Studies, University of Exeter for the Training Agency, December 1989.
15 Alan Mumford, Peter Honey and Graham Robinson, *Director's Development Guidebook—Making Experience Count*, IOD and Department of Employment, September 1990.
16 Bob Garratt, *Creating a Learning Organisation: A Guide to Leadership, Learning and Development*, Director Books, 1990.
17 Charles Batchelor, 'Thinking of tomorrow instead of just today', *Financial Times* (March 6 1990), 14.
18 Sir John Harvey-Jones, *Making it Happen: Reflections on Leadership*, 3rd impression, Fontana/Collins, March 1989, p. 211.
19 Colin Coulson-Thomas, *Human Resource Development for International Operation*. A survey sponsored by Surrey European Management School. Adaptation Ltd, 1990.
20 Colin Coulson-Thomas, *Professional Development of and for the Board*. A questionnaire and interview survey undertaken by Adaptation Ltd of company chairmen. A summary has been published by the IOD, February 1990.
21 Colin Coulson-Thomas, *Creating the Global Company: Successful Internationalization*, McGraw-Hill, 1992.

8 Developing the boardroom team

In the previous chapter we focused upon the development of individual directors. We now turn our attention to the board as a team. We have seen already that the effectiveness of a board should not be assumed.

In many companies, the board itself is perceived as a constraint upon change.[1] Surveys on both sides of the Atlantic have shown that the behaviour of many boards has severely depleted the managerial spirit.[2] The conduct of the board and a perceived gap between its words and its deeds can lead to various arenas of conflict within a company.

One study has suggested that almost 50 per cent of chairmen and CEOs are dissatisfied with the performance of their 'top teams'.[3] In this chapter, among the approaches that can be adopted, we shall look at how a board might be developed as a team while discharging certain of its responsibilities. In Chapters 9 and 10 we shall examine further steps that could be taken to remedy an unsatisfactory situation.

The exercises in this chapter are concerned with identifying and overcoming barriers to board performance, encouraging group discussion within the boardroom, and the communication of corporate vision.

Barriers to board effectiveness

So what are the barriers to improved board performance? There are many of them, and they vary from company to company.

The effectiveness of a particular board could be reduced by several overlapping and interrelated factors. The possible 'inhibitors' could include board practice, structure or conduct, the chairmanship of the board, inadequate attention, a short-term focus, divisions or a clash of personalities.

A board might not be clear about its functions. Its members may confuse the distinction between direction and management. Vision, values, goals and objectives could be vague or inappropriate. Crucial elements needed to implement strategies might be missing. People may not be empowered or equipped to act.

Some boards are manipulated or deceived, while others are naive. There are boards that are reluctant to confront reality, and others that can craft a strategy but then find it difficult to 'implement'.

A board could lack self-discipline or rigour. There are boards that operate on the basis of assumption and opinion, rather than understanding and fact. David Thompson, chairman of Rank Xerox UK, has observed that: 'Most boards concentrate on the urgent rather than the important, mainly because the urgent is more easily understood.'

Helping boards

Boards are not easy to help. We shall see in Chapter 14 the extent to which different boards can vary. Homilies, panaceas, simplistic approaches or standard solutions may achieve little beyond distracting the naive and raising false hopes.

Every board is made up of a particular combination of personalities and interests and may face specific demands and pressures from stakeholders, while the situation and circumstances of the company may be distinct from those faced by any other board. A board is a living entity, and its various features and elements, and the pressures it is under, need to be understood if whatever support that is provided is to satisfy its requirements.

Our understanding of how boards operate is plagued by myth and misunderstanding. It is important that a board is seen as it is, rather than as it ought to be. Deficiencies cannot be tackled if the realism and honesty to acknowledge them is lacking, and there is insufficient commitment to act.

There are many things that may need to be done to improve the performance of a particular board. Exercise 8.1 lists some questions that could be asked to help identify some possible 'next steps'.

Exercise 8.1: Improving board performance

To help identify some 'next steps' actions, consider the following questions:

1 **What are the main barriers, obstacles or inhibitors of improved board performance? (Group or categorize them, e.g. people problems, procedure problems, etc.)**
2 **Does the prioritization reflect the nature of the board, and the situation and circumstances of the company?**
3 **How open has the group been in identifying its deficiencies? (What is being concealed, perhaps because of the sensitivities involved?)**
4 **What are the sources of the problems? (Have root causes been identified?)**
5 **Are there particular myths, shared by certain members of the board, that need to be confronted? (Identify assumptions that should be challenged.)**
6 **What deficiencies should be addressed by individual development activity, and which by activities involving the board as a team?**
7 **Who should be responsible for particular activities? (While the chairman may assume overall responsibility, individual directors could also assume responsibilities in order to involve as many members of the board as possible in the planning of development activities.)**

A key question to ask at the end of a review like that of Exercise 8.1 is: How committed is the board to action? A board that appears to lack the sustained commitment necessary to change attitudes and behaviour, or shows complacency in the face of what has emerged, may need to be challenged with a direct question such as: 'Are you serious?'

Once the key problems and their root causes have been identified, appropriate action can be taken. Too much should not be expected of director development alone. Thus the composition, procedures or structure of the board might have to be altered. Roles and responsibilities, or the conduct of meetings, could also be changed. The development counsellor or adviser should have the breadth of perspective to understand the distinct contribution of director development within the overall portfolio of actions and activities that are initiated.

Teamwork in the boardroom

How receptive are directors likely to be to initiatives to improve teamwork in the boardroom? In a survey of 218 directors, over three-quarters of whom were either the chairman or the chairman and CEO of their companies, 'teamwork' emerged as the principal boardroom issue (see Table 3.1). The survey was undertaken by Adaptation Ltd for the IOD.[4]

Participants made it clear during the course of survey interviews that they were not just thinking in terms of teamwork in the boardroom. Teamwork at all levels in the organization was thought to be important, as was the example set, or lead given, by the board in respect of its own role-model behaviour.

The composition of the board in terms of the attributes and qualities of its individual members should match its functions. A balanced board made up of complementary skills, experiences and talents can provide a firm foundation for teamwork.[5]

Selecting good people with matching qualities will not of itself lead to success. Sir John Harvey-Jones believes the size of the board, where it meets, seating arrangements, how information is presented, the degree of informality, and the use of humour can all contribute to effective teamwork.[6]

Executive and non-executive directors

A board composed entirely of executive directors could become introverted and subservient to the wishes and drives of a strong CEO. When non-executives are introduced, care should be taken to ensure that both executive and non-executive directors understand each others' role. A UK study by PRO NED and the Stock Exchange suggests that many non-executive directors are viewed with suspicion by their executive colleagues.[7] When their role is not understood, they may be regarded as a threat.

Whereas the non-executive director may wish to contribute to the formulation of strategy, executive directors may see the function of the non-executive director as largely one of commenting on the strategy

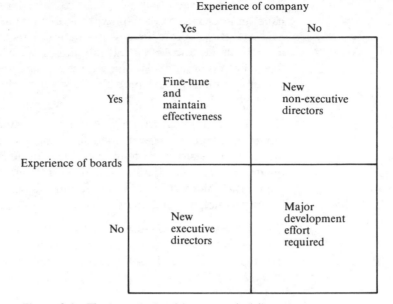

Experience of company

	Yes	No
Yes (Experience of boards)	Fine-tune and maintain effectiveness	New non-executive directors
No	New executive directors	Major development effort required

Figure 8.1 The 'executive' and 'non-executive' dimension

produced by the executive team. Peter Morgan, director-general of the IOD, has warned that a board should not be allowed to split into 'the doers and the checkers'.[8]

Executive directors sometimes find the non-executives' lack of knowledge of the company and its problems an irritant, while the non-executives might become concerned about the introversion of the executive directors, and their lack of wider boardroom experience. The biggest development challenge is provided by those who lack both company and boardroom experience (Figure 8.1).

Too much teamwork?

The search for unity, shared values and common approaches should not be carried to an extreme. We have seen in earlier chapters that directors need to retain a degree of objectivity and detachment, and that the board should not be allowed to become a 'cosy club'.[9]

David Thompson, chairman of Rank Xerox UK, warns: 'Of course boards should operate as a team, but not to the degree that team building suppresses the opportunity to challenge and say the unthinkable. Teams like to pull in the same direction, and are not a fertile breeding ground for the radical.' Teams can sometimes find it difficult to take the 'big steps' unless a 'champion' fires their imagination.

Personal attributes and qualities can help or hinder teamwork. We saw in Chapter 2 that tolerance, tact, patience and the ability to command the respect of colleagues in the boardroom are all qualities of the competent director. Empathy, awareness and sensitivity are also needed to forge relationships.

Roger Graham, chairman of the BIS Group, expects new directors to have 'an approach to dealing with people inside and outside the business as if they were your best customers. This means understanding people's needs and wants and fulfilling them wherever possible. Where this is not possible explaining why and managing their expectations.' Within the boardroom, there should be mutual understanding and 'give and take'.

Harmony in the boardroom should not be assumed. Ambition and the pursuit of corporate power does not cease with a directorial appointment. Within a group, there may well be private agendas, 'undercurrents' relating to present differences, and resentments that result from past feuds. The chairman or CEO might believe that a degree of rivalry is healthy or helps to maintain control.

The BIM report, *The Responsive Organisation*, makes the point that: 'effective team working cannot be assumed. It needs to be consciously developed. The board itself should review how effectively it is working as a team.'[10]

Learning as a team

The board itself, as we saw in the last chapter, could be used as an action learning environment.[11] Annual and strategy reviews, visioning exercises, SWOT and issue monitoring assessments, and 'helps' and 'hinders' analyses are among the many opportunities for the board to operate and learn as a team.

Every opportunity should be taken to pose, or revisit, 'first principles' questions. For example, the determination or review of vision and mission provides an opportunity to address some fundamental questions about the purpose of a company.[12]

A variety of reviews, including certain of the exercises in this book, could achieve particular objectives while at the same time allowing members of a board to increase their understanding of each other. Other options include 'away days', 'outward bound' type activities, 'peer reviews' or facilitated discussions.

Discussion of selected examples of corporate practice, perhaps using an external development as a catalyst, can help a board clarify its own views on a particular issue. For example:

- A board may find itself somewhat inhibited when discussing its own remuneration arrangements. In late 1991 Ultramar, an energy company, reduced the compensation of its directors as part of a package of moves in defence of a hostile takeover bid from Lasmo. The move included a reduction in the term of notice of termination of board appointments. A case like this could be used as a peg for the discussion of such issues as the impact of director service contracts upon director motivation.
- Those who can formulate strategy are well represented on many boards. However, such boards may not be satisfied with their ability to 'implement'. The need to balance strategy formulation with implemen-

tation skills can become more urgent and intense in a changing business and corporate environment, if a gap is not to emerge between aspiration and achievement. What could be learned from a benchmark company, for example Rank Xerox, winner of the first European Quality Award?

Other subjects for discussion could be derived from the results of director and board surveys examined in the course of this book. For example:[13]

- There is little evidence of a standard board predominating in terms of either size or composition. The total number of directors appears to be constrained by supply rather than demand. In many cases, chairmen would make additional appointments to the board if people with the required characteristics could be identified. Members of a board could be invited to consider whether their search for suitable candidates should be extended beyond the senior management team.
- There is also little evidence of experimentation with new ways of organizing boards. A board might wish to consider whether the volume, urgency and complexity of its business would justify the establishment of a 'director's network' to ensure that directors 'keep in touch' between formal meetings of the board. (The benefits of such a network, which can be particularly valuable from the point of view of the non-executive director, were examined in Chapter 7.)

Distinction between direction and management

Many management processes that 'begin and end' in the boardroom may involve the active participation of managers in various parts of the corporate organization. Boundaries between roles and processes can become blurred. From time to time, it may be necessary to clarify where the responsibilities of the board end, and where those of managers begin.

At a number of points in this book we have returned to the question of the distinction between direction and management. It can be particularly beneficial for the members of a board (and members of the senior management team) to explore and share their understanding of the points of similarity and difference. Selected results from one group exercise are shown in Example 8.1. Not all readers will agree with the distinctions made, but they illustrate the extent to which such an exercise can give rise to further opportunities for discussion.

When such an exercise is undertaken by both directors and managers, the results can be compared and discussed by both groups. The more a board invites comment and criticism from management, the more it will learn, and the better understood and respected it is likely to be.

A close relationship between executive director members of the board and the senior management team, and mutual respect and understanding, are the hallmarks of the effective executive team. Exercise 8.2 presents another set of questions that could be used by a board that is ready to take an honest look at itself.

Example 8.1 *What managers and directors contribute to an organization*

MANAGERS	DIRECTORS
Doers—paid to take decisions and manage, within a framework established by the board	*Thinkers*—paid to watch, assess and establish framework
Short term—the horizon is the next task deadline	*Long-term*—need to plan ahead
Subjective—life entwined with the corporate organization	*Objective*—should keep an independent perspective, view the organization as would an outsider
Involved—expected to be committed to the organization and its products	*Detached*—expected to arbitrate between stakeholders, rather than overtly identify with particular interests
Rational—trained to think about management problems in a logical way	*Intuitive*—need empathy and awareness to build relationships
Focused—tend to concentrate on departmental tasks and outputs	*Diffused*—have many and varied tasks, involving different dimensions and elements
Specialist—operate within a particular business unit or management discipline	*Generalist*—need to have a perspective of the company as a whole
Depth—know about the company's products and industry in detail	*Breadth*—concerned with many situations and relationships
Responsible—may work within a hierarchy, constrained by policies and procedures	*Accountable*—set their own constraints, but are also subject to legal requirements and possibly conflicting stakeholder objectives
Means—activity, role or process may become an end in itself	*End*—relevance derives from corporate vision, goals, values or objectives

Exercise 8.2: The degree of common understanding within the executive team

The views of senior managers (or those of a wider group of employees) on the following questions could be sought by means of an appropriate survey, or a a session within the framework of the company's management development programme:

1 How would you describe the board in terms of the characteristics of a person?
2 How secure or insecure are members of the board?
3 Is the board an assembly of individuals, or is it a team?
4 How loyal or disloyal are the members of the board towards each other?
5 Do those who attend board meetings respect confidentiality, or does the board 'leak like a sieve'?
6 Does the board share, empower and involve, or does it just direct?
7 To what extent are the interests and priorities of the board synonymous with those of the company?
8 Do directors and managers share the same corporate vision, goals, values and objectives?
9 Is there a conflict of interest or perspective between board and management?
10 Does the board listen to management and understand their perspective and concerns?
11 What should be done to achieve a more productive relationship between the board and management? (How might the achievement of business objectives, and the delivery of value to customers be improved?)

Certain questions in Exercise 8.2 touch upon sensitive matters. The issues raised are also important if the board is serious about becoming more effective. Any 'problem areas' that arise from such questioning ought to be flushed out and dealt with by determined and appropriate action on the part of the chairman. Nettles need to be grasped if a board is to become, and remain, effective.

Responsibility for board effectiveness

The chairman carries a particular responsibility for how effectively the board operates as a team and the extent to which the individual and collective potential of the members is harnessed and applied to a vision, values and goals that satisfy the requirements of stakeholders. Sir Adrian Cadbury considers chairmanship to be an art that requires a degree of sensitivity, as the effective chairman has to balance a number of interests.[14]

The 'business of the board' has to be managed by the chairman. Individual directors may be concerned to 'have a say', and their contributions should be encouraged. At the same time, and following a reasonable debate, the chairman will be seeking to arrive at a collective view. Certain discussions may need to be continued, perhaps on a further occasion, until there is perceived to be sufficient support for a matter to be implemented or otherwise dealt with in a definitive manner.

The view of the IOD is that:

a board of directors will only function effectively if it is given a sense of purpose and direction by its chairman. . . . The way that a chairman leads and man-
ages the board, organises its work and sets its priorities will be a major factor in
the board's relative success. . . . How the board comes together as a team will
depend very largely on his skill and leadership.[15]

The commitment of both chairman and board members is required.
John Adair has suggested that 50 per cent of the success in creating an
effective team is due to the leader and the other 50 per cent results
from the efforts and contribution of the team.[16]

Communication skills

According to a survey of company chairmen,[4] 'good communication at
all times' is the most frequently cited means of improving teamwork in
the boardroom. The interviews that were conducted suggest that
processes, attitudes and approaches, rather than structures and channels,
need to be changed in order to improve communication.

There needs to be a high level of trust and mutual respect, and a sharing
of goals and values, if discussions in the boardroom are to be open and
frank. Directors tend to be practical realists. Many harbour few illusions,
and have modest expectations of colleagues. Collective empathy and
unity may not occur spontaneously, even though the potential for syner-
gistic and productive cooperation is latent. It may need to be developed.

A board, and individual directors, may have to communicate with various
stakeholders that have an interest in the company:

The modern company is not a machine to be run or driven by its board but
rather it is a complex organism, a network of interests cooperating in some
areas and conflicting in others. One of the jobs of the board is to arbitrate
between the various interests in the company, . . . and to allocate scarce values
and resources. In essence this is a political activity. Its critical component is
communication.[17]

Visions, goals and objectives may all remain as 'scribblings on flip
charts', 'words on paper', or 'lines in the plan' unless they are communicated and shared. If this is not done, nothing much may happen, and a
wide gap between aspiration and achievement should be assumed. Individual directors may be expected to possess the ability to establish and
build relationships with those stakeholders for which they have a
special responsibility.

A wide range of people in the network organization require communication skills. The BIM report, *The Responsive Organisation*, suggests that
more 'work will be undertaken in teams with clear accountabilities and
a focus upon delivering what constitutes value in the eyes of the customer', and that 'team work and communication skills will be
highly prized'.[10]

A lack of communication skills has been identified as the main barrier
to both internal and external communication.[18] The requirement is for a
change of attitudes, approach, perspective and behaviour rather than

technical skills *per se*. Prior to initiating communications activity, the members of a board should first think through why they are communicating, and what is being communicated to whom.

Facilitating skills   Boards that define corporate objectives and priority tasks in the form of measurable outputs, and allocate responsibilities for their achievement to particular directors, are creating projects that need to be managed. Executive directors increasingly require project management and other facilitating skills.

As boards focus increasingly upon the implementation of strategy and corporate transformation, individual directors may be made accountable for particular change projects. Exercises in the boardroom to agree the 'vital few' actions that are necessary to tackle particular barriers, or achieve key objectives, also create projects for which individual directors may assume responsibility.

Corporate organizations are themselves transitioning from functional bureaucracies to more flexible and responsive networks of project groups, task forces and teams. Increasingly, individual directors are likely to be held responsible for portfolios of projects undertaken by cross-functional and multi-locational groups.

Are there specific project management competences? The main project management competences according to a survey undertaken by Adaptation Ltd for the Association of Project Managers (APM) are ranked in Table 8.1 in order of 'very important' replies.[19]

'Understanding the anatomy of a project' is considered to be the most important project management competence. A competent director should have the ability to 'see a project as a whole'. Eight out of ten respondents consider 'communication' to be 'very important'.

Interpersonal skills and communication within a group can also be important determinants of team effectiveness. The importance of communication skills has already been stressed, and is a theme of a number

Table 8.1 Competences for project management

Competence	Ranking (%)*
Understanding the anatomy of a project	88
Communication	81
Decision making	69
Control of change	62
Planning and scheduling	60
Cost-planning and control	55
Management of contracts	36

* Ranking in terms of 'very important'.

of surveys concerned with groups that come together for specific purposes, such as a board or project group. For example:

- Participants in a survey of chairmen undertaken for the IOD[4] were asked to identify any 'other skills' they thought were important in the training and development of directors. Communication skills appeared as one of the top five 'specific competences' required in the development of directors.
- When respondents in the APM survey[19] were asked to specify which 'qualities' they considered to be most desirable in project managers, communications skills was placed at the top of the list of 'very important' replies. The ability to communicate is important in its own right and is also a key element in certain facilitating competences.

We saw in Chapter 7 that the deficiencies in communication skills that need to be addressed are those concerning attitudes, approach, perspective and behaviour. These are often most apparent, and best dealt with, in a team context.

Vision and mission

Let us now turn to an extended example. A key priority for the board should be the determination of a 'purpose' for the company, and the articulation and communication of a distinctive vision (to be discussed in Chapter 12). Survey evidence has shown the importance of a clear, distinctive and compelling vision:

- We saw in Chapter 3 that a 1991 Adaptation Ltd survey suggests that a 'clear vision and mission' is the principal requirement for management of change.[18]
- A 1991 BIM survey-based report[20] has found that, in the creation of a new philosophy for managing the flat organization, 'every respondent assessing it believes clear vision and mission to be important'. About three-quarters of them consider it 'very important'.

This evidence is of some importance, as the board should be the authoritative source of a company's vision and mission. Both need to be shared with all those whose cooperation is required if implementation is to become a reality.

Integrating learning and working

We saw in Chapters 6 and 7 that directors have a preference for 'learning while doing', and for learning as a group. Agreeing, communicating and sharing a compelling vision and mission represents an opportunity to build both team and communication skills. A number of training packages[21] have been developed to help teams of directors and/or managers define and agree their vision, mission and strategy, and their communication objectives.

The focus of such an approach to integrating learning and working could be a preparation for media interviews. In this area, a 'development need' may already have been recognized, and there are advantages in a team approach:

- Many directors receive public speaking or media training, but only as individuals, and only when the need for communication skills arises. As a result, an opportunity to develop the board as a team is missed.
- Traditional communication skills courses tend to focus upon *how* to communicate, rather than *what* to communicate and *to whom*. Fundamental messages such as the vision, goals, values and objectives of a company should not be developed spontaneously by an individual director. They should be formulated and agreed by the board.
- In communicating with the media, it is important that both directors and key members of a management team speak with one voice, and have a shared understanding of the real nature of communication problems, priority messages and key targets.

As companies experience the transition from bureaucratic to network organizations, a clear and compelling vision becomes even more important. Without it, the network can disintegrate or fall apart as its members 'do their own thing', and empowered groups rush off in all directions .

The benefits of group learning

A workshop and supporting workbook package, such as *The Complete Spokesperson*,[21] recognizes that the most effective form of learning is that which is motivated or has a particular purpose. In the process, the effectiveness of the team and interpersonal skills of directors, particularly in relation to communicating with the media, can be increased.

Bringing a workgroup together to discuss a problem area can be very conducive of teambuilding. The board could spend a day analysing image problems, setting communication objectives, identifying priority audiences, defining corporate personality, creating messages and preparing to meet the media. The programme could be tailored to the needs of particular companies, and could include mock interviews. The following examples illustrate the use of such an approach:

- The board of one company had completed an exercise to draw up a corporate mission statement prior to undertaking a media training session. While trying to explain the mission of the company, the directors concluded that it was not effective as a guide to action. The decision was taken not to launch a major advertising programme until the mission had been reviewed.
- Another board, on reviewing a company's corporate personality, concluded that it was closely associated with a 'headquarters' building. This had become an icon that symbolized the company. Unfortunately, in the age of the 'lean organization' it had come to represent bureaucratic overhead. It was decided to seek a new 'building icon', and a research and development centre and an international training centre were suggested as possibilities.
- In the course of a mock interview, the CEO revealed his thoughts on the merits of a management buy-out from the group of which the company was a part. Other directors had been thinking along similar lines, but had not been aware of the CEO's interests. During the course of the day several directors learned of a number of new devel-

opments as a result of the CEO's frank responses to questions. A more open relationship between the CEO and other board members was subsequently established as a result of the group session.

- In some cases, workshop sessions have provided a board with its first opportunity to make a frank assessment of the company's external profile and define the corporate personality it is seeking to achieve. As one chairman said: 'We have never looked into a mirror before.'

- As a result of workshops, many boards recognize that a compelling vision and mission has a value beyond contacts with the media. It can also help a company to 'differentiate' itself from 'competitors', when it is communicating with employees and both existing and potential customers.

- By endeavouring to communicate a message in a workshop environment, a board may secure new insights into fundamental business problems. One marketing director concluded: 'Until you try to communicate it yourself, you don't realize how tough it is to sell an "intangible". We know it works, but it's very technical. In the time allowed I could not put it across. I feel I now understand better what our people are up against. We need a new approach to the marketplace.'

- A number of boards have re-thought their marketing strategies as a result of finding it difficult to explain what is distinctive about their products and services. In general, directors who participate in workshops conclude that more effort needs to be devoted to differentiating their companies from competitors in the marketplace.

- Other boards have concluded that more attention should be given to two-way communication and 'listening to both customers and employees'. Directors from business sectors in which customers are treated as 'outsiders' or 'cannon fodder' to be bombarded with advertisements and direct mail shots, sometimes find it difficult to enter into a dialogue and be spontaneous.

- Some boards have been galvanized during workshop interviews by direct questions concerning the ability of a company to deliver. According to one chief executive officer: 'We thought we were great. We had paid the best consultants to sweat blood crafting some really good messages. It's only when you face a direct challenge that you realize you may not be able to deliver. I don't know what needs to be done, or by whom, to make it happen.'

The proper use of relevant learning tools and appropriate learning approaches on group learning exercises can create a virtuous learning cycle, and lead to a learning culture within the boardroom (Figure 8.2). Within a learning culture, there is greater commitment to evaluating and employing the learning tools that best suit the situation and context. Learning approaches may be refined in the light of experience of their use, while success reinforces the learning culture. The board becomes a learning board.

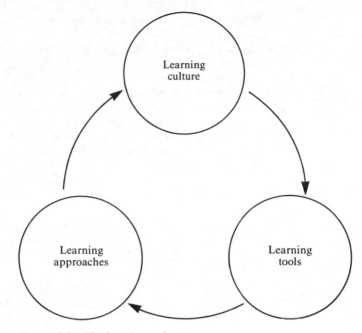

Figure 8.2 *The learning cycle*

Communicating the vision

The most exciting vision in the world will not motivate anyone if it is not communicated and shared. The authority of the vision will derive from its agreement, or endorsement, by the board, and its impact will depend very much upon the extent to which the board is thought to be committed to it. Hence, the responsibility for initiating the communication of the vision lies with the board. Exercise 8.3 suggests some questions that should be addressed by the board.

Exercise 8.3: Communicating the vision

The communication of a vision can be counter-productive if it is inappropriate or thought to be 'meaningless'. The following questions are typical of those that should be considered by the board:

1 Is the vision just 'words on paper', or 'floating about', or does it relate to actual or potential requirements in the marketplace?
2 Does it differentiate the company from other organizations? (Is it distinctive and memorable, or bland and instantly forgettable?)
3 Does the vision represent a realistic step forward from an existing image or 'corporate personality'?
4 Will the vision achieve a rapport with stakeholders and other interested parties?
5 Will the vision message encourage a response and lead to action?
6 Will its communication aid understanding, and help to build relationships with those with whom it is shared?

7 Will people link the vision with the company? (For example, will they say: why them?)

8 Could it happen, or is it always likely to remain a dream? (Is it credible?)

9 Will the vision just create an awareness of needs that other organizations will satisfy?

10 Is the vision a 'so what?' statement, or does it make people sit up, interest them, and motivate them to act? (Will it act as a catalyst to action that will lead to the furtherance of corporate goals, values and objectives?)

11 Does it stretch people? (Is the vision sufficiently ambitious?)

12 Is the vision too detailed? (Will it stand the test of time? Does it limit, constrain, exclude or constrict, or is it flexible and open?)

13 Whose vision is it? (Is it shared and widely 'owned'?)

14 Why should anyone care about it? (Does it reach the 'heart' as well as the 'head'?)

15 Is the vision likely to live and spread by word of mouth? (Is it in a form that can be communicated easily? Will people want to communicate it?)

Exercise 8.3 contains many questions, but this reflects the central need for a company to have a distinctive purpose. According to Peter Drucker: 'Only a clear definition of the mission and purpose of the organisation makes possible clear and realistic business objectives.'[22]

Advantages of board workshops

The survey for the IOD[4] suggests that directors have a strong preference for learning from each other. Board workshops can encourage greater openness and mutual trust. The experience of participants confirms that motivated learning—i.e. that which has a particular focus and is perceived as both relevant and practical—is the most effective.

Getting the board to work together on a particular task outside the normal boardroom environment—and perhaps assisted by an experienced facilitator—can yield a number of incidental development benefits. For example, in the case of vision and communication sessions:

- Participation in a workshop can give directors a grip on an area of corporate activity, such as a company's external communications, as a result of encouraging them to discuss and think through what they are seeking to achieve. This can be done against the background of a shared understanding of the current situation, which may not be possible during normal board discussions.
- Participants collectively consider issues and develop skills that can be of great importance in safeguarding and building a corporate image and reputation. The time devoted, free of agenda pressures, to thrashing out objectives and priorities has been found to be particularly beneficial. Subsequent activity can build upon the firmer foundations of consensus.
- The emergence of agreed priorities and messages appears to give workshop participants greater confidence. They tend to feel less exposed when they know that what they may say to the 'external world' is likely to have the support of board colleagues.
- Many boards are not 'self-aware'. Participation in a workshop can enable

directors to better understand how their corporate vision, values, goals, objectives and culture are perceived by others—for example, by certain stakeholders. Some boards exaggerate, and have a very subjective, narrow and unbalanced view of their impact upon the 'external world'.

- Members of boards are frequently unaware of the extent to which they make use of 'in words', or have developed a 'corporate view'. Having distanced themselves, while preparing to give their own assessments of interview performance, participants often find that, from an external perspective, conduct that is normal within the group can confuse or even alienate.

- Participation in interview sessions makes directors aware of what they are communicating 'beyond the words'. How they appear—for example, as slick or smooth, or standing against a luxurious backdrop while advocating economies—may undercut the purpose of communication. The 'image' rather than the 'content' may remain with the viewer or listener. Symbols can influence attitudes more than words.

- Sessions concerning the evaluation of communication effectiveness, and learning from experience, can encourage boards to apply the approaches developed for other corporate activities. Participation may cause directors to consider consciously how they might best learn from their experience, and review periodically what they have learned, in addition to examining the more usual performance measures.

Individuals and the group

Participation in a board workshop, such as the example we have been using concerning communication with the media, can enable directors to learn more about themselves, and each other, in relation to the group:

- Many directors have great difficulty in succinctly describing the essential purpose of their company. Ideally, all members of a board should be able to state in one or two sentences the essence of their company's vision, purpose, goals, values, mission and objectives. The form of words used should act as a guide to action for employees, and enable a journalist to differentiate a company from its competitors.

- Other directors are extremely garrulous in interview situations. Individuals who act like clams when dealing with colleagues and subordinates will sometimes 'open up' and 'reveal all' when seeking to impress a journalist. This can be dangerous when price-sensitive information is involved. Participation in the workshops can enable team members to obtain new insights into each others' qualities.

- How actual and potential directors conduct themselves in mock interviews can be of value to chairmen and chief executive officers contemplating senior appointments and reviewing the allocation of roles within the boardroom team. Interview and external communication skills can be of great importance in some directorial roles.

In addition to building confidence and specific communication skills for dealing with the media, some 'vision and communication' type workshops appear to enhance team awareness and team competences to such an extent as to suggest their use as a valid alternative to explicit 'team building' activities.

An experienced development professional will be aware of the many general factors to consider when organizing a board workshop. These will range from room layout to catering arrangements. While points of detail need to be addressed, the mechanics of making an event happen should not be allowed to squeeze out a continuing focus upon the purpose of the event.

A board workshop should be held at a location that is free of interruption. The corporate or board calendar should be consulted when dates are selected. One 'vision and communication' workshop was held within days of a quarterly 'cut off'. Throughout the day, two of the directors present were preoccupied with chasing and receiving information concerning sales against budget.

An effort should be made to anticipate considerations that may be unique to a particular form of board workshop. For example, in relation to media training type sessions:

- A 'strong' CEO may inhibit the contributions of certain board colleagues. One way of encouraging others to participate in mock interviews is to give an initial and tough interview to the CEO. Directors participating in subsequent interviews could be questioned on topics related to their experience or responsibilities.
- Experience suggests that later interviewees can benefit from reviews of the performance of those who have gone before. For this reason, assessments and discussion should be held at the conclusion of each interview. Learning can then be cumulative throughout the course of a workshop session.
- Two workshop leaders or facilitators may be better than one. During the course of mock interviews one person could play the role of journalist or interviewer while the other concentrates upon the assessment of performance.
- It is important that during the course of a board workshop all directors are involved. *The Complete Spokesperson* package[21] contains a number of data modules. When interest appears to be waning, or a change of pace is desired, a workshop leader could invite participants to complete one or more of these. This could create more interaction within the group, and draw in those who have not actively participated.

Workshop topics need to be selected with care. Directors can resent the commitment of time to activities that are not perceived to be productive. It helps if the subject matter of a directors' workshop is both intrinsically important, and capable of leading to a tangible output that relates to a key responsibility of the board. Hence the use in this chapter of an example concerning the articulation and communication of a compelling vision. This should be seen as a priority task of the board.

Overcoming barriers to implementation

The ultimate measure of how effectively a board operates as a team is the extent to which it is able to make things happen. A mature and secure board is willing to confront reality. It accepts that obstacles and opponents of change exist, and rather than avoid barriers or pretend they do not exist it actively identifies and confronts them.

A useful board technique is to list separately all the factors that are likely to help or hinder the achievement of a particular goal, objective or task. This enables barriers to be identified, and an overview of what is likely to be involved in implementation to be obtained. Activities can then be identified that build upon helpful factors and alleviate those that are unhelpful.

The value of 'helps and hinders' analysis is that it can enable a board to identify the full range of actions that may need to be initiated. Very often, boards only identify some of the relevant factors, and although these may be addressed, those that are overlooked may prevent the occurrence of desired outcomes.

Training and development is an example of an activity that may do little to contribute to the achievement of corporate goals.[1] Many companies obtain a negligible return from considerable expenditure on training activities of a high standard that do not tackle hidden obstacles to performance. Much training is undertaken on a departmental basis, and may, or may not, be applied to the support of the cross-functional and inter-organizational processes that generate customer satisfaction and deliver business objectives.

Checklist

1 However competent the members of the board of your company may be as individuals, do they work well together as a team?
2 Do they share a common vision, goals, values and objectives?
3 Do they recognize, respect and complement each others' qualities and contributions?
4 Has the board of your company discussed its own performance, and prioritized the barriers, obstacles or inhibitors to greater effectiveness?
5 Is there a satisfactory degree of mutual respect and common understanding among management and the board?
6 How united is the board as a team, and how united do 'outsiders' perceive it to be?
7 Does the board really understand the concerns of management?
8 Do communications from the board address 'root causes', and relate to and reflect corporate goals, values and objectives?
9 Have the 'audiences' been defined and prioritized, are messages clear, concise, and relevant, and are appropriate channels being used?
10 Has the board articulated, agreed and shared a clear, distinctive and compelling vision?

11 What would, could or should anyone do differently after having been exposed to the message? Will people 'believe in it'?

12 Is the board willing and able to confront the various barriers and obstacles to the achievement of corporate vision, values, goals and objectives?

13 Are all the elements, actions, processes and empowerments in place to enable the board to achieve its key objectives?

Notes and references

1 Colin Coulson-Thomas, *Transforming the Company: Bridging the Gap between Management Myth and Corporate Reality*, Kogan Page, 1992.

2 Clare Hogg, 'Making middle managers miserable', *The Times*, Appointments, (19 December 1991), 30.

3 Andrew Kakabadse, *The Wealth Creators: Top People, Top Teams and Executive Best Practice*, Kogan Page, 1991.

4 Colin Coulson-Thomas, *Professional Development of and for the Board*. An Adaptation Ltd survey for the Institute of Directors. An executive summary has been published by the IOD, February 1990.

5 Philip Sadler, 'On shaping the balance of power', *Director* (March 1992), 25.

6 Sir John Harvey-Jones, *Making it Happen: Reflections on Leadership*, 3rd impression, Fontana/Collins, March 1989, pp. 233–84.

7 PRO NED, *Research into the Role of the Non-Executive Director*, PRO NED, 1992.

8 Peter Morgan, 'Cadbury presumptions on the role of directors challenged by IOD', Letter to the Editor, *Financial Times*, (31 July 1992), 15.

9 Ada Demb and F-Friedrich Neubauer, *The Corporate Board: Confronting the Paradoxes*, Oxford University Press, 1992.

10 Colin Coulson-Thomas and Richard Brown, *The Responsive Organisation: People Management, the Challenge of the 1990s*, BIM, 1989.

11 R.W. Revans, *Action Learning*, Blond & Briggs, 1979; and Alan Mumford, Peter Honey and Graham Robinson, *Director's Development Guidebook: Making Experience Count*, Director Books, 1990.

12 Alfred W. Van Sinderen, 'The board looks at itself', *Directors and Boards*, (Winter 1985), 20–3.

13 Colin Coulson-Thomas and Alan Wakelam, *The Effective Board: Current Practice, Myths and Realities*. An IOD discussion document, 1991.

14 Sir Adrian Cadbury, *Company Chairman*, Director Books, 1990.

15 'Could you be a chairman?', Chairmanship, *Boardroom Agenda*, No. 3, (August 1992), 18–19.

16 John Adair, *Effective Teambuilding*, Gower, 1986.

17 Colin Coulson-Thomas, *Public Relations is Your Business: A Guide for Every Manager*, Business Books, 1981, p. 59.

18 Colin and Susan Coulson-Thomas, *Communicating for Change*. An Adaptation Ltd survey for Granada Business Services, 1991.

19 Colin Coulson-Thomas, *The Role and Status of Project Management*. A survey undertaken by Adaptation Ltd for the APM, 1990; and, 'Project management: A necessary skill?', *Industrial Management and Data Systems*, No. 6 (1990), 17–21.

20 Colin Coulson-Thomas and Trudy Coe, *The Flat Organisation: Philosophy and Practice*, BIM, 1991.

21 For example, see Peter Bartram and Colin Coulson-Thomas, *The Complete Spokesperson*, workshop and workbook, Policy Publications, 1990; and (handbook) Kogan Page 1991; and Colin Coulson-Thomas and Didacticus Video Productions Ltd, *The Change Makers: Vision and Communication*. Booklet to

accompany integrated audio and video tape training programme by Sir John Harvey-Jones, Didacticus Video Productions Ltd, 1991.

22 Peter Drucker, *Management: Tasks, Responsibilities, Practices*, Heinemann, 1974.

9 Evaluating performance

Establishing relevant criteria

There are all sorts and conditions of company. While there are millions of companies around the world, over a million of them being registered at the UK's Companies House alone,[1] most of those concerned with director development are likely to be focused upon the requirements of the board of a single company, or of members of the various boards within a single group.

The point that every company is unique has been made a number of times during the course of this book. Each company has directors who, as Graef S. Crystal suggests,[2] should 'earn their keep'. Beyond this, what represents effective performance should reflect the situation and circumstances of each case. Criteria for judging performance need to be established that are relevant to a particular context in which a group of people face a set of challenges and opportunities that may change over time.

What represents 'good performance' can depend upon one's priorities and interests. Thus, each group of stakeholders may have its own basis for judging board performance. While recognizing that different perspectives exist, in this chapter we shall consider the evaluation of the performance of both individual directors and the board as a whole from the 'point of view' of the company.

The exercises in this chapter are concerned with forming an overview of board performance, and assessing directorial effectiveness and contribution in relation to the functions and key responsibilities of the board. In particular, they include the assessment of the ability of the board to 'make it happen'. Evaluations tend to focus on the dynamics of the board, such as the degree of openness and extent of participation, rather than upon the outcomes, i.e. what was achieved.

Approaches to performance evaluation

Published information, such as annual reports and accounts, may be an imperfect guide to directorial performance.[3] Even if this information were more revealing, the extent to which a board—or the valiant efforts of a management team in spite of a board—contributed to documented outcomes may still not be clear. Also, a measure such as a relatively high dividend pay-out could be an indication of a short-term focus rather than 'good performance'.

What other indicators are there? One obvious place to begin is with the strategy of a company and the role played by the board.[4] For example, what role did the board actually play in the formulation of strategy? Did it initiate, or act as a rubber stamp?

An attempt could be made to benchmark performance against that of other and 'comparable' boards. Such an exercise can be difficult to arrange. Other boards may not be prepared to be sufficiently open, and a fair comparison may not be possible when the nature of the challenges faced by different boards can vary so much.

When external data such as industry league tables are used, it needs to be remembered that not all boards start from the same position. As one interviewee put it: 'Some boards are lucky, while others have a devil of a job. . . . Some situations would defeat anyone.' Improvements, or movement, may be important, rather than absolute position.

A board could participate in a mutual peer review or 'exchange directors' in order to obtain an external assessment. However, it is sometimes difficult to open up board meetings to external scrutiny when sensitive and pressing matters are under consideration. It may also be necessary to sit through more than the occasional meeting if a balanced and fair assessment is to be made.

A better solution might be for the chairman to invite one or more non-executive directors to take a special interest in the effectiveness of the board. An 'assessment committee' of non-executive directors could be formed to advise the chairman on how the effectiveness of the board, and the contributions of individual executive directors, might be improved. Comments on board performance could be sought from important stakeholders and independent analysts.

Evaluating structure

Board structures can and do vary as a result of a number of factors (considered later in Chapter 14). Structure should match the requirements of the corporate situation, business context and legislative framework. An appropriate structure for one board might not be a desirable option for another. Attitudes and behaviour, as we saw in Chapter 4, are more significant than structure, although both could be influenced by structure.

The overwhelming majority of listed UK companies appear to have established an 'audit committee', and a 'remuneration committee' with a preponderance of non-executive directors.[5] However, less than one in ten participants in a survey of 'chairmen'[6] mentioned non-executive directors as a 'resource' for improving board effectiveness.

Principles of corporate governance, or best practice, could be applied to the composition, structure and operation of the board:[7] for example, do the executive directors determine their own rewards or defer to a remuneration committee, or are agendas and papers sent out in good time? There are clearly a great many similar questions that could be asked.

There is some evidence that the structure and style of a board,[8] and particularly the position of the CEO in relation to the board,[9] can have an impact upon board effectiveness and contribution.

Evaluating conduct   An assessment could be made of the extent to which a board takes a long-term view, or is overwhelmed with short-term accommodations. Drucker recognized in the 1940s that a board has to achieve and maintain a balance between: (a) a long-term strategy based upon the core purpose and capability of the corporation; and (b) the achievement of satisfactory levels of short-term performance.[10] Doing both at a time of economic adversity is sometimes easier said than done.

Particular aspects of a board's role could be assessed. For example, one could examine the clarity of a vision. Walton puts particular importance upon the ability to explain, persuade and arbitrate between many competing interests when assessing corporate leadership.[11]

The selected focus could reflect the challenges facing the board, or how the board responded to a particular crisis.[12] Thus where change needs to occur, the extent to which the executive directors are leaders rather than managers could be especially important.[13]

One could examine the extent to which a board is able to turn intention into reality. A company is a community of people who have come together in order to increase their collective capability to turn aspiration into achievement. Of course whether or not implementation is desirable is dependent upon whether a vision, and goals, values and objectives are appropriate and relevant.

Conduct, and particularly intentions, can be obscured by rhetoric. There may be gaps or inconsistencies between what a board says and what it does. Some boards confuse or deceive themselves as well as others. In order to focus upon reality, it may be necessary to strip away a certain amount of mythology and concentrate upon fact.[14]

Evaluating effectiveness   Exercise 9.1 suggests the use of a number of questions to determine a board's approach to the evaluation of directorial competence and board effectiveness, and clarify the attitudes of its members towards the assessment of individual contributions and team effectiveness.

Exercise 9.1: How effectiveness is evaluated

For someone who is relatively new to a company, the first task may be to identify the views of the board concerning the existing approach to the evaluation of directorial competence and board effectiveness. A short checklist could be used to determine: (a) how the effectiveness of individual members of the board, and of the board as a whole, is evaluated; and (b) how the process of evaluation might be improved. Individual directors could be questioned about their effectiveness in their current directorial role and how this might be improved.

A comprehensive approach would be to start with the function of the board and the criteria that have been established for the competence of directors and the effectiveness of boards, and draw up some form of checklist. An example is given in a 'companion' book, *Creating Excellence in the Boardroom*.[15]

Approaches, attitudes and processes

When using any form of checklist, it needs to be borne in mind that, increasingly, effective direction is a question of processes for visioning, policy deployment, enabling, supporting, empowering, monitoring and learning rather than the taking of discrete decisions.

The qualities sought in competent directors (Chapter 2) and the approach taken by an effective board (Chapter 4) suggest that attitudes and behaviour, rather than structure, may be the key to performance. The author's view for over a decade has been that:

> Too great a concern with structure is a reflection of mechanical thinking, which leads to the search for an ideal structure. Viewing the company (and board) as an evolving organism leads to the conclusion that no one form of structure is likely to be the best for all companies. . . . While communication and structure interrelate, structure should be the servant of communication and not *vice versa*.[16]

Demb and Neubauer have pointed out that similar approaches are sometimes adopted by different board types.[17] The need to confront pervasive challenges in the business environment is forcing responses that have common elements, and is resulting in certain forms of behaviour quite independently of the formal structure of the board.

The approach to evaluation adopted by one company is illustrated in Figure 9.1. In this instance, the monitoring focuses upon visioning outputs, corporate goals, and how resources are combined and utilized to further them. The acid evaluation test is ultimately the extent to which the various programmes initiated by the board contribute towards the achievement of the corporate vision.

The difficulty of establishing assessment criteria

Do not be disappointed if sensible and usable evaluation criteria appear elusive. Agreeing the basis of measurement is often far from easy. The board has many functions, and views may vary on such matters as how to 'trade off' the interests of different stakeholders, or how demanding or 'stretching' objectives should be.

One may need to get very close to a board in order to assess it. It may be necessary to participate in a debate in order to judge how open it is. Reference has already been made to the possible existence of gaps between what the board says and what it does.

The seasoned observer looks for revealing symptoms. What makes the members of the board sit up, and what makes them fidget? Is the board firefighting or looking ahead? Is it confronting reality, or concerned with 'cosmetics' and appearances? Is the discussion about numbers and

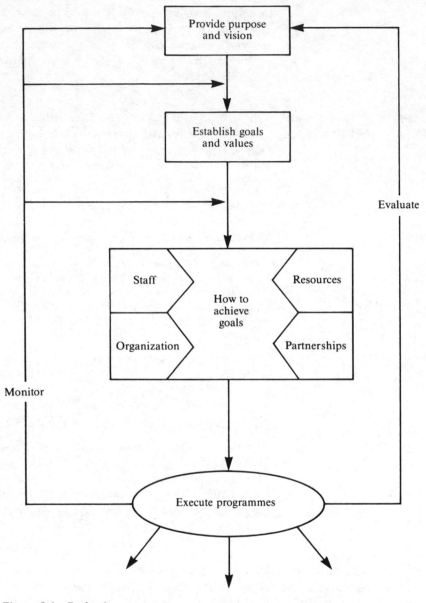

Figure 9.1   *Evaluation process*

'saving face', or about people and customer satisfaction? Regardless of the rhetoric, how much is the board really willing to share?

Just raising the question of evaluation can trigger a useful debate. For example, is the board complacent or overly ambitious? Could more demanding targets be set if the board became more proactive and determined in rooting out and tackling obstacles and barriers to achievement? Exercise 9.2 suggests some questions that could be used to encourage discussion in the boardroom.

Exercise 9.2: Establishing board prioritization and focus

The board may be busy, but is it concentrating upon the key priorities? Many boards do not focus on the 'vital few' tasks that need to be done to achieve corporate objectives. The following 'illustrative' questions are among those that could be used to assess how disciplined and rigorous a board is in its focus upon the customer:

1 Does the board listen to customers and understand what constitutes value to them?
2 Have the key cross-functional management and business processes that generate and deliver this value been identified?
3 Are they monitored and understood, and who in the boardroom is responsible for them?
4 Has the board ensured that people are empowered, equipped and motivated to operate these processes successfully?
5 Does the board actively seek to identify and overcome the obstacles and barriers to the delivery of value to customers?

The responses to such questions as those in Exercise 9.2 enable the board that is serious about satisfying customers to be distinguished from the board that is merely paying lip service to the customer.

Hugh Parker came to the conclusion that it is impossible to 'define precisely a set of criteria for board performance that can be strictly applied to all boards'.[18] Criteria should only be established if they are likely to be helpful to the board.

Measurements that could be of relevance are analyses of, or movements in indices of, customer and employee satisfaction. Both could be independently assessed, and particular targets could be set that take into account the results of benchmarking against best practice.

Whatever approach is adopted, it should be agreed with the chairman and board. Members of the board should understand the basis of their individual and collective assessments. In an ideal situation, the remuneration of the board could be linked to an assessment of its overall performance.

Evaluating the individual director

A distinction needs to be made between individual and group performance. A competent director could serve upon an ineffective board. The effective board should be a mechanism for complementing, and building upon, individual strengths within the team, and ameliorating individual weaknesses.

According to a survey of chairmen[6] the evaluation of the effectiveness of individual directors appears overwhelmingly informal. Only one in eight participants claim that their boards operate any form of periodic and formal appraisal.

We saw in Chapter 5 that the selection of directors is largely based upon their personal qualities, as demonstrated by a past track record. However, only about a fifth of respondents evaluate directorial effectiveness in terms of the demonstration of personal qualities and competences.[6] It would appear that directors are selected according to one set of criteria, and assessed (if they are assessed at all) by a different set.

Where it occurs, assessment is largely in terms of managerial rather than directorial criteria. Executive directors are assessed in terms of how well they manage their functional departments, not on the basis of their contribution to the work of the board.[6] Such an approach can encourage people to concentrate upon their managerial responsibilities at the expense of their directorial duties.

Exercise 9.3 suggests an approach to assessing directorial competences, based upon our examination of the knowledge and skills that a competent director ought to possess (see Chapters 2 and 3).

Exercise 9.3: Assesssing individual directorial competences

One approach to involving directors in the evaluation of their own directorial competences is (a) to draw up a matrix of directorial knowledge and skills, and (b) to ask members of the board to undertake a self-assessment of their own competence against the standards established in the matrix. An example of such an approach is illustrated in the appendix to this chapter. This is given by way of an example, and should not be taken as a model. Priority skills will vary to a degree from board to board.

In Chapter 3 various areas of legal and financial knowledge, personal skills and competences, and boardroom issues concerning both the board and individual directors are identified. Particular areas of knowledge and skill that are especially relevant to the requirements of a specific board could be incorporated into a self-assessment questionnaire.

The example of a self-assessment questionnaire illustrated in the appendix to this chapter contains an overall summary, and requires each director to verify that the company's 'matrix' of directorial competences has been read and understood. The latter item enables the chairman to verify that, at minimum, each director has been made aware of, *inter alia*, the accountabilities and function of the board, the duties and responsibilities of a director, and the standards of competence that might reasonably be required and are actually expected.

A number of matrices of directorial skill requirements are in existence, and more authoritative definitions of directorial competence are under preparation. These need to be treated with some caution, as what constitutes a competent director can depend in large part upon the nature, situation and circumstances of a company.

The survey of chairmen already cited[6] suggests that the criteria used to assess directors are not being employed to influence their behaviour in the boardroom. For example, there was not a single reference to being a 'team player' or contributing to the board as a team. This is surprising, given that we saw in the previous chapter that, in an earlier survey, 'teamwork' emerged as the principal boardroom issue.

It would appear that chairmen regard corporate performance as largely the result of the work of the 'board as a team' rather than the contributions of individual directors. Hence, they are assessed by departmental activities and outcomes, although a view can be taken of the extent to which individuals are 'team players'.

Many chairmen believe that they and the CEO are primarily responsible for the extent to which the board operates effectively as a team. Thus they assess individual board members according to the particular responsibilities that are allocated to them.

The board and implementation

Earlier in this chapter, we saw that one company evaluates its performance largely in terms of relating the outcomes of corporate programmes to the corporate vision (Figure 9.1). While the execution of programmes might be in the hands of management, their performance will reflect the framework and context established by the board, and the extent to which the people of the organization are equipped, empowered and motivated to act and achieve.

The board should recognize its own responsibility for turning aspiration and intention into achievement and reality. The effectiveness of a board could be assessed in relation to a major corporate programme. The assessment could cover the board's understanding of relevant issues and the relevance of its actions. A possibility might be a quality programme, as creating a quality- or customer-focused organization requires sustained commitment on the part of the board.

Few companies can deliver the whole of the value added sought by customers without understanding cross-functional business processes or working closely with other organizations in the supply chain. However, many boards composed of directors who are engrossed in their 'departmental' responsibilities are almost entirely blind to 'cross-functional' and 'inter-organizational' opportunities.

Each organization and board needs to formulate and—in the light of experience and changes of circumstance—refine its own approach to quality. Regardless of the allocation of quality responsibilities, the whole board needs to be committed to quality. All directors should feel responsible for quality. At the same time, it may make sense to give individual directors a facilitating or leadership role in respect of the implementation of certain aspects of the quality process.

Moving from assessment to action

Unless the effectiveness of the board is assessed, and deficiencies are identified, it is not easy to undertake remedial or corrective action. According to the survey of chairmen,[6] 'training' closely followed by 'changing the composition of the board' are at the head of a 'top ten' list of 'suggested ways to improve the effectiveness of the board'.

Reference has been made previously to the observation that three-quarters of the respondents in the 'chairman' survey[6] believe that the effectiveness of their company's board could be improved. There could potentially be a very significant role for director development if the assessment of development needs were more rigorous, and if the credibility and quality of development services were improved.

Checklist

1 Does the board of your company regularly assess its own performance?
2 How relevant are the approaches that are adopted? Is a holistic view taken?
3 How appropriate are the criteria that are used to assess the contribution and effectiveness of (a) the individual directors and (b) the board as a whole?
4 Do they reflect the situation and circumstances of the company?
5 Are performance outcomes related to corporate vision, values, goals and objectives?
6 How objective, dispassionate and independent is the assessment? Are non-executive directors involved?
7 Have other models of board operation or structure been considered, i.e. has a 'first principles' review taken place?
8 What positive and negative symptoms are apparent in board attitudes and behaviour?
9 Is the board focusing upon essentials and the longer term?
10 Who is responsible for the effectiveness of the board as a team, and how is this effectiveness measured?
11 Does the reward and remuneration system encourage board members to concentrate upon their managerial responsibilities at the expense of their directorial duties?
12 What, if anything, has changed as a result of the evaluation (if any occurs) of contributions in the boardroom and the performance of the board?
13 What is the relationship between director development activities and the assessment of contributions in the boardroom and the performance of the board?

Notes and references

1 Companies House, *Annual Report 1991–92*, 1992; and Andrew Jack, 'Agency has surplus of £1.56m', *Financial Times* (4 August 1992), 8.
2 Graef S. Crystal, 'Do directors earn their keep?', *Fortune International* (6 May 1991), 56–8.
3 Terry Smith, *Accounting for Growth: Stripping the Camouflage from Company Accounts*, Century Business, 1992; McBride's Design Consultants, *Annual Report Survey*, McBride's Design Consultants; and Andrew Jack, 'Shareholders show little faith in annual reports, says survey', *Financial Times*, (17 August 1992), 1.

4 Shaker A. Zahra and John A. Pearce, 'Determinants of board directors strategic involvement', *European Management Journal*, **8**, No. 2 (June 1990), 164–73.

5 Korn/Ferry, *Boards of Directors Study UK 1992*, Korn/Ferry International, 1992.

6 Colin Coulson-Thomas and Alan Wakelam, *The Effective Board: Current Practice, Myths and Realities*. A IOD discussion document, 1991.

7 See, for example, Committee on the Financial Aspects of Corporate Governance ('The Cadbury Committee'). Draft report issued for public comment, Committee on the Financial Aspects of Corporate Governance, 27 May 1992.

8 Abbass F. Alkafaji, 'Effective boards of direction', *Industrial Management and Data Systems*, **90**, No. 4 (1990), 18–26.

9 John A. Pearce and Shaker A. Zahra, 'The relative power of CEOs and boards of directors associations with corporate performance', *Strategic Management Journal*, **12**, No. 2 (February 1991), 135–53.

10 Peter F. Drucker, *Concept of the Corporation*, John Day, 1946.

11 R.E. Walton, *Innovating to Compete*, Jossey-Bass, 1987.

12 Brian Boyd, 'Corporate linkages and organisational environment, a test of the resource dependence model', *Strategic Management Journal*, **11**, No. 6 (October 1990), 419–30.

13 J.P. Kotter, *A Force for Change: How Leadership Differs from Management*, The Free Press, 1990.

14 Myles L. Mace, *Directors: Myth and Reality*, Division of Research, Graduate School of Business Administration, Harvard University, 1971; and Colin Coulson-Thomas, *Transforming the Company: Bridging the Gap between Management Myth and Corporate Reality*, Kogan Page, 1992.

15 Colin Coulson-Thomas, *Creating Excellence in the Boardroom*, McGraw Hill, 1993.

16 Colin Coulson-Thomas, *Public Relations is Your Business: A Guide for Every Manager*, Business Books, 1981, pp. 59–66.

17 Ada Demb and F-Friedrich Neubauer, *The Corporate Board: Confronting the Paradoxes*, Oxford University Press, 1992.

18 Hugh Parker, *Letters to a New Chairman*, Director Publications, 1990.

Appendix   DIRECTORIAL COMPETENCE SELF-ASSESSMENT FORM

Personal information

Name of director: ....

Directorial role and responsibilities: ....
....

Address: ....
....

Telephone number: ....

Self-assessment of directorial knowledge and experience

Instructions to directors: Please read through the corporate matrix of directorial competences and indicate with a tick how you rank, for each section of the matrix, your knowledge and experience on a scale of 1 to 10. The number 10 indicates the greatest level of skill or experience, while the number 1 indicates the least level of skill. (The groupings: Low (1–3), Medium (4–7) and High (8–10) could correspond with the categories on the directorial competences matrix.)

For each section of the skills matrix please indicate which subsection or subsections you consider to be the most significant and why.

1 **Role of the board**	Low			Medium				High		
	1	2	3	4	5	6	7	8	9	10
Knowledge										
Experience										

Most significant and why: ....
....
....
....

2 **Duties and responsibilities of directors**	Low			Medium				High		
	1	2	3	4	5	6	7	8	9	10
Knowledge										
Experience										

Most significant and why: ....
....
....
....

3 Financial accountability and reporting	Low			Medium				High		
	1	2	3	4	5	6	7	8	9	10
Knowledge										
Experience										

Most significant and why: ....
....
....
....

4 Personal skills and competences	Low			Medium				High		
	1	2	3	4	5	6	7	8	9	10
Knowledge										
Experience										

Most significant and why: ....
....
....
....

5 Strategic awareness	Low			Medium				High		
	1	2	3	4	5	6	7	8	9	10
Knowledge										
Experience										

Most significant and why: ....
....
....
....

6 Business development	Low			Medium				High		
	1	2	3	4	5	6	7	8	9	10
Knowledge										
Experience										

Most significant and why: ....
....
....
....

7 Boardroom issues and processes (etc.)	Low			Medium				High		
	1	2	3	4	5	6	7	8	9	10
Knowledge										
Experience										

Most significant and why: ....
....
....
....

Summary self-assessment of directorial competence

Having assessed your knowledge and experience under each section of the directorial skills matrix, please indicate how you would rank your overall **competence** on a continuum Low–Medium–High in each of the nine elements of the following summary matrix. (Elements chosen to encourage thought.)

Legal and financial	Personal skills	Boardroom issues
Low Medium High	Low medium high	Low Medium High
Duties and responsibilities	Strategic awareness	Board structure
------------	------------	------------
Role of the board	Business development	Boardroom dynamics
------------	------------	------------
Financial accountability	People and group	Roles and responsibilities
------------	------------	------------

Self-assessment of strengths and weaknesses

What do you consider are your strengths as a director?

....
....
....
....
....

What do you consider are your major weaknesses as a director?

....
....
....
....
....

Competence development history and future priorities

Please list any steps you have taken to develop your directorial knowledge and/or experience:

....
....
....
....

Please list any steps you plan to take to develop your directorial knowledge and/or experience:

....
....
....
....

Please describe any boardroom role or task you would not feel competent to undertake:

....
....
....
....

Attestation

I have read and understand the company's matrix of directorial competences, and hereby certify that in my judgement my responses to the above questions represent a true and fair view of my competence, and of my strengths and weaknesses as a director.

Signature of director: ....

Date: ....

10 The next steps

For most companies, given the almost complete absence of director development, there are 'next steps' to be taken. However, they must be appropriate steps. There are pitfalls and siren voices to avoid, and apathy and misunderstanding to overcome.

Standard solutions can be particularly dangerous. The development needs of individual directors and the board as a whole will reflect the nature, situation and circumstances of the company, and any particular deficiencies that have been identified.

Ideally, the development activity undertaken should help the board to 'grow the business'. It should also support corporate transformation[1] and renewal.[2] Increasingly, boards are having to assume responsibilities in relation to the direction and leadership of fundamental change, and they need to understand how this differs from traditional management.[3]

Proceeding with caution

Throughout this book we have (a) focused on various aspects of development needs (or the 'training requirement') and (b) considered numerous exercises to determine and prioritize barriers to performance and effectiveness, and the activities that are needed to overcome them. Scepticism, caution and uncertainty have been encountered at several points. Single solutions, fads and panaceas should be avoided.[4]

In many companies there is resistance to change. This may take the form of not wishing to 'distract', 'bother' or 'disturb' the board. The following interview comments reflect the mood of many chairmen:

I am interested rather than enthusiastic. The need for development is clear, but I have yet to be convinced that any action we might take will yield clear benefits.

The board is the one group I do not wish to use as a guinea pig. There are so many catchy ideas around looking for opportunities to be tested.

The board going on a course sends out signals. There are both positive and negative aspects to this, potential advantages but also risks.

The executive members of some boards, particularly those with active institutional shareholders and demanding non-executive directors, may face 'external' pressures to change.[5] However, many boards have to provide their own motivation, and much will depend upon how willing the chairman is to 'grasp the development nettle'.

The previous chapter, and particularly the exercises, summarized many of the issues raised in the course of this book. In this chapter we examine some 'next steps', with a particular emphasis upon 'making it happen'. The exercises have been designed to consolidate and focus upon the way ahead.

Directorial development priorities

What are the development priorities, and what should they be? First, let us examine the 'next steps' of companies in general. Again, some clues are suggested by the results of recent surveys.

The priorities placed upon the training and development of directors in various areas by participants in a survey of chairmen[6] are shown in Table 10.1. This ranks the areas in terms of 'very important' responses.

The area of greatest priority for the training and development of directors—which, by a significant margin, is given a 'very important' rating by almost six out of ten respondents—is 'strategic/business understanding'. In another survey undertaken by Adaptation Ltd with the IPM Research Group,[7] strategic awareness and understanding again emerged as the primary requirement.

While people at various levels may be involved, and may participate, in the strategy process, the board should give a lead in the determination and implementation of strategy.[8] This activity relates to a central function of the board (to be discussed in more detail in Chapter 12).

The need for 'financial understanding' (Table 10.1) was justified by those interviewed in terms of the accountability of the board to shareholders, and the fiduciary responsibilities of directors. These are aspects of the legal duties and responsibilities of directors., which have been given a relatively low priority, reflecting the view of many of those interviewed that while these issues are important, members of the board are able to draw upon the specialist legal and procedural expertise of the company secretary and various professionals as and when advice is needed.

Table 10.1 Professional development priorities: training and development

Area	Ranking (%)*
Strategic/business understanding	57
People skills	42
Management skills	39
Financial understanding	37
Negotiating skills	28
Knowledge of legal duties and responsibilities	18
Technical understanding	15

* Ranking in terms of 'very important'.
Note: Some respondents considered more than one area to be 'very important'.

Strategic awareness and understanding

A number of the participants in the survey of chairmen[6] were asked what they meant by 'strategic/business understanding'. Their responses included:

A knowledge and understanding of the company's long-term vision, so that the whole board is pulling in the same direction.

An understanding of the company's long-term objectives, and the strategies being used to meet the objectives.

An ability to forecast client and customer needs, via an understanding of *their* strategies.

An ability to see the business from the investor's point of view.

Being able to think strategically.

Forward planning and strategic planning.

The prominence given to strategic awareness is consistent with the essence of the distinction between direction and management. Survey evidence stresses the requirement for directors to look ahead, and with the perspective of the 'company as a whole'.[9]

People skills and personal qualities

Directors are members of a boardroom team. The second training and development priority for participants in the 'chairman' survey[6] was a range of 'people skills' (Table 10.1). Those interviewed stressed:

- the importance of personal qualities, rather than professional expertise and technical knowledge, as a distinguishing characteristic of the director;
- the need for empathy and awareness of others in the context of the boardroom, and the ability to win the trust and respect of colleagues;
- the value of listening, and the necessity of establishing and nurturing relationships with various stakeholders.

Awareness, perspective and personal qualities are the product of a great many factors, of which development activities could be but one. Selection criteria and the tone and 'culture' of the boardroom may result in a collective set of approaches and attitudes that are not easily changed.

Implementation

A board that 'works well' as a team, and can determine what needs to be done, must next address the question of implementation. We have already seen in earlier chapters that many boards are better at crafting strategies than at putting them into effect.

The importance given by participants in the 'chairman' survey[6] to 'management skills' (Table 10.1) reflects the fact that executive directors are both directors and managers. Several of those interviewed referred to various 'making it happen' skills as 'management' skills. One could argue that certain of the skill requirements that were identified for making sure that strategy is not only articulated but implemented could be considered 'directorial'.

It would appear that many chairmen of larger companies are taking the view that their boards need to become more actively involved at driving change through the corporate organization. Sir John Harvey-Jones chose to entitle his book of 'reflections on leadership', *Making it Happen*.[10] The appendix to this chapter lists some questions that could be used by a board to identify what needs to be done to 'make it happen'.

Establishing where to begin

Directors tend to be busy people. Hence development activity should focus upon requirements that relate to key business priorities and objectives rather than general qualities that are 'nice to have'. Without a sense of relevance and current importance, commitment may be difficult to achieve, and there may be a tendency to postpone action.

To help identify where one should begin, the contents and exercises of this book could be used. An attempt has been made to structure the book in a logical way to enable it to be of value for this purpose.

- Is the board aware of, and does it understand, the challenges and opportunities facing itself and the business (Chapters 1 and 11)? Where more than incremental change is required, and the drive and impetus from the boardroom is lacking, some awareness building exercises, or issue review sessions, could be beneficial.
- Is the role and function of the board understood, and are all directors aware of their legal duties and responsibilities (Chapter 12)? The board that is 'unable to see the wood for the trees' may need to be focused upon its responsibility for determining, monitoring, reviewing and ensuring the implementation of objectives and strategy. Executive directors with functional responsibilities might need greater strategic awareness and general business understanding.
- Do the members of the board understand the distinction between direction and management (Chapter 13)? Certain directors may neglect their directorial duties in order to cope with the flow of day-to-day problems. A session on how to achieve more of a balance between the two might be advisable, though tact may be needed where it is felt the directors may resent criticism.
- Is the nature of the board, and its size, composition and structure, appropriate given the situation and circumstances of the company and the development needs of the business (Chapter 14)? Some new blood, or even a board of a different type, may be needed before there is an acceptable team to develop. On the other hand, it is not unknown for a demanding development programme to be used to identify members of the board who are 'coasting' or 'passengers'.
- How competent are the individual members of the board (Chapter 2)? Do they have sufficient legal and financial knowledge, and an awareness of various matters concerning directors and boards (Chapter 3)? Certain directors may need individual development programmes. Skill requirements should not be defined so tightly as to inhibit flexibility as a business evolves.
- How effective is the board as a team (Chapter 4)? Some form of team-building activity may be needed if the personalities, skills and

experiences of the various members are to be harnessed and integrated.

- Is there a clear and open route to the boardroom (Chapter 5)? It may be necessary to agree the qualities that are sought in members of the board. There might be a requirement for formal criteria which could be used to assess new directors, and help existing directors to better understand what is expected of them.

- How are directors prepared for their directorial roles (Chapter 6), and how should they be prepared (Chapter 7)? It may be necessary to introduce both formal and informal development activities and learning opportunities.

- What should be done to help the directors to work together more effectively as a team (Chapter 8)? Some form of director's network could be of value.

- How is individual effectiveness and team performance in the boardroom assessed (Chapter 9)? The chairman may need to be counselled on how to evaluate directorial contributions and development needs, and set development objectives.

- Does the board get to the heart of the problem? Are barriers to the achievement of board objectives identified and overcome? It may be necessary to facilitate some form of 'help' and 'hinder' review, or barrier analysis.

When working through such a list of questions, a sense of perspective should be maintained. The aim of the exercise is not to list requirements that could be addressed, but to identify those that really ought to be tackled.

It is especially important that the focus of action should be identified. For example, David Thompson, chairman of Rank Xerox (UK), identifies a key question: 'Do boards spend enough time identifying what the problems really are, as opposed to what they think they are?' 'Groupthink' and misperception should be avoided.

Exercise 10.1 suggests how the areas requiring particular attention might be identified.

Exercise 10.1: Identifying the focus of action

Before a programme of next steps can be drawn up, areas in which action is needed must be identified. As has been stated so many times in this book, these will reflect the situation and circumstances of the company. For example:

1 A chairman might be happy with an existing board, but concerned about where the next generation of directors is to come from. In this case, the exercises of Chapter 5 could be used to widen the search, and open up new and clearer paths to the boardroom.

2 Another chairman may have been happy in the past with his or her board, but might now face the prospect of coping with a major international expansion. In this instance the priority may be to use the exercises of Chapter 14 to review the composition of the board. The demands placed upon the board

may have changed out of all recognition since the last review was undertaken.

The 'focus of action' could be identified by using: (a) the broad content of the chapters in this book to identify the general areas that need most attention; and then (b) using individual exercises within the 'highlighted' chapters to draw up a priority list of specific matters that need attention.

The 'next steps' agenda

It would be presumptuous of me to draw up a master list of next steps. The particular requirements of each company and every board must be thought through and kept under continual review.

The basics (which will be discussed in Chapters 11 to 14) should not be overlooked. For example, it should not be assumed that all members of the board fully understand either the distinction between direction and management, or the extent of their legal and financial duties and responsibilities. All directors could at least be encouraged to undertake an initial overview course on the role of the board, and the accountabilities, duties and responsibilities of company directors.

A number of next steps could arise out of the various deficiencies in current practice that have been identified in the course of this book. For example, the following matters were identified by one board as particularly significant:

Director development has had a relatively low priority. The board should acknowledge the need for, and invest in, the professional development of both existing and potential directors. [In this case it was felt that 'public acknowledgement' would 'demonstrate that the board means business'.]

The development needs of directors differ from those of managers. Company courses and other activities for the development of boardroom knowledge and skills should be distinct from, but complementary to, those concerning management competences.

Too little thought is being given to board succession and the next generation of directors. A 'search team' should be established to consider the possibilities. [Boards need not limit their search for potential directors to those who happen to be members of a company's senior management team.]

All new appointees to the board should be fully prepared for the role of company director. Potential directors need to know what is required.

Someone on the board needs to be a champion of director development. The chairman should act as a catalyst in assessing boardroom development needs and ensuring that appropriate action is taken.

The company lacks director development expertise. The board would benefit from access to an experienced counsellor or facilitator who could work with both individual directors, and the board as a whole, in the assessment of boardroom performance and the development of directorial competence.

The board should devote more attention to management and business processes, and especially to those that cross functions. The two priorities are to identify those processes that deliver customer satisfaction, and to ensure that the company has effective processes for ongoing learning, adaptation and change. [This particular board found that, because of the company's 'departmental' form of organization, no-one was responsible for cross-functional processes.]

Director development does not occur in a vacuum. It needs to support other board activities, initiatives and priorities. A broad view, and holistic perspective are also desirable in order to understand how different factors are interrelated.[11] Exercise 10.2 suggests one approach that could be taken to encourage a board to adopt a broad and holistic approach. As an alternative, the questions in the appendix to this chapter could be addressed.

Exercise 10.2: Corporate governance in perspective

One way of broadening the perspective of a board concerning 'what could be' is to compare the situation of a company board with those of the governing bodies of other types of organization. The process of finding out about other models of corporate governance can itself be a useful learning experience.

Health authorities, universities, schools, local authorities, public corporations, professional associations, etc., all have governing bodies. Compare and contrast type questions could include:

1 What are the consequences of incorporation by Royal Charter, as opposed to under the Companies Acts?
2 Should the board enter into a mutual 'peer review' arrangement with an organization other than another company?
3 What lessons in terms of relationships with customers might be learned from observing the responsibilities and conduct of the council of a professional body towards its 'members'?
4 What might be learned from other approaches to developing competent directors and effective boards?
5 How does the receipt of a substantial element of public funding affect accountability?
6 How might members of the board benefit from service upon some form of public sector board, or the governing body of another form of organization?
7 Are there other 'walks of life' from which good candidates for non-executive director appointments could be drawn?

The board of a public company could examine various discussion papers and guidelines on the principles of corporate governance that are issued from time to time. A 1992 UK example is the draft proposals of the 'Cadbury Committee'.[12] As one might expect, given the many perspectives from which such proposals are judged, initial reactions to them have been mixed.

Professional development cautions and warnings

For many years director development has been a 'cinderella' subject. Either the 'need' has not been recognized, or commitment to development action has been lacking. Difficulty has been experienced in assessing deficiencies, defining requirements, and identifying appropriate 'solutions'.

There could now be a danger that a growing awareness of the extent of the 'development gap' in the boardroom could lead to inappropriate activity. In the course of this book we have drawn upon relevant surveys (see section 1 in the Bibliography) in order to illustrate that there is often a wide gulf between theory and practice, much inconsistency, and a severe shortage of relevant expertise.

Enthusiasms can and do lead companies and their boards astray. For example, let us consider the question of directorial competence:

- A passion for the detailed definition of directorial competences could set in concrete 'what is' rather than 'encourage what ought to be'. 'What is', or current practice, might not be appropriate, or even desirable.
- The lack of innovation in the structure and operation of boards needs to be recognized. Those who define directorial competences within a particular national context should learn from best practice, and take account of experience elsewhere in the world.
- If competences are to have authority and be credible, they should be defined by those with directorial experience, and under the auspices of an organization of standing.
- The definition of competences should not be so extensive that the 'basics', or the essence of what is distinctive about direction, are overlooked.

Exercises to define competences have a tendency to result in voluminous lists of requirements, as those reviewing draft documentation 'think of some extra points to add'. A degree of pragmatism and common sense can sometimes be overlooked.

Programme availability

As far as formal courses for directors are concerned, a lack of provision might be preferable to initiatives that are inappropriate. There are institutions that would like to offer more in the field of director development. However, some are more cautious than others:

- Those who are responsible are often restrained by a shortage of people who are able to deliver courses of the required level and quality. Tailoring an approach to the needs of the members of a particular board may require special skills, and can demand both insight and preplanning.
- In contrast, less scrupulous organizations sometimes 'retread' elements of existing management programmes and 'repackage' them as short courses for directors. Going for a relatively cheap and available package can often turn out to be a 'false economy'.

A 'solution' that has superficial appeal is to integrate the development of directorial competences into regular management courses—for example, the elements of an MBA programme. If this is done, care should be taken to ensure that students taking such courses fully appreciate the distinction between direction and management.

Another possibility would be for a wider range of professional bodies to develop courses and learning materials for those concerned with the direction of particular functions. Alternatively, or additionally, such a need could be met by a wider provision of courses by the IOD. It is important that any courses that are provided make clear the distinct nature of 'direction', and the duties and responsibilities of the director towards the company as a whole.

Creating separate modules for programme elements concerning directors and boards makes it easier to establish a distinct directorial perspective. One UK national framework for the assessment and mutual recognition of course modules already exists in a network of collaborative arrangements that the IOD has established with a number of business schools and colleges.

A focus upon the role of the board, directorial qualities, and the duties and responsibilities of the company director might be more appropriate in the period before, and just after, a boardroom appointment. In order to offer such a programme, use could be made of suitable people on a flexible basis. Why 'make do' with the services of a permanent employee when an appropriate authority could be contracted to deliver a short course?

Flexibility could also be applied to the learning process, in recognition of the fact that directors are busy people. Respondents in one survey we have considered[13] showed an interest in distance learning. However, they expressed a preference for informal contact with other directors.

The known scepticism and caution of the directorial skills marketplace has inhibited several institutions from making the relatively large investments needed to develop distance learning packages. If other materials of this type are to be produced, it is likely that they will be used to support the informal learning of individuals and to complement formal programmes designed to encourage participation and interaction.

Informal learning

Formal learning has its limitations. We saw in Chapter 5 that little weight is attached to academic, professional and technical qualifications when boardroom appointments are made. The emphasis during the selection process tends to be on personal qualities. However, once people are on a board, they may become aware of the need for particular knowledge or a skill that should be met by formal development or otherwise.

It is likely that the 'next steps' of most boards will include informal learning,[14] the value of which was highlighted in Chapters 6 and 7.

Many directors naturally learn informally, for example, in discussion with each other. Rather than traditional 'subject teachers', directors require development advisers, counsellors, mentors and facilitators. A good facilitator is able to guide the development of individual directors and of the board as a whole.

Many directors need to be made more aware of the development opportunities in the normal business and corporate environment. Directors should learn from those situations with which they are actively involved. The boardroom itself should be perceived as a rich learning environment.

While informal learning can and does occur, many directors could be more deliberate in their learning. They could (a) consciously review experiences to determine what lessons can be learned and (b) actively seek learning activities, perhaps setting out in advance to structure particular situations or directorial tasks as learning opportunities.

The role of the chairman

It is important that the chairman is involved in any assessment of areas of development focus and the determination of next steps. This book has consistently argued that the chairman of the board should assume responsibility for ensuring that individual board members are competent, and that the board as a whole is effective.

The chairman is also in a position to have a direct influence on attitudes and behaviour through his or her approach to the chairmanship of the board. For example, requiring inputs to the board to present trends, variations, root causes and corrective actions can encourage a focus upon fact and reality. Rank Xerox adopts this approach. It makes it more difficult to 'play up' good news and conceal the bad, while actions that do not impact upon trends become more visible. Behaviour can be influenced to a degree by the frequency, format and conduct of meetings.

There appears to be a widespread feeling among chairmen that the effectiveness of boards could be improved.[6] In Chapter 6 it was suggested that in order to overcome a degree of scepticism, director development needs a champion in the boardroom. This book advocates that the chairman should adopt such a role.

A review by the chairman should be far-reaching and encompass more than just development requirements. There will be those who judge the company, and whether or not and to what extent to establish a relationship with it, according to their perception of the calibre of its board.[15]

Exercise 10.3 could be used to help determine the chairman's role in respect of a particular board.

Exercise 10.3: Chairman's role checklist

This chapter suggests certain aspects of the role of chairman that the board as a whole may wish to discuss. It obviously helps if the board itself is committed to director development. Certain basic questions that the board might address can give rise to further considerations. For example:

1 Should the chairman require the board as a team to undertake an annual review of its function and purpose, and of the collective and individual roles and responsibilities of board members? (When? How? To be implemented by reorganization, etc.?)

2 Should the chairman initiate and undertake with the board an annual review of its size, composition, operation and effectiveness? (When? How? A separate exercise, or to be linked with the review of function and purpose? With all reviews: is external help needed?)

3 Should the personal effectiveness in the boardroom, and contribution to the board, of all directors be assessed once a year by the Chairman? (When? How? Again, does individual contribution need to be seen in the context of function and purpose? Is a review timetable needed?)

4 Should the chairman ensure that all candidates for boardroom appointments are made aware of the qualities sought in, and the distinct duties and responsibilities of, the company director? (By what means? How does one 'test' awareness?)

5 Should the chairman insist that all newly appointed directors are properly prepared for their role as a company director, and that, following an appointment to the board, they take steps to ensure that their directorial knowledge and skills remain current and relevant? (Again, by what means? How does one assess the development process itself?)

There are many other supplementary questions to those in Exercise 10.3 that will need to be asked if director development is to occur, and be relevant to the needs of both the board and the business.

The board and corporate transformation

Let us turn now to the question of corporate transformation. The composition, skills and approaches of a board that have enabled it to adjust over time on an incremental basis, may not be able to cope with framebreaking redefinition, restructuring and reorientation. One of the major contemporary challenges facing many boards is how to bring about significant change.

The desire for change appears to be genuine. Many boards have a broad understanding of what needs to be done, and are seeking to build more flexible and responsive organizations. However, intentions are not matched by achievements. While the desire for corporate transformation is strong, little progress has been made. Attitudes and behaviour within corporate organizations are proving stubbornly resistant to change.[1]

While coping with incremental adjustments to discrete challenges, boards are finding it difficult to take more fundamental steps.[16] Why is this? Why is a consensus in the boardroom on the need to change, so rarely matched by an awareness of how to implement the changes that are desired?

The changing business environment

Corporate transformation is not sought for its own sake, but in order to respond to challenges and opportunities in the business environment. In order to survive, in Rosabeth Moss Kanter's phraseology, giants are having to learn to dance.[17]

What are the change priorities? While acknowledging their accountabilities to a range of stakeholders, and particularly to share-holders, the boards of 'benchmark' companies appear to be putting a higher priority upon their relationships with customers and employees. Central elements of BIM surveys in recent years have been the importance of (a) the key 'internal' issue of motivating, developing and harnessing the talents of people, and (b) the key 'external' issue of building closer relationships with customers.[18] As one managing director stated: 'Financial performance follows customer satisfaction, and employee involvement and satisfaction. If you go straight for it, financial success can prove elusive. It is difficult to sustain good "ratios" for very long if the customers and employees are dissatisfied.'

While stressing the importance of customers and employees in corporate videos and speeches, many boards persist in linking remuneration and advancement to the achievement of narrow, and sometimes inappropriate, financial targets rather than measures of customer satisfaction and employee involvement and satisfaction. Not surprisingly, the people of the organization take their cue from the actions of the board, and not from the words.

The corporate response

Corporate transformation is not just being discussed in the boardroom, it is being actively sought. A considerable amount of 'change' appears to be occurring within the organizations participating in *The Flat Organisation* survey:[19]

- Approaching nine out of ten of the participating organizations are becoming slimmer and flatter; while, in some eight out of ten, more work is being undertaken in teams, and a more responsive network organization is being created .
- Over two-thirds of participants acknowledge that functions are becoming more interdependent, and procedures and permanency are giving way to flexibility and temporary arrangements. Over half consider that organizations are becoming more interdependent.

The 1991 BIM report[19] reveals that there is a clear commitment to fundamental change, which in many boardrooms is now regarded as a necessity rather than as a matter of choice. However, in almost all the organizations examined in the course of the survey, the securing of significant changes is proving more protracted than was first imagined. Why is this?

The failure of implementation

Many attempts at corporate transformation are having counter-productive consequences, and the perceived gap between aspiration and achievement has caused a degree of cynicism and despair. Many transformation programmes are incomplete. Vital change elements or pieces of the transformation jigsaw puzzle are missing, without which success is unlikely to occur.[1]

Boards are responsible for a widespread failure to deliver. People within organizations are perceiving gaps between the rhetoric and the actions of the board and the role-model behaviour of its members. In many companies a variety of arenas of conflict exist, and there is distrust of the board among the management team. A Cranfield study has revealed that over two-thirds of UK general managers do not trust the board, while in Germany the figure rises to over nine out of ten.[20]

These findings are disturbing, given the responsibility of the board and senior management team for providing leadership in the establishment of a healthy corporate culture.[21] There are many reasons for the failure of implementation.

- Responsibilities are given to managers, and other employees, who are not equipped to cope with them.[19]
- While CEOs and members of boards stress the need for delegation and the importance of improving the quality of management, individual managers are not being equipped to handle the new demands that are being placed upon them.
- Boards are not finding it easy to provide people with 'prospects', or a vision of their career or personal future, in an organization without a traditional hierarchy and 'layers to climb'.
- Many companies are 'downsizing' or 'flattening' without first identifying those activities and processes that deliver value to customers. Their boards lack adequate criteria for determining who should go and who should stay.
- Problems are not anticipated, and likely barriers are not identified and removed. There are boards that pretend problems do not exist, and ignore or conceal difficulties.
- Boards should not be surprised by obstacles. For example, they should assume a degree of opposition and 'dragging of feet' on the part of those who do not perceive the sought-after changes to be in their best interests.
- The short-term actions of many boards, in response to economic recession, are not always consistent with either a company's vision, or the building of long-term relationships with its customers.

As a result of missing 'change elements', many corporate change initiatives are built upon foundations of sand.[1] It is little wonder that such wide gaps often emerge between rhetoric and reality.

Many boards are unimaginative when seeking 'solutions' to the various problem areas that have just been raised. For example, consider the question of motivation and prospects in the flat organization. According to one managing director: 'We suspended all our natural prejudices and benchmarked ourselves against our local college, and also local professionals. . . . They've never had much hierarchy as such, yet their people feel they are getting ahead . . . they work on more difficult problems.'

Understanding where you are

Corporate transformation can involve radical change and substantial upheaval. No individual should undertake a demanding programme of exercises, and break old habits, in the drive to become leaner and fitter, without first obtaining a health check. This also applies to companies.

- Without understanding your current situation, how can you determine what approach or routine is right for a company?
- How can you decide how far to push the company and the people associated with it?
- What dangers might result from failing to recognize areas of weakness or to properly prepare?

Prior to initiating a major corporate programme, a board should undertake some form of assessment of what is required and what it needs to cope. The current situation in terms of both the requirement for, and potential for, change need to be understood along with the likely barriers to change.

Exercise 10.4 suggests possible areas to address when carrying out some form of 'corporate health check'. Trained facilitators could be used to guide structured review sessions, and detailed frameworks for such an exercise exist.[22]

Exercise 10.4: Carrying out a 'corporate health check'

The need for corporate transformation, responsiveness and flexibility is clear and agreed. Uncertainty exists in (a) deciding the approaches or techniques that are relevant, (b) how best to proceed, and with what priorities, and (c) how to bring achievement closer to aspiration and turn vision into reality. The board should consider whether or not to undertake a comprehensive and penetrating 'corporate health check' to address the following questions:

1 Has an honest assessment been made of the situation or context within which change needs to occur?
2 Where should the board begin? (Many boards are mesmerized, uncertain or confused, and do not know what to do next.)
3 Have the key cross-functional and inter-organizational processes that identify and deliver the value that is sought by customers been identified? (Does the board itself 'add value' to these processes?)
4 What pieces of the transformation 'jig-saw' are missing? (Throwing more people and resources into the transformation task may increase frustration if (a) key obstacles are not removed; or (b) key enablers are not put in place.)
5 What approaches, techniques and tools are most appropriate to the situation in which the company finds itself? (Be selective.)
6 Which of these have been tested and shown to work? (A role for 'benchmarking'?)

7 **What are the most likely implementation obstacles and barriers?**
8 **Are experienced analysts available who could work with the board to determine where the company is in relation to where it needs to be?**

If a review similar to that presented in Exercise 10.4 is far-reaching, then gaps, barriers and deficiencies should be identified. There are some who may feel that a focus upon obstacles and barriers is 'negative'. Where there are vested interests, those in favour of the status quo are likely to resist. According to Tom Peters: 'Good intentions and brilliant proposals will be dead-ended, delayed, sabotaged, massaged to death, or revised beyond recognition or usefulness by the overlayed structures at most large and all too many small firms.' [23]

Among other 'health check' outputs, the board should secure an action programme and timetable that is tailored to the particular situation and circumstances of the company. The action programme should detail the next steps to be taken, including the techniques and tools that could be used to overcome implementation barriers.

By carrying out a systematic analysis, the board should be able to proceed with greater awareness and confidence. Through their participation, the directors should have obtained a shared overview of what is required. This could lead to a greater degree of unity in the face of the problems and challenges likely to arise during the implementation phase.

The importance of a clear vision

We saw in Chapter 3 that one of the key functions of the board is to provide a company with a sense of purpose, and a compelling and distinctive vision. Among the participants in the survey for *The Flat Organisation* report:[19] 'Every respondent assessing it believes clear vision and mission to be important; and about three quarters of them consider it "very important" '.

Sir John Harvey-Jones believes: 'a vision should present an attractive and clear view of the future which can be shared. It must motivate, be ambitious and should stretch people to achieve more than they might ever have thought possible.'[19]

We saw in Chapter 4 (Table 4.1) that (a) 'clear vision and strategy' and 'top management commitment' are jointly ranked as the most important requirements for the successful management of change; and (b) the vision must be shared, the purpose of change communicated, and employee involvement and commitment secured. A board must articulate and communicate a clear vision.

Another survey by a team from Cranfield has found that vision is one of five key skill areas required of people at the top of organizations, the others being the quality of relationships among this group, understanding the structures of organizations and how to change them in order to better meet business needs, communications skills, and the ability to invite feedback.[20] All these qualities relate to the sharing and implementation of a vision.

The gap between aspiration and achievement

While there is agreement on the importance of vision, *The Flat Organisation* report[19] goes on to reveal the relatively common phenomenon of a gap between vision and reality: 'While clear vision and mission are thought to be essential, in many companies both are regarded as just "words on paper", and they do not act as a guide to action.'

This finding ought to be of particular concern to those boards that have devoted some effort to communicating a vision or mission throughout their corporate organizations. Sir John Harvey-Jones warns: 'There cannot be a gap between words and deeds. If there is, cynicism will result.'[19]

The gap between aspiration and achievement cannot be closed by rhetoric. Missing change elements have to be put in place. Commitment needs to be matched by the use of approaches and processes that can 'make it happen'. Many boards make tactical adjustments, and simple or 'cosmetic' changes. However, attitudes, behaviour and values are difficult to shift. While it may be possible to change them,[1] the board may need to adopt a longer term perspective.

Review of board requirements

The point was made in Chapter 9 that what constitutes an effective board depends upon the interests and perspective of the party undertaking the assessment. From the viewpoint of a substantial company that aspires to total quality or corporate transformation, the effective board is composed of a united team of competent directors who share and can communicate a common quality or transformation vision.

The first step in formulating and communicating vision and strategy is for the chairman to ask the following questions:

- Do the members of the board share a common vision? If fundamental change is to occur there must be an agreed vision of a better future.
- Are they committed to an agreed strategy? The directors should be committed to both a clear and compelling vision, and a common and realistic strategy for its achievement.
- How effective are they at communicating with customers, employees and business partners? A clear and compelling vision has to be communicated and understood if it is to be shared, and if it is to motivate.
- The quality priority is the quality of management[24] (so much so that TQM could stand for **The Quality of Management**). Is there an explicit commitment to improving the quality of management and the quality of management and business processes?

Moving from rhetoric to reality

Are there role-model companies from which the essence or secrets of directorial effectiveness might be divined? The quality culture can be created, but only when 'all the elements of the jig-saw puzzle are in place'.[1]

The members of an effective board ought to have the perspective to see the broad picture and to assemble all the 'pieces of the puzzle'. However, 'role model' or 'benchmark' boards are scarce:

- Most companies are 'missing some pieces'. Their boards are generally looking for them in the wrong places.
- Few companies understand the processes that deliver business objectives or value to customers, and many boards add little value to them.
- Within corporate organizations, there are obstacles and barriers, frequently unrecognized, that are preventing the 'breakthroughs' that could lead from rhetoric to reality.

So what change elements might be missing? Let us examine what can be learned from the experience of benchmark companies:

- A clear and shared vision that is rooted in the customer is essential.
- Board and top management commitment to change is crucial, and needs to be visibly sustained and communicated.
- Members of the board should act as role models.
- The vision must be shared, the purpose of change communicated, and employee involvement and commitment secured.
- The board should never forget that returns to the 'owners' or shareholders derive from satisfied customers and employees.
- Problems should be tackled, not shifted, avoided or hidden; while 'things that go wrong' should be regarded as opportunities to learn.
- Boardroom debate and management action should be based upon fact and understanding, and not on opinion and speculation.
- More than vision, talk and targets may be required—e.g. people may need to be motivated to give priority to the requirements of customers.
- Activity for its own sake is of little value if it does not add value for external customers; i.e. motivation needs to be harnessed and applied to customer-related tasks.
- Individual employees have to understand what they must do to contribute to the achievement of corporate objectives.
- People need to be empowered, equipped and motivated to cope with change.
- The root causes of implementation obstacles and barriers, and potential arenas of conflict, should be identified and tackled.
- Rather than 'make do' with inadequate or 'standard' external services, or widely used 'remedies' of dubious value, a benchmark company should be prepared to think through its problems and devise its own solutions.
- Appropriate implementation tools are required, and, in particular, those that can be used to identify and re-engineer the management

and business processes which are most crucial to delivering value to external customers.[25]

- Members of the board should be responsible for key management and business processes, and, ultimately, the board should consist of cross-functional process owners with a company-wide perspective rather than functional heads with a 'departmental view'.[1]
- Closer and partnership relationships are required between internal departments and external companies.
- A company should actively learn from those who have developed ways of breaking through many of the more common implementation barriers, and continually push out the boundaries of what can be accomplished.

The achievement of significant culture change can be achieved, but boardroom resolutions, however perceptive and incisive, are not enough. The onus is upon the board to be absolutely tenacious in confronting and overcoming implementation obstacles and barriers.

Key lessons   The key lessons of what it takes to bring about fundamental change are considered in another book on the subject of transforming the company.[1] A holistic approach is required.

The failure to achieve corporate transformation usually results from gaps or missing elements in the corporate transformation strategy that is adopted, and to bridge the gap between rhetoric and reality it is necessary to ensure that all the change elements that make up the transformation jig-saw puzzle, or the essential building blocks, are in place (Figure 10.1).

The nature of the missing elements will vary from company to company, but a combination of these elements must be assembled and deployed in such a way as to overwhelm any obstacles and barriers to change. A company that selects the change elements to adopt, will probably fail. The picture is not complete until every piece of the jig-saw is in place.

Rather than struggle with the simplistic notions of vested interests and enthusiasts, companies and their boards should be more open to, and more prepared to share, the insights of those in 'real companies' who are successfully overcoming today's barriers in the contemporary market environment. A company should establish its own standards to equal or exceed those of the best in respect of all aspects of its operations. An ambitious board could use Exercise 10.5 to develop a business excellence action plan.

Exercise 10.5: Developing a business excellence action plan

The search for business excellence is an unending quest. There is always another company that is better at something. A business excellence action plan could be developed as follows:

- **A number of key factors that might indicate business excellence could be identified.**

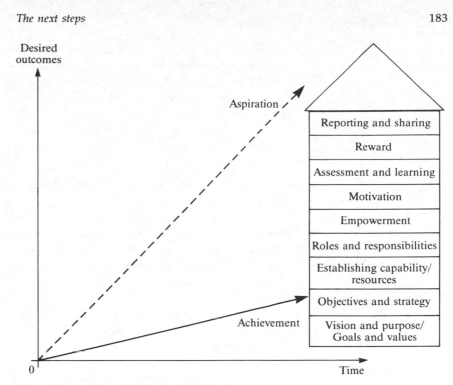

Figure 10.1	*Assembling the building blocks*
	Source: Transforming the Company, 1992

- For each factor, benchmark status could be defined in terms of a desired situation that is expressed as a quantified target.
- In respect of each factor, those with relevant responsibilities could be asked to indicate how close the company is to benchmark status.
- Specific actions could then be determined which would take the company from where it is to where it would like to be.

The following are examples of some of the key factors that should be borne in mind by a board that is determined to achieve and retain 'benchmark' status:

1 Awareness and understanding of the needs and interests of stakeholders.
2 Clarity of vision, goals, values and objectives, and the extent to which they are shared.
3 Commitment to 'making it happen'.
4 The priority that is given to the customer among business objectives.
5 Customer-focused organization, processes and reward.
6 A focus upon 'outputs' and knowledge, rather than 'inputs' and physical and financial resources.
7 Processes for allocating departmental and individual roles and responsibilities.
8 The establishment and monitoring of precise output objectives.
9 Measuring performance from a customer perspective (e.g. return on time, rather than return on net assets).
10 Employee involvement and empowerment (e.g. self-managed work groups).
11 Commitment to learning and continuous improvement.
12 Use of relevant tools, techniques and approaches.

In the final analysis boards, too, are likely to be judged by 'results' of some form, whatever viewpoint one adopts. For example, most of the key processes for delivering business objectives and value to customers, and achieving corporate change, should begin in, end in, or pass at some point through, the boardroom. Are directorial and managerial roles and responsibilities in respect of these processes clear? Is the board adding value to them, and will 'director development' enable it to contribute more?

The effective board 'makes it happen'. In the harsh reality of a competitive marketplace there is little requirement for either 'cosmetic' corporate transformation programmes or 'dream' boards. A board should be united, committed and focused; holistic in its approach to change; and determined to ensure that the 'vital few' actions are in place to tackle the major barriers to the attainment of a shared corporate vision.

Checklist

1 Is the capability of the board relevant to the strategic challenges and opportunities the company faces?
2 How committed is the board to taking practical steps to improve its own effectiveness?
3 Is its approach comprehensive and holistic, but at the same time focused and realistic?
4 Has a list of development priorities been drawn up?
5 Do planned development activities reflect the nature, situation, circumstances and business development needs of the company?
6 Do they relate to, and support, the company's vision, and its goals, values and objectives?
7 In particular, do they tackle priority deficiencies and obstacles to the achievement of corporate vision, goals, values and objectives?
8 Have the implications been thought through, and is an action plan in place?
9 Does this cover formal and informal learning activities?
10 What basis has been established for assessing the relevance and quality of any 'external' sources of development expertise that have been identified?
11 Does the board think through what is required prior to initiating major corporate programmes?
12 Are the crucial enablers always put in place, barriers and obstacles identified, and actions initiated to tackle them?
13 Are the management and business processes of the company kept continually under review to ensure that they focus upon whatever constitutes value for customers?
14 Ultimately, has the board given the company a sense of will and purpose?
15 Has a distinctive and compelling vision been articulated, agreed, communicated and shared?

Notes and references

1 Colin Coulson-Thomas, *Transforming the Company: Bridging the Gap between Management Myth and Corporate Reality*, Kogan Page, 1992.
2 Robert H. Waterman, *The Renewal Factor*, Bantam, 1987.
3 J P Kotter, *A Force for Change: How Leadership Differs from Management*, The Free Press, 1990.
4 C.K. Prahalad, 'Developing strategic capability: An agenda for top management', *Human Resource Management*, **22**, No. 3 (Fall 1983), 237–54.
5 Geoffrey Mills, 'Who controls the board?', *Long Range Planning*, **22**, No. 3 (1989), 125–32; Allen Sykes, 'Corporate governance, bigger carrots and sticks', *Financial Times* (31 October 1990), 19; and Judith H. Dobrzynski *et al.*, 'Taking charge', *International Business Week*, (3 July 1989), 36–43.
6 Colin Coulson-Thomas and Alan Wakelam, *The Effective Board: Current Practice, Myths and Realities*. An IOD discussion document, 1991.
7 Colin Coulson-Thomas, *The Role and Function of the Personnel Director*. An interim Adaptation Ltd survey carried out in conjunction with the Research Group of the Institute of Personnel Management, 1991.
8 Brian Houlden, *Understanding Company Strategy: An Introduction to Thinking and Acting Strategically*, Blackwell, 1991; and Adrian Davies, *Strategic Leadership, Making Corporate Plans Work*, Woodhead-Faulkner, 1991.
9 Colin Coulson-Thomas, *Professional Development of and for the Board*. A questionnaire and interview survey undertaken by Adaptation Ltd of company chairmen. A summary has been published by the IOD, February 1990.
10 Sir John Harvey-Jones, *Making it Happen: Reflections on Leadership*, Fontana/Collins, 1988.
11 Peter Senge, *The Fifth Discipline: The Art and Practice of the Learning Organisation*, Doubleday/Currency, 1990.
12 Committee on the Financial Aspects of Corporate Governance. Draft report issued for public comment, Committee on the Financial Aspects of Corporate Governance, 27 May 1992; and Norma Cohen, 'Cadbury proposals prove unpalatable', *Financial Times* (3 August 1992), 5.
13 Alan Wakelam, *The Training and Development of Company Directors*. A report on a questionnaire survey undertaken by the Centre for Management Studies, University of Exeter for the Training Agency, December 1989.
14 Alan Mumford, Peter Honey and Graham Robinson, *Director's Development Guidebook: Making Experience Count*, Director Publications, 1990.
15 D. Hambrick and P. Mason, 'Upper echelons: The organisation as a reflection of its top management', *Academy of Management Review 1984*, **9**, No. 2, 193–206.
16 M.L. Tushman, W.H. Newman and D.A. Nadler, 'Executive leadership and organisational evolution: Managing incremental and discontinuous change', in R. Kilman and T.J. Covey (eds) *Corporate Transformation*, Jossey-Bass, 1988.
17 Rosabeth Moss Kanter, *When Giants Learn to Dance*, Simon & Schuster, 1989.
18 Colin Coulson-Thomas and Richard Brown, *The Responsive Organisation, People Management: the Challenge of the 1990s*, BIM, 1989; and *Beyond Quality: Managing the Relationship with the Customer*, BIM, 1990.
19 Colin Coulson-Thomas and Trudy Coe, *The Flat Organisation: Philosophy and Practice*, BIM, 1991.
20 Andrew Kakabadse, *The Wealth Creators: Top People, Top Teams and Executive Best Practice*, Kogan Page, 1991.
21 Edgar H. Schein, *Organisational Culture and Leadership*, Jossey-Bass, 1985.
22 See, for example, Adaptation/Rank Xerox, *The Business Excellence Health Check*. A six category 'corporate health check' of 41 items, Adaptation Ltd and Rank Xerox (UK) Ltd, 1992.
23 Tom Peters, *Thriving on Chaos*, Alfred A. Knopf, 1987.

24 Colin and Susan Coulson-Thomas, *Quality: The Next Steps*. An Adaptation Ltd survey for ODI , Adaptation Ltd, 1991; Executive summary available from ODI Europe, 1991.

25 Peter Bartram, *Re-inventing the Company: The use of IT to Re-engineer Corporate Processes*, Business Intelligence, 1992; and Roger Woolfe, *The Role of Information Technology in Transforming the Business*, Butler Cox Foundation, 1991.

Appendix: how to make it happen

The failure of many companies to turn aspiration into achievement often results from gaps or missing elements in the corporate transformation strategy that is adopted by the board. A list of questions along the lines of the following could be used to identify the broad location of areas of deficiency:

(a) The vision

1 Is there a shared and compelling vision?
2 Is the vision rooted in the customer?
3 Is there sustained 'top management' commitment?
4 Do directors and senior executives exude role-model behaviour?

(b) The customer

1 Is priority given to the customer?
2 Is the board motivated and the company 'run' according to customer-related objectives?
3 Is performance measured in terms of its impact upon the customer?
4 Are corporate processes and procedures focused on the customer?
5 Is sufficient importance attached to establishing and sustaining relationships?

(c) The people

1 Are employees involved and committed?
2 Is reward strategy consistent with corporate goals and objectives?
3 Are people actually remunerated to generate value for customers?
4 Is empowerment for real—e.g. is work undertaken by self-managed work groups?
5 How appropriate are attitudes, values and perspectives in terms of the achievement of the vision?

(d) The processes and the tools

1 Are people equipped to cope?
2 Is there active learning from others, e.g. benchmarking?
3 Are relevant tools and approaches used?
4 Have the key cross-functional management and business processes that determine and deliver value for customers been identified?
5 Are they re-engineered, as appropriate, in order to focus more clearly upon customer requirements?
6 Who is responsible for them within the boardroom?

7 Is the company competing on response, delivery or learning time, and are learning and working integrated?

Once areas of deficiency have been identified, appropriate director development responses can be determined. For example, perhaps the board would benefit from an 'away day' specifically on corporate transformation and the role of the board in relation to its achievement.

PART THREE

Background and fundamentals

11 The development challenge

The bewildered board

The boards of many companies face a bewildering array of challenges, and have much to think about, quite apart from their own development. Directors are busy people. Even when they recognize the need for development, 'next steps' will have to compete with other claims upon their time.

Consider the following small selection of comments from busy directors:

We have not been sitting around discussing our own development needs . . . [because] . . . priority has been given to the needs of the business. Ultimately, we will be judged by the performance of the business. The results of the business are visible. Who other than us knows or cares how we operate in the boardroom?

I am beset with problems from all directions. We face stiff competition . . . [etc.]. At this moment in time, going on courses and holding workshops is a luxury we cannot afford. . . . I worry about the signals [director development] would give out. Assuming we can coordinate diaries there are always urgent matters to discuss.

Development is fine in theory, but we have to recognize our needs and agree it is important. Before acting we need to be convinced that what is on offer will help. . . . We do not really believe that what we have seen would help us. You cannot understand the pressures we face unless you are in there with us in the boardroom.

These sentiments, and others like them, have been expressed by the members of several boards that have subsequently undertaken some form of development activity. Initially, there is: (a) a concentration upon other, frequently short-term, priorities; (b) a reluctance to recognize a development need; (c) a degree of caution regarding the commitment of limited time; and (d) considerable scepticism towards the relevance of development services on offer, and the credibility of those seeking to supply them.

To be accepted as a catalyst, coach or facilitator of director and boardroom development, it is usually necessary to establish a position of trust and respect. An understanding of the pressures faced by the board, and from a directorial perspective, can help in the building of a rapport. It can also provide a more realistic understanding of the background against which development needs to occur.

In this chapter, we shall examine the essence and purpose of the company, sensitivity to the business environment, and understanding of the market and business environment in which the company operates. We shall also consider the extent of focus upon the customer, whether corporate organization is an obstacle to or enabler of customer satisfaction, and relationships with the people of the organization.

There is more to director development than courses, workshops and 'action learning'. A development coach who has a strategic perspective and gains trust and respect can work with a board over a period of time, and do much to help it become more effective. To sustain the relationship, such a person needs the capability to grow and develop with the board as situations and circumstances change. Those boards who tackle the many questions in this chapter should secure an enhanced appreciation of their own attitudes and priorities.

Essence and purpose

It should not be thought that every company has a distinct and compelling reason for survival. Every day, companies go into liquidation because they no longer have a sense of purpose. If this is not provided by the board a company is likely to wither and die.

Exercise 11.1 could be used to assess the extent to which the directors have collectively provided a company with a will and purpose to continue. The questions could be considered by the directors individually, and/or discussed by the board at an 'away day' session.

Exercise 11.1: The essence and purpose of the company

Ask the members of the board to address the following questions:

 1 Why does the company exist? Why should it continue to exist?
 2 Given a choice, why should a customer be interested in the company?
 3 Does it really address needs in the marketplace?
 4 Why do people work for the company rather than for a competitor?
 5 How would you persuade someone to invest in the company?
 6 What has the world gained from the company's existence?
 7 What is the essence and purpose of the company?
 8 Is there anything particularly distinctive or special about the company?
 9 What would be lost if it ceased to exist?
10 What would be different if one could 'start again'?

Depending upon the responses to such questions, a follow-up discussion could focus upon:

- Whether the overall pattern of responses is encouraging or discouraging, and the implications and action that needs to be taken.
- In particular, what could be done to create a more compelling rationale for sustaining relationships with external stakeholders.
- The extent to which the responses might enable the board to formulate and agree a shared purpose.

- What might be done to create a more distinctive essence and purpose that would differentiate the company in the marketplace?
- To what extent is the 'essence of the company' rooted in the reality of conditions, circumstances and requirements in the marketplace?

If the directors do not agree and cannot articulate and share a distinct purpose for the company, its activities may well be based upon foundations of sand. It will become increasingly difficult to differentiate the company from other suppliers in a competitive marketplace. It is important that a board should address and periodically review such fundamental questions as those in this exercise.

The requirement for a distinctive purpose and sense of mission is easier to state than to achieve, and there are many factors that need to be thought through.[1] Hence, the board should be prepared to commit the time it takes to produce an agreed purpose, vision and mission that is compelling and capable of being shared and understood.

Communicating a vision or mission that is bland, not thought through or 'words on paper' can be counter-productive.[2] The board may have a requirement for facilitation support from someone experienced in the boardroom use of visioning techniques.

The business environment

A board that is not sensitive and aware of the business context within which a company operates is fatally flawed, regardless of its other attributes. The essence and purpose of a company must derive from opportunities, needs and requirements in the business environment. Ultimately it is the board's responsibility to determine the extent to which a company has a purpose.

Before a board and its members can be developed there must first be some recognition of a development need. One place to begin is the context in which a company operates, and the strategic awareness of the directors. To what extent do the individual members of the board, and the board as a whole, understand the nature of the business environment?

This question is not easily answered. According to David Thompson, chairman of Rank Xerox UK: 'The problem for boards is to be able to keep up with the momentum of change eg most Personal Computers are obsolete on the day they are launched. Investment and marketing plans for the old Eastern Europe are valid for weeks not years.'

It should not be assumed that directors are sensitive to, or monitor, developments in the external business environment. Many do not systematically consider fundamental developments. Their focus is almost exclusively upon board papers and the agenda for the next meeting, rather than upon what the agenda ought to be.

Exercise 11.2 could be undertaken as part of an annual strategy review. In a 'companion' book, *Creating Excellence in the Boardroom*, various changes in the business environment are presented, and the 'variety and fundamental nature' of these 'are such as to suggest a transition has occurred to a new era'.[3] These discontinuities could be used as the basis for boardroom discussion.

Peter Drucker has referred to the current period as the 'age of discontinuity'.[4] A board that does not address relevant changes, both incremental and revolutionary, is 'hiding its head in the sand'.

Exercise 11.2: Sensitivity to business environment issues

The board could be presented with some aspects of the changing business environment, or it could brainstorm its own list of fundamental developments. The following questions could then be asked:

1 Which of the developments in the business environment are of the greatest significance?
2 Can these more significant 'issues' be ranked in order of priority?
3 Which of the more significant developments can be considered a 'help' or positive factor, and which a 'hinder' or negative factor?
4 What are the implications for the company and its stakeholders, particularly customers, employees and owners?
5 What, as a consequence, will become more or less difficult?
6 What new opportunities are likely to be created?
7 In which areas is the company most vulnerable to external developments?

The questions of Exercise 11.2 should be reviewed at least once a year by the board. At the end of a discussion, an assessment should be made of the overall sensitivity of the board to developments in the business environment. If the board is blind, blinkered or asleep, the company will be in danger.

A development need might arise for a programme of, say, monthly boardroom briefings on major issues and challenges. Some boards arrange these briefings to coincide with their meetings; while other boards prefer to keep them separate to avoid distraction from the business of normal meetings. The use of internal staff to synthesize and report on developments could also help key managers to become more aware of external issues, while independent inputs can ensure objectivity and could open the company up to more challenging viewpoints.

Peter Morgan, director general of the Institute of Directors, believes:

The central issue is that directors should respond effectively to the threats and opportunities continually present in the company's environment due to the changes brought about by market forces in the free market economy. . . . Anticipating and reacting to market forces converts the challenge of survival into the opportunity to prosper. The successful control of this process of surviving and thriving is what distinguishes the direction of a business from the administration of a bureaucracy.'[5]

The effective board ensures that 'external' as well as 'internal' developments are systematically monitored, their impacts upon the company analysed, and corrective action taken as appropriate. The board of Xerox Corporation actively seeks and commissions assessments and reviews that challenge its view of the world. The issue monitoring and management system of an international company needs to cover local, regional (e.g. European) and global developments.[6]

In the absence of any discussion in the boardroom, who else is examining where and when the more significant developments in the external business environment will impact upon the company? Can corrective action be taken at the point of impact? Some companies are 'out of control'. Those that are oblivious to major threats and opportunities are the most vulnerable to competitive attack.

There will be some directors who question the value of 'general discussions'. Hence, reviews and exercises should focus on impacts upon the company, and what the company should do in response. According to one director who was interviewed on the subject of 'issue monitoring and management': 'We spend too much time on the immediate, and not enough looking ahead. We have always put off this sort of exercise. There is never a slack time, you just have to do it.'

Bringing discussions closer to home

Many directors 'sit up' when the discussion shifts to matters with which they are familiar. Informal chats 'at the bar' at the conclusion of review exercises frequently turn to what is happening in the immediate marketplace, and the activities of the company's competitors.

While developments in the immediate market environment, and a company's particular business sector, should be seen against the broader context of the total environment in which the company operates when its purpose, vision, or mission are reviewed, the incorporation of more familiar areas into the 'away-day' or 'away-weekend' agenda can encourage interest and involvement.

The conclusion of a review of general and fundamental trends in the business environment may be a good time to turn to the company's particular market environment. Questions similar to those below could be used to build the understanding of the board:

- What major changes are occurring in the marketplace?
- What is happening to customer expectations?
- How are developments effecting the relationships between customers and suppliers?
- What are the consequences, dangers and opportunities for suppliers?
- How do, or could, suppliers differentiate themselves from competitors?
- What are the key requirements for success?
- How does the company equate to the key 'success factors'?
- What are the company's major deficiencies, and how might they be remedied?

Some boards have a tendency to view the world as they would like it to be, rather than as it is. Factors and developments that do not accord with existing views are ignored, challenged or 'played down', while those that confirm their beliefs and prejudices are exaggerated or 'uncritically adopted'.[7]

The use of an external, or independent, and robust facilitator can help to ensure that significant inputs are not 'screened out' or 'rationalized away'. Again, the use of internal staff to support a review can help to share understanding and build the relationship between the board and the management team.

A board also needs to understand the dynamics of the business sector in which a company is operating. To do this, it could ask such questions as:

- What is happening in the sector in terms of market trends, customer requirements and supplier reactions?
- What are the conditions and requirements for success in the sector?
- Are there emerging, or new, bases for customer segmentation?
- What new forms of relationship are, or could be, forged between customers and suppliers?
- What are the main sector drives and pressures?
- What changes are occurring in the structure of the sector, the dynamics of competition and the relationships between the 'key players'?
- Are new patterns of relative advantage and dependence emerging?

If members of the board find it difficult to respond to the above questions, this could indicate that they may be focusing too closely on internal and immediate issues, and neglecting the external and strategic dimension. Rather than distribute background papers that may not be read, briefings could be arranged on developments in the business sector.

Depending upon the circumstances, there is much the board could learn from an 'overview' provided by a trade or sector journalist, or a leading edge customer. Inviting members of the board to suggest briefing topics can encourage them to broaden their perspective and become more actively involved in their own learning.

A key issue for the board is the extent to which the capability, culture and resources of the company match the success requirements of its chosen business sector. Where gaps are identified between what is needed and the capacity to act, appropriate remedial and development action should be initiated. For example, a board might wish to consider whether the company's position would be strengthened by some form of collaboration, or a programme of selected arrangements.

Staying close to the customer

It is the customer that is the source of value and not the board. The customer decides whether or not what is produced is consumed, and whether or not the capability, culture and resources of the company are relevant. The company that loses sight of the customer is doomed, hence a lack of customer focus becomes a high priority for remedial action.

A customer focus should not be assumed. While claiming to give a priority to customer satisfaction, or 'building longer term relationships with customers', many boards pay 'lip service' to the importance of the 'external' customer while focusing predominantly upon the company's own internal requirements.

A board should be judged by its actions rather than by its words. For example, the corporate video may well call for more customer care, but such an 'appeal' is unlikely to be heeded where reward and advancement is linked to 'return upon net assets' rather than customer satisfaction. A board that understands the perspective of the customer is more likely to identify the gaps between, or the incompatibilities of, different policies.

Exercise 11.3 contains questions that could be used to assess the extent to which the board is focused upon the customer, and views issues from a customer perspective.

Exercise 11.3: Customer focus and perspective

A focus upon the customer in the boardroom, and a customer perspective, should not be assumed. The following questions could be posed:

1 Who represents the customer in the boardroom?
2 How much time does the board spend discussing the customer, and how much time do individual members of the board spend with customers?
3 What has the company done, or what should it do, to learn from the customer?
4 How highly does customer satisfaction rank among the company's business objectives?
5 Can all members of the board list the main elements of customer satisfaction, and the major sources of customer dissatisfaction?

The responses to Exercise 11.3 will suggest the action that needs to be taken. Encouraging members of the board to raise questions, to move one step at a time, and to consolidate changes of perspective and awareness as they occur, is the role of the coach rather than the traditional trainer. However, some specific skill needs could arise at this stage. For example, in order to help identify what is to be done, the board might benefit from a brief presentation on benchmarking or how to learn from best practice.[8]

Delivering value to the customer

If a company is to satisfy its customers, it will require more than a board that is 'focused upon the customer'. The board will need to put in place the various change elements required to turn its own concern and rhetoric into corporate reality. To do this the following questions should be addressed:

- Who in the company does, and should, add value for customers?
- Who is motivated, and encouraged in terms of reward and remuneration, to add value for customers?

- What are the 'vital few' things that need to be done to improve customer satisfaction significantly or to reduce customer dissatisfaction?
- Are roles and responsibilities allocated on the basis of those things that need to be done to build customer satisfaction?
- Are the company's management and business processes—particularly those that cross departmental and functional boundaries—aligned and focused upon the priority requirements of customers?
- Are employees empowered to harness the resources of the company, independently of their location, in order to add value for individual customers?

Working through a list of such questions should be of value in enabling a board to identify what needs to be done. Just considering the various areas that need to be addressed makes the point that 'single solutions' are unlikely to work. There is rarely an easy route to customer satisfaction in a competitive business sector.

A board that finds it difficult to take a 'process' view of the company, might benefit from a presentation on management and business process simplification and re-engineering. This is best done by someone from a real and benchmark company who has successfully completed a project, and is willing to share the results and the lessons.

Those to avoid are people who might use the occasion as an opportunity to attempt to 'sell' something to the board. The directors may well resent that someone has sought to 'take advantage', and the experience could lower the standing of those seeking to develop them.

Organization, people and processes

Having understood what is happening in the business environment, the board needs to ensure that the company is able to cope. If the board has not already done so, it should focus on its responsiblities for ensuring that the company's organization, people and processes enable it to respond to challenges and opportunities in the external business environment, and particularly customer requirements.

Many directors might argue that the company has 'survived' hitherto by taking *ad hoc* steps to cope with particular challenges. However, given both the number and the fundamental nature of many of the developments that are occurring, the board needs to be capable of handling both incremental and discontinuous change.[9]

In the case of some boards, and especially those with a predilection for 'firefighting', it may first be necessary to make them more aware of the issue. Exercise 11.4 could be used to focus the board upon the requirements for organizational change, if it has not already done so.

Exercise 11.4: The board and corporate organization

Certain of the following questions could be used to initiate a board discussion or review:

1 **What priority is the board placing upon the achievement of a more flexible and responsive organization?**
2 **What are the main requirements for coping with the major challenges and opportunities the company faces in the business environment?**
3 **What are the main organizational requirements for success in the market-place?**
4 **Identify the major deficiencies or gaps between where the company is and where it needs to be in order to cope with external challenges and achieve marketplace success.**

The questions of Exercise 11.4 could keep a board busy for the whole of an initial review meeting. There are other questions that will need to be asked at subsequent sessions; for example:

- Have the key corporate transformation tasks and requirements been defined in clear output terms?
- Does the 'blueprint' of what is sought encompass the key management and business processes that will deliver the value that is sought by customers?
- Have corporate transformation roles and responsibilities been agreed in the boardroom, and allocated among the directors?
- Have an understanding of the transformation objectives, and the allocation of responsibilities for their achievement, been communicated and shared throughout the company?
- Has the board determined the resources and processes that will be required to facilitate and support the transformation programme?
- Has the board identified and addressed any overlaps or gaps in responsibilities or likely deficiencies in motivation or resources?
- Has the board identified, and is it 'keeping its eye upon', those 'vital few' initiatives that will probably determine whether or not transformation is achieved?
- Have all the people in the organization been encouraged, empowered and equipped to cope with the transformation tasks they are expected to perform?
- Is the board satisfied that people are motivated to succeed?
- How realistic is the corporate transformation timetable, and is progress being monitored by the board?
- Are all members of the board united behind, and totally committed to, the achievement of a corporate transformation?

Again, the responses may flush out areas of relative uncertainty. There is likely to be much that the members of a board determined to achieve a corporate transformation will need to absorb. It is important that they learn from those with benchmark experience who are prepared to 'tell it as it is', rather than present a sanitized version of events wrapped in a 'soft sell'. The obstacles and barriers are what the board really needs to focus upon in order to 'make it happen'.

The transformation challenge

The smaller company may find it relatively easy to change direction if a vision is shared and the commitment to succeed is sustained. Transforming the larger organization is more of a challenge.

We saw in Chapters 9 and 10 how difficult it can be for a board to bring about changes of attitudes and behaviour within a corporate organization. Schein[10] sees the achievement of culture change as a key element of corporate leadership, and suggests that sensitive antennae and considerable flexibility may be required during the process of transformation—for example, reward and motivation strategy may need to be modified as a shift of attitudes occurs.

Evidence suggests that the desire for corporate transformation is not matched by an understanding of how to bring it about.[2] We saw in Chapter 10 that significant changes of attitudes and behaviour are unlikely to occur unless a combination of change elements are put in place to meet the situation and circumstances of the particular company.

The board and the building of relationships

The quality of the relationships a board establishes with people will be a critical determinant of how effective it is. Parry Rogers has served on the boards of such companies as IBM UK, Plessey and ICL. He believes that 'virtually every decision in the boardroom has a human implication or consideration'.[11]

Two groups that no board can afford to ignore are the customers and the people of the organization. Les Jones, personnel director of Rank Xerox UK, believes:

there are two prime goals that organisations will be striving to achieve in the 1990s, preferred supplier status and preferred employer status. I doubt if one can be achieved without the other. Customer satisfaction has to be complemented by an employee satisfaction process. Preferred employer strategy can only be achieved through an integrated approach and strategic focus at board level.[11]

The extent of the director and board development challenge will also depend greatly upon the board's relationship with key stakeholders. Exercise 11.5 could be used to assess the board's current position.

Exercise 11.5: Relationships with people

The following questions could be used to explore the extent of a board's commitment to building relationships with people:

1 Has the board identified, and established relationships with, the key stakeholders in the company?

2 **Do all the directors understand the needs, interests, perspectives, attitudes and values of these key stakeholders?**
3 **Has the board identified the 'vital few' things that are really important to them?**
4 **Have roles and responsibilities relating to establishing and maintaining relationships with these groups of people been agreed by the board and allocated between individual directors?**

Whether or not a board that is committed to achieving a satisfactory relationship with the various groups of people that have an interest in the company will succeed can depend upon many factors. For example:

- Are communications with these groups two-way, i.e. does the board, and do its individual members, listen?
- Are the relationships that have been established based upon mutual trust, respect and understanding?
- Does the board recall, and monitor the implementation of, its various 'commitments' to different groups of people?
- Do all directors act as role models when dealing with the various groups with an interest in the company?
- Do members of these groups understand what is expected of them, and are they properly equipped and supported?
- To what extent do they understand and share the vision, mission, goals, values, and objectives of the company?
- Has the board articulated the values, and clearly formulated the rules of conduct, that should apply to relationships between people?

These are penetrating questions, and some directors are more willing to 'stare into the mirror' than others. The responses could suggest the need for relationship building or communication skills. Some of the deficiencies that can emerge are not easy to address. Director development of itself may not be sufficient to bridge all the gaps that emerge between an actual situation and what is desired.

Facing the challenge

In many companies satisfactory relationships based upon mutual trust and understanding have not been forged, and people are not being equipped, empowered or motivated to do what is expected of them.[2] This is not a new problem. Chester Barnard recognized the need to 'make it happen' in the 1930s, and stressed the important contribution of shared values and co-operative activity to the achievement of business results.[12]

Throughout this book it is suggested that the chairman should take personal responsibility for the competence of directors and the effectiveness of the board. It may be the chairman alone who can assemble and juggle with all the options. These could include changing the composition or structure of the board.

The various exercises of this book are concerned with what, for many companies and their boards, represent areas of actual, persistent and pressing development need. The director development challenge in the case of many boards is to help the directors individually and collectively to close the gap between where they are and where they would like to be. Too many strategies and plans remain as words on paper, and too many brave initiatives and programmes have foundered upon the rocks of inadequate preparation and implementation.

Checklist

1 Who really cares whether or not the company continues to exist?
2 If it did not exist, would it be brought into existence?
3 Who would lose most if the company ceased to exist?
4 What is special about the company, e.g. what 'justification' might persuade a Minister to visit the company?
5 What would you do differently if you owned the company?
6 Is the board aware of (a) developments in the business and market environment and in its own business sector, and (b) the likely impacts of these issues on the company?
7 Why should the customer 'feel good' about the company, or have any particular interest in it?
8 Has the board really thought through what it is trying to achieve in the areas of corporate renewal and transformation?
9 Do all the directors share a common understanding of what is sought?
10 What is the board doing to learn from the experience of transformation?
11 How much effort does the board devote to building and sustaining satisfactory relationships with various stakeholders in the company?
12 Is the board able to deliver all that it has promised to each group of stakeholders?

Notes and references

1 A. Campbell, M. Devine, and D. Young, *A Sense of Mission*, Hutchinson and *The Economist*, 1990; and A. Campbell and K. Tawadey, *Mission and Business Philosophy*, Heinemann, 1990.
2 Colin Coulson-Thomas: *Transforming the Company: Bridging the Gap between Management Myth and Corporate Reality*, Kogan Page, 1992; and 'Strategic vision or strategic con?: Rhetoric or reality?', *Long Range Planning*, **25**, No. 1 (1992), 81–9.
3 Colin Coulson-Thomas, *Creating Excellence in the Boardroom*, McGraw-Hill, 1993.
4 Peter Drucker, *The Age of Discontinuity*, Heinemann, 1989.
5 Peter Morgan, *Why an Institute of Directors?* Lecture to the Cardiff Business Club, 3 February 1992, p. 14.
6 Colin Coulson-Thomas, *Creating the Global Company: Successful Internationalization*, McGraw-Hill, 1992.
7 Leon Festinger, *A Theory of Cognitive Dissonance*, Stanford University Press, 1962.
8 Robert C. Camp, *Benchmarking: The Search for Industry Best Practices that Lead to Superior Performance*, Quality Press, 1989.

9 M.L. Tushman, W.H. Newman, and D.A. Nadler, 'Executive leadership and organisational evolution: Managing incremental and discontinuous change', in R. Kilman and T.J. Covey (eds) *Corporate Transformation*, Jossey-Bass, 1988.
10 Edgar H. Schein, *Organisational Culture and Leadership*, Jossey-Bass, 1985.
11 Colin Coulson-Thomas, 'What the personnel director can bring to the boardroom table', *Personnel Management* (October 1991), 36–9.
12 Chester Barnard, *The Functions of the Executive*, Harvard University Press, 1938.

12 Directors and boards

In the course of this book we have encountered some failings of boards and typical frustrations of directors, and looked at the business and market environment within which a company and its board operates. But, what should they be doing?

Before considering the question of boardroom competences and qualities, someone new to director development must first determine the function of the board. What is the purpose of the board, and to whom is it accountable?

The legal duties and responsibilities of directors are extensive, and an accessible summary is presented in the IOD's periodically updated *Guidelines for Directors*.[1] Here, we only need enough of an 'overview' to enable the counsellor and developer at board level to (a) understand what directors and boards have to be equipped to do and (b) enable them to identify an actual state or situation that has not reached expectations.

In this chapter we shall consider the identification, prioritization and review of accountabilities in order to allocate roles and responsibilities within the boardroom, test the perceptions and understanding of directors of their own roles and that of the board, and identify development needs. We shall also consider a checklist of items for possible action by the chairman.

The exercises in this chapter are designed to help a board clarify its role and responsibilities, and ensure that the ethical dimension is not over-looked. Many boards find it helpful to have their roles and responsibilities reviewed, and similar exercises facilitated by experienced counsellors who can help to ensure (a) that the processes, approaches and techniques used are satisfactory and (b) that agreed outputs are recorded in a form that enables them to be understood and acted upon.

The role of the board

The legal and formal accountabilities of a board to stakeholders are established by the legislative and regulatory framework within which the company has incorporated. However, a board that concentrated solely upon a narrow legal interpretation of its responsibilities could fail in the marketplace as a result of not meeting the expectations and requirements of many groups that might consider themselves as having an interest in the company.

Views differ as to what the role of the board should be beyond its minimum legal and financial accountabilities. What is common practice, and attainable, varies from board to board, and to some extent by country. Let us examine some particular viewpoints.

- Lorsch and MacIver adopt a relatively 'detatched' approach and describe the function of the board in terms of overseeing management, reviewing performance, and ensuring that the various activities of a company are socially responsible and in compliance with the law.[2]
- A more 'proactive' view is taken by Bob Tricker. He has described the function of the board in terms of establishing strategic direction and overseeing company strategy, assessing and monitoring performance, and also—especially in the case of executive directors—becoming involved in action to ensure implementation.[3]

Sir John Harvey-Jones takes a holistic and demanding view of the role of the board. Early in his book, *Making it Happen*, based upon his own experiences, he writes: 'I start with the view that the final responsibility for the future of the company depends upon the board as a whole, and therefore the direction in which the company is to be led is the unique responsibility of the board.'[4]

The directorial view

What do individual directors think is the function of the board? The provision of strategic direction and representation of the interests of stakeholders are claimed as preoccupations. The following are typical responses from executive directors concerning the role of the board:

Establish aims, goals and values; set overall policy and strategy; and provide clear direction.

To create the broad vision and direction for the Company.

Determine the strategic direction of the company, and review operational performance in the interests of the shareholders.

To increase shareholder value in absolute terms and in relative terms to those attained by competitors.

Supervisory oversight of the strategic direction of the group, and a 'control' on executive management.

These comments from executive directors appear to exclude any significant directorial contribution to 'making it happen'. Perhaps this is seen as a 'managerial' rather than a 'directorial' responsibility by those who are both board directors and managers of particular departments, functions or business units.

When asked about key activities of the board, the following are among typical responses:

Defining strategy and monitoring its implementation.

Setting objectives, making decisions, setting standards, communicating overall philosophy.

Set culture—standards, quality, etc., define and communicate mission and key success factors.

To ensure an executive team capable of maximizing profitability and achieving long term business growth.

Planning for continued profitability and growth; ensure effective control, discipline and communication; encourage innovation and new ideas.

Again, it would appear that 'making it happen' is not seen as the responsibility of the board. We shall see in the next chapter that grasping the essence of the difference between direction and management is important if a board is to be effective, and its members are to contribute.

Experience in working with teams of directors has shown that the 'benchmark' boards that are most successful with the implementation of strategy (a) understand the distinction between direction and management, while at the same time (b) realize that there is much that a board can do to help turn aspiration into achievement.

The view from the chair

An 'IOD' survey[5] has found that the primary function of the board, from the perspective of the chairman, is setting the policy, objectives, strategy or vision of the company. If one includes the 'direction' of policy and strategy, then seven out of ten respondents described the function of their boards in proactive terms of establishing policy, objectives, strategy or vision.

The next largest group of replies in this survey of chairmen could be categorized as a reactive or monitoring function of controlling or reviewing strategies, objectives, shareholder requirements, or staff. If one adds those who specifically referred to monitoring the performance of top executive management, then over seven out of ten of the respondents referred to a reviewing, monitoring and controlling role.

A suggested view

My personal view is that the function of the board is to:

- understand the context within which a company operates, and the interests, attitudes, perspectives, needs and requirements of the various stakeholders;
- determine what needs to be done, by providing an organization and its people with a distinctive purpose and clear vision, and establishing broad and achievable goals, and specific and measurable objectives;
- create the capability to do what needs to be done, by assembling the people, finance and other resources that are required, not for their own sake, but in order to implement the agreed strategy and achieve corporate goals and objectives;
- decide how to do what needs to be done, by agreeing roles and responsibilities, and allocating them within the board and among the people of the organization;

- ensure that what needs to be done actually is done, that outcomes meet expectations and stakeholder requirements, and that the highest standards of quality and excellence are achieved;
- ensure that what is done, and how it is done, satisfies legal and other requirements;
- report to shareholders and other stakeholders upon what has been achieved.

The implications of the above functions are considered in greater detail in the companion book, *Creating Excellence in the Boardroom*.[6]

Stakeholders to whom the board is accountable include the shareholders, customers, suppliers, employees, the government and the general public. The emphasis and stakeholder priorities vary by country of incorporation and operation:

- In the UK and US, many directors are reluctant to be 'distracted' by accountabilities other than to shareholders.
- In many EC member states the interests of other stakeholders such as 'social partners' assume a higher priority, while a Japanese board may give greater attention to the pursuit of the business philosophy of the company.

The surveys upon which this book is based (see Bibliography, section 1) suggest that directors need to become more involved in identifying and overcoming obstacles and barriers to implementation. In too many companies, a considerable gap has appeared between aspiration and achievement. What is regarded as a lack of commitment, and what are perceived as gaps between 'what a board does and what it says', are undermining confidence and leading to internal conflicts.

Time devoted to directorial duties

A question for many individuals, in view of the demanding nature of the functions of the board, is how much time they should devote to directorial duties, as opposed to other responsibilities. Let us look at meetings of the board.

- A majority of single-tier boards appear to meet on a monthly basis.[5]
- In countries in which they are a requirement, the meetings of many supervisory boards are held on a quarterly basis.[7]

Of course there is more to being a director than attending meetings. Preparation and thinking time need to be taken into account. A survey, predominantly of executive directors, undertaken by Alan Wakelam[8] found that six out of ten appear to spend less than a third of their time on direction. The rest of their time is spent upon management or other activities.

A Korn/Ferry survey of larger UK companies suggests that non-executive directors spend 10–12 days per annum on their directorial duties,[9] while an average of 14 days per annum has been suggested for US directors.[2] The reality of a limited commitment of time needs to be faced by those concerned with director development.

The management of time is a particular problem for the director with heavy executive responsibilities. Those whom the counsellor might advise to take on additional responsibilities—such as a non-executive directorship or public appointment—in order to broaden their perspective can experience even greater pressure upon their time.

According to one CEO:

You don't demonstrate [directorial] commitment by long hours of work. Volumes of papers and background shouldn't make you feel good. What matters is quality of input where it counts . . . [i.e.] rapidly getting to the heart of the problem. [This requires] insight, instinct if you like, . . . a nose for what is important, and what it is really all about. Some people go straight to it, others take a bit more time.

Directors should be encouraged to discuss problems such as the 'shortage of time', and share any insights they may have concerning how best to cope. At least they will learn they are not alone. At best they will be encouraged to focus upon the essence of the directorial role, prioritize, and concentrate upon the 'vital few' actions the board and its members need to take to support the achievement of collective goals and agreed objectives.

Board and management relationship

A key element of the Credo of the IOD is that: 'for companies to prosper directors must balance the interests of all the parties associated with the enterprise (the so-called stakeholders)'.[10] The success with which a board discharges its various responsibilities can depend very much upon the quality of its relationships with various groups of stakeholders. We considered the importance of relationships with customers and the people of the organization in the previous chapter, and we shall return to the latter in the next chapter.

Stakeholder priorities can vary according to the type of company, and over time. The board of a listed or quoted company, for example, may need to pay more attention to its relationships with investors and analysts than that of a company owned by its directors. Both might need to concentrate particularly on the creditors of the company at a time of financial crisis.

Of especial and continuing importance on an operational basis is the relationship between board and management team. This can change over time according to situations and circumstances. Typically, the board formulates an overall strategy for the achievement of defined objectives, while the detailed development and implementation of strategy is undertaken by a management team that is accountable to the board. The board establishes the goals, policies and values that define the framework within which management operates. In larger companies, plans and proposals produced by management are reviewed and, if necessary, approved by the board, which then monitors performance against agreed targets, taking corrective action as required.

In practice, some boards become over-dependent upon, or lose the initiative to, the management team. For example, many boards are reactive rather than proactive in the determination of strategy.[11] Some boards will 'rubber stamp' proposals that are submitted by the management team.

A complacent or apathetic board may not represent fertile soil for development activity. Hence, the emphasis put at the start of this book upon getting to know the directors and their individual motivations and commitment. The most receptive board is often that which has already decided to review or enlarge its role.

A board that decides to 'get more involved', should not become so immersed in detail as to lose its objectivity and overview perspective. Demb and Neubauer have pointed out that at times the director has to tread carefully in order to maintain a balance between commitment and detachment.[7]

The CEO and the board

The relationship between the CEO and a board is of crucial importance. An effective CEO has an open and two-way relationship with the board, and ensures that the affairs of the company are conducted in accordance with the framework of vision, goals, values and strategy established by the board.

The CEO, as leader of the executive team, can act as a 'gatekeeper', a critical interface, between the board and management. A strong CEO can dominate a board, and drive challenge and debate out of the boardroom. A weak CEO can become the Achilles' heel of the board, and the source of misunderstanding and lack of management unity and purpose.

Particular attention should be paid to the appointment of a new CEO. Vancil identifies the selection and appointment of a CEO as a prime opportunity for a board to influence the future direction and performance of a company.[12] At the same time, the CEO may have a significant influence upon the appointment of directors, so there is a degree of interdependence, and the balance of power between CEO and board may continually change.

A board should take care not to become the poodle of a strong CEO. According to Sir John Harvey-Jones: 'It is a sad commentary that in many cases and places, board members have failed to observe their responsibilities, and powerful chief executives have, to a large extent, hijacked their boards.'[4] Similarly, the development adviser or counsellor, whose role is dependent upon the continuing goodwill of a chairman or CEO, may need both courage and integrity to push for what is thought to be right, rather than what is known to be acceptable.

A survey of directors by a team at Cranfield has suggested that a top team rather than an outstanding CEO, may be the key to sustained corporate success.[13] This underlines the importance of an effective board, and of establishing a productive working relationship between the board and the management team. Where such a relationship does not exist, the board could not be said to be effective.

When examining the performance of top management, executive directors need to be aware of their distinct roles as managers and directors, and when acting in the latter category they need to be objective and independent. In the case of those directly involved in the day-to-day conduct of business, this will not be easy and will require detachment and self-discipline.

While considerable responsibility for a range of operational matters may be delegated to management, the board cannot avoid its ultimate responsibility for the company. Thus the board may insist upon the review and approval of key management appointments, and retain responsibility for the organizational framework of accountabilities, processes, and values and corporate culture within which the executive team operates.

An initial review of the board

Do not assume that all the directors understand the role of the board. Identifying gaps in understanding is not always easy, particularly in the case of a board that is reluctant to open itself to 'external' scrutiny. It may be advisable to link an initial assessment of the board to its own review process and cycle. The review process adopted by one board is illustrated in Figure 12.1.

While the board works its way through the various stages of an 'annual review', the following questions could be asked to determine: (a) a board's understanding of its own role and purpose; and (b) the extent to which it is discharging its responsibilities:

- Is there a formal statement of the function of the board, and is it agreed, understood and periodically reviewed by the board and brought to the attention of all new directors?
- Does the company have a distinctive purpose that provides a compelling reason for its continued existence?
- Has the board formulated, agreed and shared a clear and distinctive vision that acts as a guide to action and is capable of attainment?
- To whom is the board accountable, and for what?
- Does the board really understand the interests, needs and requirements of the various stakeholders in the company?
- Has the board formulated operational goals, values, objectives and policies, or are they just 'words on paper'?
- Are the various resources of the company—i.e. finance, people, organization, technology and processes—sufficient to enable it to meet its obligations and commitments to stakeholders, and to achieve its goals and objectives?
- Has a framework of values, accountabilities and processes been established that will enable the company to sustain beneficial relationships with stakeholders?

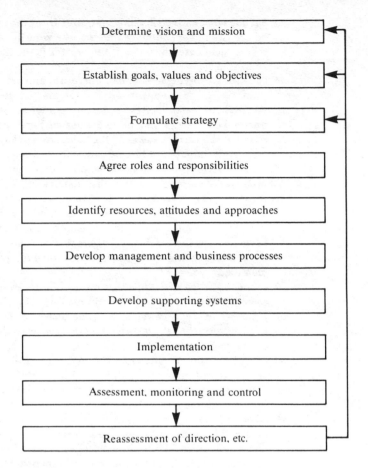

Figure 12.1 Board review process

- Does the board operate a review process that embraces its major accountabilities?

Certain of the above questions could be used as the basis of an 'away-day' exercise. For example, Exercise 12.1 is focused upon the key issue of board accountability.

Exercise 12.1: Board accountability

To ensure that a board addresses its various accountabilities in a systematic way, the following approach could be considered:

1 Brainstorm and list the various accountabilities of the board. (Do not be concerned at this stage if the list is long.)
2 Rank these accountabilities, together with the appropriate stakeholders, in order of priority. (Do not rush this. If necessary consider what each stakeholder could do to help or harm the company, and what each might do if not satisfied. Assess their relative power.)

3 Set out what each stakeholder requires from the company. (Start with, and be prepared to spend more time on, the priority stakeholders. The more that requirements are understood, the greater is the likelihood that they will be addressed.)

4 For each requirement establish minimum and achievable standards of performance. (If requirements are not understood, be prepared to investigate or undertake research. For example, a customer satisfaction survey could be undertaken to determine more precise customer requirements.)

5 Examine the current status of the company's relationship with each stakeholder group and identify areas of deficiency. (Again one could undertake research, using, for example, a customer survey to identify and prioritize sources of customer dissatisfaction.)

6 For each stakeholder group, identify the steps that need to be taken to achieve minimum and achievable standards of performance. (Be as specific as possible, using quantitative measures. Prioritize the steps that need to be taken, so that the 'vital few' actions that will make the greatest contribution towards improving the company's relationship with each group can be identified.)

7 Examine the list of actions that need to be taken to (a) determine whether there is duplication or incompatibility, and (b) assess the resources and processes that will be required. (The boards of few companies identify the key cross-functional processes that deliver or could deliver what is required or sought by stakeholders.)

8 Establish trade-off criteria and, if necessary, make a choice between possible actions according to the earlier prioritization of accountabilities and requirements. (One could distinguish on the basis of time, i.e. achieving so much in one financial year, and taking further steps the next.)

9 Allocate roles and responsibilities among the members of the board. (A particular director could be given lead responsibility for communicating with, and maintaining relationships with, each stakeholder group. Actions could be grouped according to the functional responsibilities of executive directors. Each core management and business process could be made the responsibility of an individual director.)

10 Establish an implementation and monitoring process to ensure that priority actions occur and all key requirements of stakeholders are met. (The work of the board will continue so long as stakeholder requirements change and there are still actions to implement. Accountabilities may need to be broken down and allocated between individuals and groups within the company by means of a cascade process. Changes in resources may be necessary, and management and business processes may need to be re-engineered. The board will need to establish a cycle of review meetings, 'meeting manager' accountabilities, and information requirements.)

Some boards are reluctant to confront reality when assessing their own activities and operation. How boards operate in practice is often very different from what an examination of their formal accountabilities might suggest.[14]

A board needs to understand the requirements of all significant groups of stakeholders, and to communicate and establish relationships with them. The effective board is a listening board. A degree of perceptiveness and empathy may be needed to be sensitive to differences of view and perspective within particular groups.

Accountability issues

The question of board accountability is not an idle exercise for many companies. Each of the key stakeholders in a company may be in a position to assist or hinder the achievement of corporate objectives. A board needs to be aware of actual and potential constraints upon its freedom of action. For example, while in practice a board may feel relatively free of shareholder pressures,[15] there is some evidence that institutional shareholders are becoming more restive.[16]

From time to time the interests and perspectives of different groups of stakeholder may be at variance, if not in conflict. In *Public Relations is Your Business*,[17] I have pointed out that:

The role of the board of directors is to arbitrate between these interests. Each has a form of sanction it can employ if it feels it is not getting a sufficient share of the value added generated by the enterprise. Shareholders may not respond to an invitation to subscribe for new share capital. Employees may seek employment elsewhere. Customers can buy a competitor's products. Creditors may call in existing loans or refuse to grant new ones. A government can employ sanctions to obtain its taxes. . . .

The board is faced with claims, some conflicting, from a variety of interests. Some of these publics have to be negotiated with. The board must in one way or another communicate with all of them. Satisfying a number of these interests to an acceptable degree can involve considerable political skill.

Survey evidence suggests that too much communication from boards is one way rather than two way.[18] Some remedial development work may be needed to improve the communications and listening skills of individual directors and of the board as a whole.

There also appears to be little satisfaction with the financial information that boards make available to stakeholders. One survey suggests that 'most analysts and shareholders do not believe annual reports give a "true and fair view" of a company's financial position'.[19]

Keeping to the straight and narrow path

One of the reponsibilities of the board is to ensure that legal and other requirements are satisfied, and that the business of the company is conducted in an ethical and responsible way. The experience of corporate collapses, such as that of BCCI or companies associated with the late Robert Maxwell, emphasize the extent to which the moral standards and ethical tone set by a board can pervade a corporate organization.

It is not just the directors of large companies who are at risk. For example, in the UK, by the end of July 1991, The Insolvency Service, which became an executive agency within the DTI on 21 March 1990, had succeeded in obtaining over 1000 disqualification orders on incompetent, dishonest and negligent company directors.[20]

So important is the legal and moral dimension in distinguishing the effective board, that questions similar to those in Exercise 12.2 should be used to assess whether or not a board is paying 'lip service' to the need to establish and monitor certain standards of conduct. Like other exercises in this book, the suggested review is essential, as the penalties for a failure to discharge certain duties and responsibilities can be severe.

Exercise 12.2: The legal and moral framework

The following questions should be addressed:

1 Does the allocation of roles and responsibilities make clear who is responsible for ensuring that the board meets its various legal and moral obligations and commitments? (In many companies the company secretary has specific responsibilities in this area.)
2 Is the existing allocation of responsibilities for ensuring that the board and directors are kept aware of their legal duties and responsibilities adequate? (A compliance officer might be desirable.)
3 Has the board established and communicated a framework of corporate values, and is this observed? (Many companies draw up a code of corporate conduct or ethics which covers such questions as the giving and receipt of gifts and hospitality, the exercise of influence, avoidance of conflicts of interest, and relationships with public bodies and officials.)
4 Does the board make appropriate arrangements to avoid the conflicts of interest that can arise where one or more individuals may be a director, an employee and an owner? (An example of an appropriate arrangement would be the use of a remuneration committee composed of non-executive directors to fix the pay and benefits of the executive directors.)
5 Are the members of the board covered by an appropriate directors' professional liability insurance? (A number of such policies are available from commercial suppliers.)

When undertaking an assessment such as Exercise 12.2, particular attention should be paid to the question of whether the directors are able to distinguish between the roles of 'owner', 'director' and 'manager'. There may be 'owner-directors' and 'owner-managers' who own shares in the company. It is possible for an owner executive director to be an owner, a director and a manager.

The precise legal, fiduciary, ethical and practical constraints upon a board will vary by country of incorporation, and according to the corporate constitution. For example, a UK company will have its own Memorandum and Articles of Association, and will be subject to the Companies Act, Insolvency Act, Financial Services Act and other legislation placing specific duties and responsibilities upon directors and boards.

In the case of a public sector board, some constraints upon the freedom of the directors to act might be imposed by a contractual relationship with Government, public accountability requirements, or guidance issued by a Minister or Secretary of State. The members of such a board, particularly newly appointed non-executive directors, might need to be given some induction into the strategic and accountability framework.

The attitudes, values and role-model behaviour of the board help to define the corporate culture that distinguishes a corporate organization and network and holds it together. The board should ensure that the values of the company are similar to those of the various groups with which it deals and communicates. In the case of a company that operates internationally, corporate values, ethics, style and culture must be such as to attract the interest and harness the commitment and talents of those from a variety of national, religious, ethnic and cultural backgrounds.

Directorial duties

A director owes a fiduciary duty to the company. Hence, a director should act honestly, prudently, in good faith and in the best interests of the company. The powers of the board should only be used for the purposes for which they were conferred, and care should be taken to avoid *ultra vires* actions. The director is a steward of corporate information and property, and should respect confidentiality and avoid conflicts of interest and commitments that cannot be honoured.

A director is under a duty of care not to be negligent when exercising directorial duties. The standard of skill expected will reflect the knowledge and experience of the individual director. It is recognized that a non-executive director may not be in a position to give continuous attention to a company's affairs.

This is not the place to go into detail concerning the legal duties of directors, as these are covered in the IOD guide already mentioned,[1] and other publications.[21] A board undertaking a review or exercise of the type given in Exercise 12.2 would be advised to have a qualified lawyer in attendance.

Some chairmen ask the company secretary to prepare a briefing note on 'directors' duties' for members of the board, and, subsequently to keep them up to date with current developments. There are also public courses that are of particular value to newly appointed directors. For example, the IOD offers a short 'Role of the Company Director' course on the role, accountabilities, duties and responsibilities of the company director.

Corporate governance

Various proposals have emanated from the European Commission that could have a significant impact upon (a) corporate governance and (b) the relationships between a board and various groups of stakeholders. In view of the general issues they raise, a board should have a view on such proposals, whether or not a company is incorporated within an EC member state. Their discussion can sharpen a board's awareness of its own structure and operation, and its relationship with a group such as the employees of a company.

For example, a board could consider the following EC proposals or options, which have appeared in the Draft European Company Statute (*) and the Draft Fifth Company Law Directive on the Structure of PLCs (†), and discuss their advantages, disadvantages, and implications from the perspective of its own situation and context:

- A two-tier board structure—one 'supervisory' and the other 'executive'—with between one-third and one-half of the supervisory board consisting of employee representatives with the same rights to information as any other director (†). (One-third to one-half of the members of the supervisory or administrative board to be appointed by the employees or their representatives (*).)
- A single-tier board, but with between a one-third and one-half of its members consisting of non-executive directors elected by the employees (†).
- Both the general meeting of shareholders, and the representatives of employees, to have the power to raise objections to the co-options of directors onto the board (*).
- A body representing employees (e.g. a works council) which would have certain rights to corporate information and the same rights to information as supervisory board directors (†).) (A body representing employees would have rights to certain information from the board, to require reports from the board, and to be informed and consulted before the implementation of specific decisions (*).)
- The agreement of (a) a model of employee participation (one that would provide the employees with rights to specific information, and to be informed and consulted before the implementation of specific decisions) with the employees or their representatives (*), or (b) a corporate structure that would provide for employee participation along the lines of one of the proposed models (see above) by collective agreement (†).

Establishing who is responsible for the initiation of development action

In many companies, the need to improve the competence of all or some of the directors, and to improve the effectiveness of the board is latent. Its existence and nature may not be acknowledged or recognized. If someone is concerned about the competence of directors, or the effectiveness of a board, to whom should he or she turn? Whose backing should be sought if action is to occur?

There are boards that are dominated by a powerful CEO, and many directors themselves turn in the first instance to the CEO. This may be the reality of the corporate context within which a development adviser and counsellor has to operate. My view, based upon an IOD survey, is that the chairman is the best person to judge how effectively the board is operating.[5] This viewpoint is supported by experienced chairmen of the calibre of Sir Adrian Cadbury and Sir John Harvey-Jones.[22]

The chairman should ensure that individual members of the board are competent, and that the board operates effectively as a team. A selection from the following list of items could be used to prepare a checklist for the chairman:

- Review the board's understanding of the essence and purpose of the company.
- Re-examine the company's vision, goals, values and objectives as established by the board.
- Undertake an annual review of the function, role and purpose of the board.
- Review and prioritize the collective and individual accountabilities and responsibilities of members of the board.
- Assess the extent to which assumptions and perceptions accord with reality.
- Ensure that all directors understand their legal duties and responsibilities.
- Review the size, composition, operation and effectiveness of the board.
- Assess the effectiveness, contribution and development needs of all members of the board.
- Review the commitment of the board and of its individual members.

Some chairmen prefer to use external counsellors to assist in the assessment of their boards, in order to ensure objectivity. Others put their faith in psychological and other tests that might reveal incompatibilities in the approaches, attitudes, perspectives or personalities of different directors.

The perceptions and priorities of the members of a board could be assessed by means of a survey. The results might reveal a difference between 'theory and practice', or between the views of individual directors, that could form the basis of a discussion within the board. However, bear in mind that directors are busy people and will already be confronted by many issues, and a great deal of material, that demands attention. Hence, only undertake what is essential in order to understand the particular situation.

Checklist

1 Is there a formal statement of the function of the board, and is it agreed, understood and periodically reviewed by the board and brought to the attention of all new directors?
2 Are all members of the board aware of their legal and fiduciary duties and responsibilities?
3 Are all members of the board familiar with the contents of the Memorandum and Articles of Association?
4 Are all members of the board aware of the circumstances that can give rise to legal penalties and, in particular, wrongful or fraudulent trading?
5 Are legal developments that are relevant to directors and boards brought to the attention of all directors?
6 Are all directors aware of the circumstances in which they might

experience a conflict of interest, and are such conflicts of interest declared?

7 Does the board act as an independent check upon the executive, or to what extent is it subservient to the will of the CEO?

8 Does the board understand the distinct interests, needs and requirements of each group of stakeholders?

9 Has the board established and communicated a framework of corporate values, and is this observed?

10 Do all members of the board behave as 'role-models' in respect of all aspects of their conduct?

11 Who is responsible for ensuring that the board acts in a responsible, competent, prudent and ethical manner in respect of its various accountabilities?

Notes and References

1 Institute of Directors, *Guidelines for Directors*, 4th edn, The Director Publications Ltd, May 1990.

2 Jay Lorsch and Elizabeth MacIver, *Pawns or Potentates: The Reality of America's Corporate Boards*, Harvard Business School Press, 1989.

3 Robert Tricker, *Corporate Governance: Practices, Procedures and Powers in British Companies and their Boards of Directors*, Gower Press, 1984.

4 Sir John Harvey-Jones, *Making it Happen*, Fontana Paperback Edition, 1989, p. 38.

5 Colin Coulson-Thomas and Alan Wakelam, *The Effective Board: Current Practice, Myths and Realities*. An IOD discussion document, 1991.

6 Colin Coulson-Thomas, *Creating Excellence in the Boardroom*, McGraw-Hill, 1993.

7 Ada Demb and F-Friedrich Neubauer, *The Corporate Board: Confronting the Paradoxes*, Oxford University Press, 1992.

8 Alan Wakelam, *The Training and Development of Company Directors*. Report for the Training Agency, Centre for Management Studies, University of Exeter, October 1989.

9 Korn/Ferry, *Boards of Directors Study UK*, Korn/Ferry International, 1989.

10 Peter Morgan, *Why an Institute of Directors?* Lecture to the Cardiff Business Club, 3 February 1992, p. 10.

11 J. W. Henke, 'Involving the board of directors in strategic planning', *Journal of Business Strategy*, 7, No. 2, (1986) 87–95.

12 R. Vancil, *Passing the Baton: Managing the Process of CEO Succession*, Harvard Business School Press, 1987.

13 Andrew Kakabadse, *The Wealth Creators: Top People, Top Teams and Executive Best Practice*, Kogan Page, 1991.

14 Myles L. Mace, *Directors: Myth and Reality*, Division of Research, Graduate School of Business Administration, Harvard University, 1971.

15 J. P. Charkham, *Effective Boards*, The Institute of Chartered Accountants in England and Wales, 1986.

16 See, for example, Association of British Insurers (ABI), *The Responsibilities of Institutional Shareholders: A Discussion Paper*, ABI, 1991; and Fiona Walsh, 'Sweeping out the boardrooms', *The Sunday Times* (16 June 1991), Section 4, p. 9.

17 Colin Coulson-Thomas, *Public Relations is Your Business: A Guide for Every Manager*, Business Books, 1981, p. 60.

18 Colin and Susan Coulson-Thomas, *Communicating for Change*. An Adaptation Ltd survey sponsored by Granada Business Services, Adaptation, 1991.

19 *Annual Report Survey*, McBride's Design Consultants, 1992, cited in Andrew Jack, 'Shareholders show little faith in annual reports, says survey', *Financial Times* (17 August 1992), 1.

20 John Redwood MP, *Over 1,000 Unfit Directors Disqualified*, Department of Trade and Industry Press Notice P/91/420, 31 July 1991.

21 Federation of Small Businesses, *The Penalties of Being in Business*, Federation of Small Businesses, December 1990; and Desmond Wright, *Rights and Duties of Directors*, Butterworths, 1991.

22 See, for example, Sir Adrian Cadbury, *The Company Chairman*, Director Books, 1990; Lee Iacocca, *Iacocca, An Autobiography*, Sidgwick & Jackson, 1988; and Sir John Harvey-Jones, *Making it Happen*, 2nd edn, Fontana, 1989.

13 Direction and management

We saw in the previous chapter that directors have distinct legal duties and responsibilities which are not shared by managers. For example, they are appointed by, and are accountable to, shareholders. However, people do not always find it easy to distinguish between direction and management.

Sir John Harvey-Jones believes a clear distinction can be made: 'It is fair to say that the change from being a manager or CEO of a business to joining the company's board, is one of the most profound that a business-man is ever likely to experience. The jobs are quite different and require quite different skills.'[1]

Executive directors are usually directors *and* managers. They have a collective responsibility for the overall strategy and performance of the company, and an individual responsibility as head of a function, division or business unit for the delivery of certain aspects of the corporate plan. Many are likely from time to time to be concerned that a lack of time, onerous management duties, and short-term pressures should not inter-fere with the longer term and holistic perspective that is required of a competent director.

Before drawing up any further elements of a development programme for a particular board, or for the individual members of a boardroom team, it is usually desirable to test their understanding of the distinction between direction and management. The exercises in this chapter are designed to help the adviser or counsellor, and directors themselves, with this process and to clarify the differences.

Distinguishing direction from management

How is the distinction between 'direction' and 'management' perceived by directors in general? For some two out of three respondents in a sur-vey undertaken for the IOD[2] the essence of the distinction lies in a broad, longer term or strategic awareness and perspective. To provide strategic direction, board members need to be able to see a situation as a whole, understand the context within which the company operates, and look ahead.

The following are typical responses from those asked to identify what distinguishes the director from the manager:

Strategic awareness and breadth of vision.

Broader strategic vision of the business as a whole.

Broader perspective, and wider experience.

A strategic thinker rather than an operational manager.

Helicopter vision, political awareness and business integration.

Ability to think strategically and broadly (i.e. outside own professional territory).

Objectivity and imagination, tinged with pragmatism, are required in order to formulate a distinctive vision and define a realistic strategy. Both vision and strategy may need to be shared with diverse groups.

While aware of their accountability to various stakeholders such as shareholders, the participants who were interviewed put a priority upon their responsibility to the company.

The qualities the IOD survey participants sought in new members of the board were overwhelmingly personal qualities and attributes.[2] In both this and another survey undertaken for the Institute of Personnel Management,[3] strategic awareness, objectivity, a perspective from the viewpoint of the company as a whole, business acumen, an open but responsible approach to communication, and individual qualities and attitudes emerge as more significant than specialist qualifications or technical skills.

The following are some representative comments from other directors on what distinguishes a personnel director from a personnel manager:

A director should make an impact on all of the organization's activities, not just the personnel function.

An ability to relate to broad business (as opposed to people) issues.

Ability to grasp principles of other functional areas (financial, marketing, ops, etc.).

Being a full business partner on the board.

Other comments remind us that executive directors also recognize that they may have a special contribution to make:

To define and implement the HR strategy such that it complements and supports the overall company strategy.

To ensure that personnel strategy and personnel policies help the organization to maximize the potential of its workforce to meet its business goals.

Executive directors with professional skills detect a shift of emphasis following their appointment to a board. For Richard North, who had been a practising accountant prior to becoming finance director at the Burton Group: 'The real change was moving from giving advice to becoming a party to decision making.'[4]

A director must be willing to assume personal and collective responsibility. A degree of self-control and self-discipline can also be of value in coping with the cut and thrust of healthy boardroom debate.

Understanding of the essence of direction

Director development should recognize that efforts to define and build management competences may not of themselves lead to the qualities considered desirable in company directors. Past experience may or may not be of value in terms of preparation for the boardroom. The key question is the extent to which it has led to the development of the strategic awareness, holistic perspective, and personal qualities that are sought in new appointees to the board.

Those concerned with a particular board should assess the extent to which the distinction between direction and management is understood by the members. If it is not, remedial work may need to be undertaken. The effectiveness with which a director development programme complements and builds upon an existing base of management skills and qualities can depend upon (a) the extent to which the programme focuses upon the essence of direction, and (b) how well the distinction between direction and management is understood.

Once a common understanding of the function of the board and the duties and distinguishing role and qualities of the director have been established, the specific development needs of particular categories of director such as chairman, CEO, or non-executive director can be addressed.[5]

The development foundations

How firm is the base upon which directorial competences and qualities might be built? Many of those being considered for directorial appointments may already have undergone periods of management training. These development foundations need to be understood.

- Much of the training received may not have made the distinction between direction and management explicit. John Harper, head of Professional Development at the IOD, believes that 'company direction requires qualities, competences and awareness in directors that are different from those needed by most managers'.[2]
- The relevance of what 'has gone before' can vary greatly between companies. In some, managers are given little discretion, and are provided with few opportunities to obtain an 'overview'. In others, a wide range of managers may be involved in the discussion of strategic issues, and business units may be given considerable freedom to run their own affairs.

The adviser or counsellor may be able to reduce anxieties by pointing out that (a) the identification of deficiencies in relation to a board appointment may not in any way be a reflection upon the management qualities of those concerned, which could be outstanding; while (b) certain qualities, or a particular perspective, might not be expected in someone who hitherto has not had an opportunity to develop them.

The more open people are about their experience, qualities, concerns, perceived weaknesses and development foundations, the easier it is to help them. The modest and honest individuals who are open, self-aware

and 'at peace with themselves', are more likely to represent development potential than someone seeking to conceal or impress, and eager
to please.

Orientation and focus

Orientation and focus also depend upon the context. In the smaller
business, most people may have 'their heads down', while the directors
are 'out and about' and 'do the talking'. Managers in larger organizations are often also required to understand the business environment
and be effective communicators.

The most important quality sought in members of senior management
teams in one survey of international companies[6] is 'strategic awareness',
followed by 'customer focus', 'individual responsibility' and 'communication
skills'. We have seen that these qualities are also desirable in directors.
Some three-quarters of the respondents consider 'strategic awareness' to
be a very important 'senior management' quality.

While there would appear to be an overlapping of the qualities sought
in directors and managers, the concerns and perspective of the manager
are more likely to relate to a particular business unit or function, rather
than the company as a whole. The general manager is likely to be concerned with a single business, while the board juggles a portfolio of
businesses.

John Lovering, finance director of Sears Group, found that upon coming
a director: 'The amount of time which has to be allocated to external
people increases dramatically—whether it's investment analysts or
investment bankers with deals to suggest.'[4] The manager may have little
contact with important stakeholders such as investors, and may not be
exposed to the legal risks and obligations borne by the director.

Theory and practice

Director development should confront what is, rather than what ought
to be, and there may be assumptions and perceptions to challenge.
There are many myths surrounding how boards operate, that do not
accord with reality.[7]

For example, one 'expectation' could be that the board is focused upon
the external business environment and long term strategy, while managers concentrate upon the short term and implementation. However, in
practice directors and managers are both facing pressures and requirements that are causing them to shift their focus and horizon
(Figure 13.1).[8]

In order to create more flexible and responsive organizations that are
better able to cope with the changing business environment, directors
are concentrating more upon the internal priority of creating a flatter
and slimmer structure, and more adaptable processes. At the same time,
the board of the public company experiencing the impacts of an economic recession or downturn may be concerned about the reactions of
analysts and investors to 'disappointing' financial performance.[9] Hence
more attention may be given to short-term actions to improve ratios

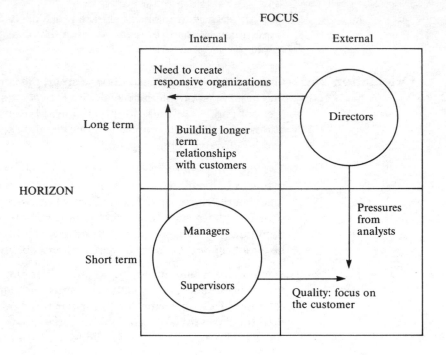

Figure 13.1   Focus and horizon

such as return on net assets, and the impact of their activities upon share price.

In comparison, managers are being expected to focus upon building longer term relationships with external customers, while total quality, process re-engineering, and other initiatives are encouraging them to think of external environments and long-term strategies.[10]

The members of a board could be given a blank matrix in the form of Figure 13.1 and asked to indicate (a) where they think they are and (b) where they feel they ought to be. This could indicate the extent to which the directorial perspective may need to shift. Comparing the results with those from a sample of senior managers could reveal incompatibilities of focus or horizon that could lead to misunderstandings and differences.

Arenas of conflict   The consequences of the changing focus and horizons of directors and boards include allegations of 'short-termism' and the existence in many companies of 'arenas of conflict'. These have development implications:

* There is some evidence that fund managers and investment analysts take a longer term view than chief executives and financial directors;[11]

so members of the board may need to be reminded that a longer term perspective should be a directorial quality.

- Boards that have a tendency to dabble, react, 'fire-fight', or 'over-rely' on management may need to be focused upon their role in the determination of strategy.[12]
- The existence of arenas of conflict can lead to a breakdown in the relationship between board and executive team, cynicism and despair, and effort may need to be applied to the re-establishment of trust and mutual respect.[10]

Tensions between a head office and operating units, or between a holding company board and the boards of subsidiary companies, can undermine a sense of common purpose. A board may need to examine whether its own role-model conduct, perceived gaps between its actions and words, or the reward criteria, performance measures or processes it has established have contributed to misunderstanding and conflict.

Development implications

Care should be taken when selecting training material and courses, to avoid those that blur the distinction between direction and management. If a board and management team are to work harmoniously together, each needs to understand the distinct perspective of the other.

The board and management team should have clear and matching roles and responsibilities and should complement each other's qualities and contributions. Where these conditions are not met, formal progammes for directors and managers could contain a discussion module on directorial and managerial roles and responsibilities, or a review forum could be held embracing directors and managers to enable mutual perceptions and expectations to be explored.

Satisfactory relationships require mutual understanding, trust and respect, and the commitment of directors and managers. The framework established by the board could empower, motivate even liberate managers, or it could constrain, restrict and frustrate them. Head office directors sometimes treat subsidiary company directors as if they were branch managers.

The board in turn may be dependent upon management for information and support. If the board is to operate effectively it is important that senior managers have the judgement to determine when a matter ought to be brought to the attention of the board.

Arenas of conflict should be confronted rather than avoided, and their root causes addressed. A board should have its 'ear to the ground' in order to identify latent conflicts. The effective board is a listening board. The competent director looks, listens and learns. Exercise 13.1 could be used with directors and senior managers to assess the extent to which arenas of conflict exist within a corporate organization.

Exercise 13.1: Arenas of conflict

Consider the changing focus and horizon of the directors and managers in your company (see Figure 13.1). Is there a potential for conflict:

1 between directors and managers?
2 between the head office and operating or business units?
3 between generalists and specialists?
4 between those who have been quality trained or 'culture changed' and those who have not?
5 between the board and various stakeholders?
6 between the company and its customers, suppliers or business partners?
7 between the board of the holding company and those of its subsidiaries?

What other arenas of actual or potential conflict are there as a consequence of changing perspectives?

Some boards have acknowledged collectively for the first time festering and debilitating differences of viewpoint as a result of carrying out a review similar to that given in Exercise 13.1. As one chairman stated, mixing metaphors: 'For too long we hid things under the carpet rather than grasp the nettle.'

In the case of each significant arena of conflict that is identified, the following questions could be asked:

- What action should the board take to improve communication and understanding in order to re-establish or build a relationship that is based upon mutual trust and support?
- Do the company's processes and procedures reduce or exacerbate the potential for misunderstanding and conflict, and should they be re-engineered?
- To what extent has the current allocation of roles and responsibilities contributed to misunderstanding and conflict, and should it be reviewed?

Strains and conflicts often result from a misunderstanding of the distinction between direction and management. The directors may become 'interfering busybodies' preoccupied with details, rather than 'strategic thinkers'. The allocation of responsibilities between board and management may be haphazard and confused. Many problems stem from people who join a board but continue to think, act and behave as managers rather than develop a directorial awareness and perspective.

Thinking 'director' or 'manager'

Many individuals with considerable experience of management education and development do not find it easy to contribute to director development. Often this is because they are not sensitive to the differences that can occur between the perspectives of directors and those of managers. Some are more subtle than others, but recognizing them and making them explicit enables aspects of the directorial perspective to be developed.

Thinking 'director', rather than 'manager', could mean aiming to please shareholders rather than a boss, or confronting trade-offs rather than pursuing a single objective. What the manager accepts as a 'given' might be challenged by the director. The manager is often expected to enthuse commitment, while a degree of detachment might be more appropriate in a director colleague. A manager may be respected for his or her knowledge, while the reputation of the director might depend upon judgement, or even a 'nose' for 'what is right'.

There will be those who question the distinctions just made. The differences suggested are necessarily general and impressionistic. There are managers who think like directors, and directors who behave like managers.

Comparing, contrasting and sharing

In practice, a variety of overlapping and differing attitudes and viewpoints are likely to be found among directors and managers, even within the same company. Are directors more, or less, willing than managers to confront reality? Role playing or the context may encourage managers to compete while directors cooperate.

Reflecting upon how directors think or behave, or should think and behave, can help clarify what distinguishes direction from management. One approach to assessing the extent of mutual understanding is suggested in Exercise 13.2.

Exercise 13.2: Directorial and managerial perceptions

Both the board and a group of managers (senior or representative) could be asked to distinguish in their own words between the perspectives and attitudes of (a) directors and (b) managers. The groups could be given some time to do this, and their conclusions could then be compared and discussed. The two groups could be brought together to explore the consequences of any differences in mutual perceptions that emerged.

'Slow starter' groups could be prompted by asking them to address a specific issue (e.g. relationships with customers; or how the board and management could work more closely together in order to deliver value and satisfaction to customers). Alternatively, they could be asked to comment on, or indicate whether they agreed or disagreed with, the attitudes identified in Example 8.1 re. 'managerial and directorial contributions'. (These attitudes and viewpoints are given for the purposes of illustration.)

The secure and open board should be prepared to share its responses to an exercise (such as Exercise 13.2) with members of the management team. The purpose of this exercise is to increase mutual understanding and identify obstacles, barriers and gaps. A key question is: Do the directors and managers in your company really understand each other's accountabilities, roles and responsibilities, attitudes and perspectives and what action should be taken to bridge any gaps in mutual comprehension and awareness?

Dr Ingham Lenton, while chairman of Compass Group plc, has taken the view that 'whilst the functions of direction and of management of a company are significantly different, they overlap and intertwine, and the quality of each is important to a business'.

Managerial and directorial attitudes

The beliefs, attitudes and values of directors could vary from those of managers (a) as a consequence of their differing accountabilities, roles and responsibilities, and perspectives, or (b) because a board has failed to share corporate values and encourage appropriate attitudes.

Managerial and directorial attitudes can be of considerable significance. Attitudes can be positive or negative, 'helps' or 'hinders'. Some attitudes can be supportive of corporate vision, goals, values and objectives, while other attitudes may be in conflict with them.

Attitudes can influence behaviour, motivation and reward and vice versa. Those who treat people—and measure and remunerate them—as 'managers' rather than 'directors' should not be surprised if they behave as managers regardless of the label attached to them. Training and development will not of itself lead to a change of attitudes if under-mined by symbols, reward, performance measurement, criteria for advancement or role-model behaviour.

Current attitudes may have their roots in past behaviour. The waves caused by long-departed directors and previous decisions can colour perceptions of, and attitudes towards, the current board. The achievement of corporate transformation may be dependent upon changing attitudes.

Identifying and learning from attitudes

Relatively few boards undertake surveys of directorial attitudes. The pattern of directorial responses to such an exercise could reveal a group problem, or that certain individuals are 'out of step' with colleagues, where the attitudes of a few directors are distinct from those of the rest of the board.

It is sometimes possible to chart where individual directors might be expected to stand on particular issues from what is known about their attitudes. Information concerning directorial attitudes should not be ostensibly obtained for one purpose and subsequently used for another.

Directors are sometimes more willing to express views and attitudes that could be construed as 'critical' or 'negative', when responses are collated by an independent third party with confidentiality guaranteed.

Where trust is forthcoming, its betrayal can make it difficult for a counselling or facilitating role to be sustained.

Where members of a board appear to be exhibiting a managerial rather than a directorial approach to its business, it might be a good idea to list expressed attitudes, and ask the board (a) to identify which are 'helps' and which 'hinders', and why; and then (b) to assemble and prioritize those directorial attitudes thought most appropriate to the board's current situation.

Within some boards, directors tend to keep their relationships relatively formal and their attitudes to themselves. Where a board is reluctant to confront its own attitudes directly, a 'straw man' list of views and opinions could be used to approach 'indirectly' the question of directorial attitudes.

Once desirable directorial attitudes have been identified, the next step is to encourage the members of a board to examine, individually and collectively, how closely their own attitudes match what is considered ideal. Deficiencies that are revealed can then be addressed by appropriate counselling and development support.

Roles and responsibilities

In many companies, the source of continuing problems can often be traced to the allocation or division of responsibilities between directors and managers. The allocation is unlikely to be clear and productive where people are confused about the distinction between direction and management. Not only the board, but also the members of the management team, need to understand the points of difference, and to what extent these may be of kind, degree or emphasis.

The distinction between direction and management is especially important to those with directorial ambitions and potential. The IOD advocates: 'Recognition of the significant difference between the role of director and that of manager, and the vital necessity of training in the particular responsibilities involved in being a director.'[13]

In some companies, an insecure board may be reluctant to encourage a group of managers, or directorial aspirants, to question the current division of responsibilities between the directorial team and management. The fear could be of criticism, challenge, the unknowns of the Pandora's box that might be opened, or even of insurrection. A less threatening approach is to explore the allocation of roles and responsibilities in relation to a 'case study' situation.

Wherever possible, case study and other material used for director development should be concerned with issues of particular interest to the board, such as, for example, the achievement of corporate transformation, or the determination and implementation of environmental or quality policy.

Checklist

1 Has the board articulated, agreed and communicated the qualities it is seeking in its directors and its managers?
2 Are the qualities that are sought discussed and reviewed periodically?
3 How do the qualities that are sought compare with those identified in benchmark companies, and in companies in general?
4 Have guidelines been drawn up to assist assessment, review and career planning, and are they observed?
5 Have the requirements been expressed in general or precise terms?
6 Does the terminology that is used capture the subtleties of the distinction between directors and managers?
7 Do definitions, guidelines, requirements and distinctions capture the essence of what it is to be a director?
8 Have the requirements relating to directors been shared with members of the management team?
9 What reactions or comments have been received from members of the senior management team?
10 Are the qualities sought in directors compatible with, and do they complement, those required of managers?
11 Is there a clear distinction between the qualities sought in directors and managers respectively, and is this understood?
12 What is the basis of the distinction at the senior management level?
13 Is there an integrated skills and awareness programme that extends from initial induction to developing directorial attitudes, perspective and qualities?

Notes and references

1 Sir John Harvey-Jones, *Making it Happen: Reflections on Leadership*, 3rd impression, Fontana/Collins, 1989, p. 186.
2 Colin Coulson-Thomas, *Professional Development of and for the Board*. A questionnaire and interview survey undertaken by Adaptation Ltd of company chairmen. A summary has been published by the IOD, February 1990.
3 Colin Coulson-Thomas, *The Role and Function of the Personnel Director*. An interim Adaptation Ltd survey carried out in conjunction with the Research Group of the Institute of Personnel Management, 1991.
4 Jane Simms and Heather Farmbrough, 'Unfit for power or on course for achievement?', *Financial Director* (September 1992), 57–60.
5 Sir Adrian Cadbury, *Company Chairman*, Director Books, 1990; G. Copeman, *The Managing Director*, 2nd edn, Business Books, 1982; and K. Lindon-Travers, *Non-Executive Directors: A Guide to their Role, Responsibilities, and Appointment*, Director Books, 1990.
6 Colin Coulson-Thomas, *Human Resource Development for International Operation*. A survey sponsored by Surrey European Management School, Adaptation, 1990.
7 Myles L. Mace, *Directors: Myth and Reality*, Division of Research, Harvard Graduate School of Business Administration, 1971; and Colin Coulson-Thomas, 'Competent directors: Boardroom myths and realities', *Journal of General Management*, **17**, No. 1 (Autumn 1991), 1–26.
8 Colin Coulson-Thomas and Alan Wakelam, *The Effective Board: Current Practice, Myths and Realities*. An IOD discussion document, 1991.

9 3i's, 'The FD and corporate governance, 3i's seventh plc UK survey', *Financial Director* (April 1992), 23–4.

10 Colin Coulson-Thomas, *Transforming the Company: Bridging the Gap between Management Myth and Corporate Reality*, Kogan Page, 1992.

11 MORI, *Shareholder Value Analysis Survey*, Coopers & Lybrand Deloitte, 1991.

12 Shaker Zahra and John Pearce, 'Determinants of board directors strategic involvement', *European Management Journal*, **8**, No. 2 (1990), 164–73; and Shaker Zahra, 'Increasing the board's involvement in strategy', *Long Range Planning*, **23**, No. 6 (1990), 109–17.

13 Blenyth Jenkins, 'Companies in need of a code', *Boardroom Agenda*, Issue 1 (February 1992), 18–19.

14 The boardroom team

In Chapter 1 we considered the need to understand the motivations of individual directors, why they sought to become directors, and what board membership means for them. In this chapter, we shall turn our attention to the nature of the particular board whose development needs are to be addressed.

There are many different types of board; for example, private and public company boards, holding and subsidiary company boards, and unitary and supervisory boards. It should not be forgotten that members of all of these boards may share certain common duties and responsibilities.[1]

Demb and Neubauer have found that there can be similarities in directorial attitudes, and in how boards operate in practice, across various board types.[2] There are also differences, and the contribution of development activities and support can depend upon the extent to which these are addressed.

There are an almost endless number of different combinations and permutations of directors that can come together in the boardroom. The exercises in this chapter are concerned with reviewing the extent to which the type of board, and its size and composition, are appropriate.

Matching the board to the company

There is an enormous number of companies: over a million are registered at Companies House alone in the UK.[3] Only 1 in 500 of these are quoted on the Stock Exchange.

It was estimated in 1992 by the IOD that all but 10 000 of these UK companies have less than 100 employees, and only some 800 employ over 1000 people and have a turnover in excess of £100 million.[4] Most companies are small businesses, with two or more directors who may rarely meet or act as a board. Most of these businesses do not have a boardroom 'team'.

An ideal or standard board does not exist. The nature of the board, its size and composition should reflect the situation and business context of the company and its development needs and prospects. The national legal framework, local practice, and corporate structure, technology or processes can all influence the nature of the board.

Table 14.1 The process of corporate evolution

Stage of evolution	Board	Concerns
Start-up	Owner-directors	Survival and growth
Small business	New appointments to complement skills of founder directors	Succession; maintain independence
Medium-sized business	Appointment of functional directors	Balance the team; build relationships
Large business	Establishment of subsidiary boards	Reorganization and transformation; 'cover' main elements of organization and key activities; arrangements and joint ventures
Public company	Appointment of non-executive directors; creation of audit and remuneration committees	Strategy, planning and issue monitoring; image and reputation; account-ability and protection of interests of widely scattered investors
International expansion	Establishment of foreign subsidiaries; appointment of non-nationals to the board	Internationalization; global alliances

A board is a living entity, and its membership, and how these members interrelate, can evolve as circumstances change. Table 14.1 presents a highly simplified summary of how a board might change as a business grows and develops, along with possible concerns at each stage of evolution. While the latter are just examples, they illustrate the extent to which the directors of an expanding business may themselves need to develop over time.

The effective board should periodically review its nature, size, composition and operation. Exercise 14.1 illustrates the sort of approach that could be taken.

Exercise 14.1: The nature of the board

The following questions could be considered by a board during the course of a
review of its nature and evolution, and an examination of how relevant and
appropriate it currently is to the corporate and market situation and context:

1 What is the nature of the board in terms of category, form and type?
2 Why is the board the way it is? (Make sure the reasons are really
  understood.)
3 When did the last significant change in the nature of the board occur and
  why?
4 Does the nature of the board reflect the type of company, and the nature of
  the circumstances the company is in?
5 Does the board 'benchmark' itself against other 'representative' boards of
  'similar' or 'equivalent' companies?
6 What other models of corporate governance and boards might be appropriate,
  and what are their advantages and disadvantages?

In undertaking a review in the manner of Exercise 14.1, the board might
require some facilitation support, preferably from someone who is
familiar with different board types and their relative suitability in
particular situations and circumstances.

Where a board exists in a wider group context, there is potential for
conflict and misunderstanding between a 'main' or holding board and
operating or subsidiary company boards. Further questions to
consider include:

- How does the board interact with other boards (if applicable) within a
  group, and when was the division of responsibilities and allocation of
  accountabilities within the group last reviewed?
- Does the structure of corporate governance that has evolved within a
  group (if applicable) enable a company to meet its various obligations
  and commitments, and is the allocation of accountabilities and
  responsibilities both clear and operationally sound?

The evolving board

The nature of many boards will undergo an evolution as a company
expands and develops; and the board and its directors needs to grow
and adapt with the business. Thus, while the founder directors of a
business may be happy to work informally, or keep matters 'within the
family', inviting one or two additional individuals onto a board may lead
to a demand for formal meetings.

As the business grows, and functional departments and business units
are set up, those heading them may obtain seats on the board and
become employee directors. Subsidiary boards could be established to
give elements of the business greater autonomy.

In the period prior to a listing, or as external finance is secured and
operations and accountabilities become more complex, the membership

Entrepreneurial small business

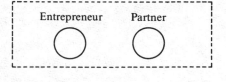

Small company

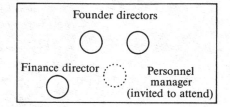

Medium-sized company
CEO and 'functional' directors

Large company
CEO and mix of 'functional' directors
and subsidiary company
managing directors

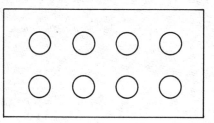

Public company

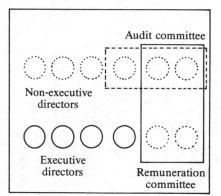

Figure 14.1   *Varieties of board*

of the board might be widened to include non-executive directors. International expansion can lead to the formation of operating companies in various countries and could result in a requirement to 'internationalize' the board.

The varieties of board that can result from the development of a UK business are shown in Figure 14.1. Each of the boards illustrated is based upon an actual company. In certain other EC member states, a supervisory board might, or would, need to be established once a company has reached a certain size.

The size of the board

An obvious question to ask is whether the size of the board is 'about right'. How many members do boards have in practice?

According to one survey, the most common size of board for the 'medium' sized UK company in the £1–10 million turnover range is six,[5] and larger companies tend to have larger boards. The examples selected for Figure 14.1 illustrate this tendency of boards to expand in size to match the growth of the directorial challenge.

Another survey of a broad sample of UK companies by Alan Wakelam found that about a half of the boards covered had three or fewer executive directors, together with three or fewer non-executive directors.[6] Many boardroom teams are relatively small and intimate.

Outside of certain service sectors, it is only in the case of the 'large' and public companies that UK boardroom teams of around a dozen or more people are likely to be encountered. Surveys of larger US companies suggest 13[7] and 14[8] as an average size of board. Such boards would be composed primarily of non-executive directors.

How big should the board be? The answer to this question will depend upon the factors we have already considered, the capabilities and personalities of the directors and the dynamics of the boardroom. There is little point in bringing extra people onto a board if the quality of chairmanship does not allow them to make an effective contribution.

The questions in Exercise 14.2 illustrate the considerations to be taken into account when reviewing the size of a board.

Exercise 14.2: The size of the board

The following questions could be used during a discussion of the size of a board:

1 Why is the board the size it is?
2 How does the size of the board compare with that of 'benchmark' companies?
3 How does the current size of the board help or hinder discussion and decision making?
4 How appropriate is the size of the board in the context of the current situation and circumstances of the company?
5 In what circumstances might additional members of the board be beneficial?
6 What impact do, might or could non-executive directors have upon the size of the board?
7 What would be the advantages and disadvantages of a smaller or larger number of directors?
8 Given the current size of the board, what factors might result in a significant improvement in the effectiveness of the board?

Sometimes, the arguments used to suggest the need for additional directors can help to indentify deficiencies that could also be met, in whole or in part, by director development. A balance may need to be struck between development and 'recruitment', depending upon the assessed qualities, capabilities and potential of an existing boardroom team.

Board size itself can be a compromise between a number of different factors. The small board, while intimate, may lack balance and an adequate range of experience. However, too large a board may find it difficult to operate as a team, and individuals may not find it easy to contribute.

The composition of the board

It is generally advisable to consider the questions of the function, nature, size and composition of a board together. However, in some circumstances, it may be advisable to invite comments on the nature or size of a board prior to examining its composition. This may allow more time for a focused discussion of each aspect, and might better prepare the board for the consideration of its composition.

When a sudden or dramatic change occurs in the circumstances of a company, the composition of a board may need to be reviewed as a matter of urgency. Some members of a board may have the capability of rising to the occasion, while others may be sidelined as a 'crisis' group is brought together to handle a rapidly changing situation.

Other reviews could be undertaken proactively to coincide with a planned corporate development. The qualities needed to preside over the affairs of an established company in a relatively protected market may be very different from those needed to bring about a fundamental transformation.

A board should never take its composition for granted, or run the risk of becoming an introverted or exclusive 'club'. From time to time 'new blood' may be needed, as after some years directors can lose their 'edge' and become complacent and less objective.

With some boards the directors are regularly re-elected until they retire. In other companies, chairmen and CEOs may be quite ruthless in their treatment of colleagues who do not perform. In the case of a takeover, an entire board may be replaced.

Factors to take into account

A board should relate its composition to its own situation and aspirations, and the following factors need to be taken into account when reviewing the composition of the board:

- Any provisions in the Memorandum and Articles of Association relating to the composition of the board and changing the membership of the board.
- Responsibilities, accountabilities, and company practice relating to the composition of the board and changing the membership of the board.
- The extent to which review criteria that are used are explicit and capable of leading to appropriate action.
- The circumstances that gave rise to the existing composition of the board and the extent to which these have changed.

- The extent to which the existing composition is perceived as a 'given' or model, or whether it is perceived as something to be changed according to circumstances and personalities.
- Views, opinions, and attitudes on such issues as (a) whether or not the roles of chairman and of chief executive should be occupied by the same or different people; and (b) whether or not membership of the board should include non-executive directors.
- Whether, and to what extent, difficiencies exist in the current composition of the board.
- What is necessary to turn the vision, goals, values, objectives and policies of the company into a reality.
- In particular, whether the composition allows a satisfactory allocation of roles and responsibilities among the various members of the board.
- The extent to which the current composition of the board could or ought to be strengthened, complemented or supplemented.
- Whether there are situations that are imminent, likely or probable that would justify a substantial reconstitution of the board, and whether any contingency plans for coping with such an eventuality exist.

The insecure and self-interested director may perceive new members of the board as a threat. More confident colleagues who put the interests of the company first may reflect upon opportunities to tap a broader range of experience and wisdom.

The views, attitudes, opinions and perspective of the existing members of a board can be very suggestive of what needs to be done. Directorial attitudes can act as a facilitator of, or constraint upon, change. Complementary qualities may be sought.

My view is that the chairman should assume responsibility for reviewing, or initiating a review of the composition of the board. According to Sir John Harvey-Jones, only the chairman 'can develop the board as a collective organization, handle, select and motivate its members, and manage its work. . . . The actual way in which it works depends entirely on the chairman.'[9]

Specialism in the boardroom

As companies grow in size and functional departments are established, there is a tendency to appoint departmental heads to the board. Such appointments should not be made unless the individuals concerned have directorial qualities and strategic awareness. To do otherwise runs the risk of introducing the 'curse of professionalism' into the boardroom. Senior professionals themselves recognize that many of their colleagues have a narrow and blinkered perspective, and that appointments to the board should reflect personal qualities rather than specialist expertise.[10]

Overall, survey evidence suggests that expert opinion tends to be treated with some caution and scepticism in the boardroom.[5] A typical view of chairmen is that 'you don't need to appoint people to the board to get the benefit of their specialist expertise'. The inputs of 'experts' with particular knowledge and/or competence can be obtained by means of hiring them as employees or consultants.

The mix of specialisms that tend to be found in the boardrooms of larger companies, and their relative 'pecking order', can vary by country. For example, Parry Rogers, who has served on the boards of IBM UK, Plessey and ICL, has pointed out that: 'not only is it normal practice for there to be a personnel director in the boardroom of major Japanese companies, but the personnel director in Japan is usually the most senior director after the chief executive, sitting in the position of influence more usually occupied here [UK] by the finance director'.[11]

Lester Thurow has pointed out that in the US boardroom, the chief financial officer or CFO ranks second only to the CEO, while the director responsible for people is regarded as relatively less important.[12] He regards the reversal of this situation in Japan as a source of competitive advantage for Japanese companies.

The functional head who is most likely to be found upon a UK board is the finance director. A survey of UK public companies has revealed that: 'In nine out of ten companies, finance is the sole responsibility of an individual board director. Apart from board representation for heads of major subsidiaries, finance is the only function assigned to be the sole responsibility of a board member in most companies.'[13]

When putting together a director development programme, it should not be thought that because there is a finance director on the board, other directors do not need to be financially literate. We saw in Chapter 3 that all directors need sufficient financial knowledge to enable them to discharge their individual and collective duties and responsibilities.

Integrating expertise and individuals into the team

Individual directors might well be working with a number of specialists (Figure 14.2). The management challenge for executive directors and senior managers is to harness and manage such expertise by means of teams, task forces and project groups so that it contributes to the achievement of business objectives. When knowledge is applied, it is important that 'gaps' do not emerge.

The role of the board, as we have seen, is to define the overall mission, goals, values, strategy and objectives of a company and monitor the extent to which various activities, including those that draw upon expert opinion, result in their attainment. The skills and knowledge of the board and the senior management team should match the business development needs of a company and the competitive context within which it operates.[14]

The board's task in relation to expertise[5] is to ensure that individual expert contributions, including those of functional departments made up of those with related expertise, combine into a unified and holistic approach to boardroom issues (Figure 14.2).

The director development challenge goes beyond the creation of 'islands of competence' or 'centres of excellence'. These have to be

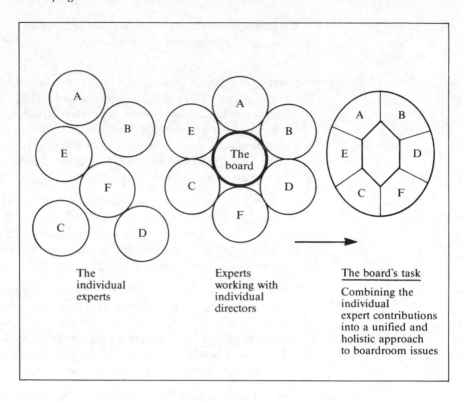

The
individual
experts

Experts
working with
individual
directors

The board's task

Combining the
individual
expert contributions
into a unified and
holistic approach
to boardroom issues

Figure 14.2   *Expert opinion*

harnessed, assembled, integrated and applied in order to facilitate and
support the work of the board. This has to be done in such a way that
its individual members approach issues from the perspective of the
company as a whole.

To assess the extent to which a board makes appropriate use of specialist expertise, the questions of Exercise 14.3 could be used.

Exercise 14.3: Specialists and experts in the boardroom

Building upon the consideration of the distinction between direction and management (the subject matter of the previous chapter), the following questions
could be posed concerning the role of the specialist or expert in the boardroom:

1 What 'specialisms' are 'represented' in the boardroom, and who is a member
   of the board by virtue of heading up a specialist function?
2 What (function) or who (person) is the most significant 'omission' in terms
   of membership of the board?
3 What does board 'membership' mean for a specialist function, and what are
   the advantages and disadvantages?
4 Are some boardroom positions regarded as 'more equal than others'?
5 Is it perceived, and where or by whom, that there are certain 'functional
   slots' in the boardroom that ought to be filled?

6 Which stakeholders (if any) would be concerned if a particular 'vacancy' on the board was not filled and why?

7 To what extent did personal qualities rather than functional management role, or professional or specialist expertise, play a part in securing boardroom seats for those concerned? (The criteria used in selecting directors was considered in Chapter 5.)

8 How might boardroom roles and responsibilities best be allocated: on the basis of relevance of expertise, function, cross-functional process, individual task, team or project accountability or another basis?

9 What areas of specialist expertise (if any) ought to be available via a member of the board, rather than through an adviser or consultant to the board?

10 What innovative or (additional) facilitating roles, and further areas of facilitating expertise, are desirable in the boardroom?

Directors need to take a holistic rather than a functional view of issues and matters that appear on the boardroom agenda. While deputy chairman of Blue Arrow Employment Group, Charles Lowe cautioned: 'A board composed of specialists is likely to lack direction even though its individual management expertise may be first class. Although a board needs a variety of talent, to be effective as directors its members must go beyond their own disciplines and use them as servants not masters.'

Increasingly, the issues with which a board is concerned transcend functional compartmentalism, and directors of change, learning, relationships, thinking, and transformation with process, facilitation, enabling and empowering skills are likely to be in increasing demand at the expense of 'traditional pillars of the professions'.

In the case of the public company, other considerations apply, and establishing an independent check upon the executive team by separating the roles of chairman and CEO, appointing robust non-executive directors, and establishing audit and remuneration committees composed largely or wholly of non-executive directors may also be an important consideration.[15] While the executive director's whole life and prospects may be intimately bound up with the company, the non-executive director can generally afford to 'stand back' and take a more detached view. This is the perspective that also needs to be adopted by the development counsellor or adviser.

Checklist

1 Is the board of your company part of the traditional 'heritage' of the company, or is it a 'living entity'?

2 How has the current form of the board evolved or come about?

3 Does the size of the board 'just happen', or is it considered, and by whom?

4 Are potential new members of the board easy or difficult to find?

5 Have any appointments to the board been made for 'symbolic' or 'cosmetic' reasons?

6 Who in the boardroom has comparative experience of other boards, and how might such expertise be acquired or used?

7 Have other models of board, and different approaches to corporate governance, been considered?

8 How does the composition of the board compare with that of benchmark companies?

9 Is there a 'pecking order' among the directors, and (if so) what does this reveal about board priorities?

10 What experience does the board, or its members, have of a larger, or smaller, number of directors?

11 Has the company reached such a watershed in its development as to suggest that a review of the nature and composition of the board would be desirable?

12 Within five years, what 'specialisms' might be 'represented' on the board if suitable candidates could be found?

13 What is the most likely 'next step' in the evolution of the board?

14 Who is responsible for initiating a review of the nature, size and composition of the board?

15 What experience do the members of the board have of such a review, and who should undertake it?

Notes and references

1 Institute of Directors, *Guidelines for Directors*, 4th edn, Director Publications, May 1990.

2 Ada Demb and F-Friedrich Neubauer, *The Corporate Board: Confronting the Paradoxes*, Oxford University Press, 1992.

3 Companies House Annual Report 1991–92, and Andrew Jack, 'Agency has surplus of £1.56m', *Financial Times* (4 August 1992), 8.

4 Peter Morgan, *Why an Institute of Directors?* Lecture delivered to the Cardiff Business Club, 3 February 1992, pp. 5–6.

5 Colin Coulson-Thomas and Alan Wakelam, *The Effective Board: Current Practice, Myths and Realities*. An IOD discussion document, 1991.

6 Alan Wakelam, *The Training and Development of Company Directors*. A report on a questionnaire survey undertaken by the Centre for Management Studies, University of Exeter for the Training Agency, December 1989.

7 Heidrick & Struggles Inc., *The Changing Board*, Heidrick & Struggles, 1987.

8 Jeremy Bacon, *Membership and the Organization of Corporate Boards*, Research Report No. 886, Conference Board, 1986.

9 Sir John Harvey-Jones, *Making it Happen: Reflections on Leadership*, 3rd impression, Fontana/Collins, 1989, p. 235.

10 Colin Coulson-Thomas, *The Role and Function of the Personnel Director*. An interim Adaptation Ltd survey carried out in conjunction with the Research Group of the Institute of Personnel Management, 1991.

11 Colin Coulson-Thomas, 'What the personnel director can bring to the boardroom table', *Personnel Management* (October 1991), 36–9.

12 Lester Thurow, *Head to Head: The Coming Economic Battle among Japan, Europe and America*, William Morrow, 1992.

13 3i's, 'Corporate strategies and the FD, 3i's sixth plc UK survey', *Financial Director* (February 1992), 24–5.

14 D. C. Hambrick, 'The top management team: Key to strategic success', *California Management Review*, 30 (1987), 88–108.

15 Committee on the Financial Aspects of Corporate Governance (chairman: Sir Adrian Cadbury). Draft report Issued for public comment, Committee on the Financial Aspects of Corporate Governance, 27 May 1992, p. 13.

Bibliography

1 'Director and board' surveys

The following selection of reports from an ongoing programme of investigations of directorial and boardroom practice represents the prime source of background evidence used in the preparation of this book:

Coulson-Thomas, C., *Professional Development of and for the Board*. An Adaptation Ltd survey for the Institute of Directors. A summary published by the IOD, London, 1990.

Coulson-Thomas, C., *Developing IT Directors*. An interim Adaptation Ltd report to the Department of Computing Science, Surrey University, 1990.

Coulson-Thomas, C. and Wakelam, A., *Developing Directors*. A survey, funded by the Training Agency, undertaken by Adaptation Ltd with the Centre for Management Studies, University of Exeter, Exeter, 1990.

Coulson-Thomas, C., *The Role and Development of the Personnel Director*. An interim Adaptation Ltd survey undertaken in conjunction with the Institute of Personnel Management (IPM) Research Group, IPM, Wimbledon, 1991.

Coulson-Thomas, C. and Wakelam, A., *The Effective Board: Current Practice, Myths and Realities*. An Institute of Directors discussion document, IOD, London. 1991.

Coulson-Thomas, C., *Development Needs of NHS Authority and Board Members*. An Adaptation Ltd report prepared on behalf of the NHS Training Directorate, London, 1992.

2 Boardroom issue surveys

The following selection of reports has also been drawn upon in order to understand the interrelationship between directorial responsibilities; board strategy, objectives, policies and issues; and the market and corporate context:

Coulson-Thomas, C., *The New Professionals*. BIM, Corby, 1988.

Coulson-Thomas, C. and Brown, R., *The Responsive Organisation: People Management, the Challenge of the 1990s*, BIM, Corby, 1989.

Coulson-Thomas, C., *Too Old at 40?*, BIM, Corby, 1989.

Coulson-Thomas C. and Brown, R., *Beyond Quality: Managing the Relationship with the Customer*, BIM, Corby, 1990.

Coulson-Thomas, C., *Human Resource Development for International Operation*. An Adaptation Ltd survey sponsored by Surrey European Management School, Adaptation, London, 1990.

Coulson-Thomas, C., *The Role and Status of Project Management*. An Adaptation Ltd survey for the Association of Project Managers, Adaptation, London, 1990.

Coulson-Thomas, C. and Coulson-Thomas, S., *Managing the Relationship with the Environment*. An Adaptation Ltd survey sponsored by Rank Xerox (UK) Ltd, Adaptation, London, 1990.

Coulson-Thomas, C. and Coulson-Thomas, S., *Implementing a Telecommuting Programme*: *A Rank Xerox Guide for those Considering the Implementation of a Telecommuting Programme*, Adaptation, London, 1990.

Coulson-Thomas, C. and Coulson-Thomas, S., *Quality: The Next Steps*. An Adaptation Ltd survey sponsored by ODI International, Adaptation & (Executive Summary) ODI International, London, 1991.

Coulson-Thomas, C. and Coulson-Thomas, S., *Communicating for Change*. An Adaptation Ltd survey sponsored by Granada Business Services, Adaptation, London, 1991.

Coulson-Thomas, C. and Coe, T., *The Flat Organisation: Philosophy and Practice* (The initial questionnaire survey was entitled: *Managing the Flat Organisation*), BIM, Corby, 1991.

Coulson-Thomas, C., *Harnessing the Potential of Groups*. An Adaptation Ltd survey sponsored by Lotus Development, Adaptation, London, 1993.

3 Related books

Some of the issues raised in *Developing Directors: Building an Effective Boardroom Team* are considered in greater detail in the following books, which also draw, in part, upon the above research programme:

Coulson-Thomas, C., *Creating the Global Company: Successful Internationalization*, McGraw-Hill, Maidenhead, 1992.

Coulson-Thomas, C., *Transforming the Company: Bridging the Gap between Management Myth and Corporate Reality*, Kogan Page, London, 1992.

Coulson-Thomas, C., *Creating Excellence in the Boardroom*, McGraw-Hill, Maidenhead, 1993.

4 Further information

Further information on any of the surveys referred to in this appendix, and details of the corporate transformation 'health check' mentioned in Chapter 10, can be obtained from Adaptation Ltd, Rathgar House, 237 Baring Road, Grove Park, London SE12 OBE, England. Tel.: 081-857 5907

Details of the BIM publications cited, and of other related BIM/IM surveys and reports, can be obtained from the Publications Department, Institute of Management, Management House, Cottingham Road, Corby, Northants, NN17 1TT, England. Tel.: 0536 204222

Details of the Complete Spokesperson workshop and workbook mentioned in Chapters 8 and 10 can be obtained from Policy Publications Ltd, 29 Tivoli Road, Brighton, East Sussex, BN1 5BG (Tel.: 0273 565505, Fax: 0273 550072).

Details of director development courses, workshops and seminars of the IOD, and related publications, can be obtained from the Centre for Director Development, Institute of Directors, 116 Pall Mall, London SW1Y 5ED, England. Tel.: 071-839 1233.

5 Selected books and articles for further reading

Adair, J., *Effective Teambuilding*, Gower, 1986.

Alkhafaji, A.F., 'Effective boards of directors', *Industrial Management and Data Systems*, **90**, No. 4 (1990), 18–26.

Aram, J.D. and Cowen, S.S., *Information Requirements of Corporate Directors: The Role of the Board in the Process of Management*. Final Report to the National Association of Accountants, April 1983.

Bacon, J., *Membership and the Organization of Corporate Boards*. Research, Report No. 886, Conference Board, 1986.

Baker, J.C., *Directors and Their Functions*, Harvard University School of Business Administration, 1945.

Bavly, D., 'What is the board of directors good for?', in B. Taylor (ed.), *Strategic Planning, the Chief Executive and the Board*, Pergamon Press, 1988, pp. 35–41.

Beevor, J.G., *The Effective Board: A Chairman's View*, BIM, 1975.

Bennis, W., *On Becoming a Leader*, Hutchinson Business Books, 1990.

Bennis, W., and Nanus, B., *Leaders: The Strategies for Taking Charge*, Harper & Row, 1985.

Boone, L. and Johnson, J., 'Profiles of the 801 men and one woman at the top', *Business Horizons* (February 1980), 47–52.

Byrd, R.E., 'Corporate leadership skills—a new synthesis', *Organisational Dynamics*, **16**, No. 1(Summer 1987), 34–43.

Cadbury, Sir A., *Company Chairman*, Director Books, 1990.

Charkham, J.P., *Effective Boards*, The Institute of Chartered Accountants in England and Wales, 1986.

Committee on the Financial Aspects of Corporate Governance (chairman, Sir Adrian Cadbury). Draft report issued for public comment, Committee on the Financial Aspects of Corporate Governance, 27 May 1992.

Coopers & Lybrand Deloitte, *Becoming a Director?: What You Need to Know*, Coopers & Lybrand Deloitte, 1991.

Copeman, G., *The Chief Executive*, Leviathan House, 1971.

Copeman, G., *The Managing Director*, 2nd edn, Business Books, 1982.

Coulson-Thomas, C., 'Career paths to the boardroom', *The International Journal of Career Management*, **2**, No. 3 (1990), 26–32.

Coulson-Thomas, C., 'Company directors, the myths and the realities', *Administrator* (May 1991), 4–6.

Coulson-Thomas, C., *Creating Excellence in the Boardroom*, McGraw-Hill, 1993.

Coulson-Thomas, C., *Creating the Global Company: Successful Internationalization*, McGraw-Hill, 1992.

Coulson-Thomas, C., 'Customers, marketing and the network organisation', *Journal of Marketing Management*, **7**, (1991), 237–55.

Coulson-Thomas, C., 'Developing competent directors and effective boards', *Journal of Management Development*, **11**, No. 1 (1992), 39–49.

Coulson-Thomas, C., 'Developing directors', *European Management Journal*, **8**, No. 4 (December 1990), 488–99.

Coulson-Thomas, C., *Developing IT Directors*. An Adaptation Ltd report to the Department of Computing Science, Surrey University, 1990.

Coulson-Thomas, C., *Development Needs of NHS Authority and Board Members*. An Adaptation Ltd report prepared on behalf of the NHS Training Directorate, July 1992.

Coulson-Thomas, C., 'Directors and IT, and IT directors', *European Journal of Information Systems*, **1**, No. 1 (1991), 45–53.

Coulson-Thomas, C., 'Direct yourself to the IT board', *Computer Weekly* (8 February 1990), 15.

Coulson-Thomas, C., 'From personnel professional to successful personnel director: developing competent directors and effective boards'. Seminar paper prepared for the 1991 Annual Conference of the IPM, Harrogate, 24 October 1991.

Coulson-Thomas, C., 'IT directors and IT strategy', *Journal of Information Technology*, **6** (1991), 192–203.

Coulson-Thomas, C., 'Preparation for the boardroom', *Training and Development*, **8**, No. 12 (December 1990), 18.

Coulson-Thomas, C., *Professional Development of and for the Board*. A questionnaire and interview survey undertaken by Adaptation Ltd of company chairmen. A summary has been published by the Institute of Directors, 1990.

Coulson-Thomas, C., 'Strategic vision or strategic con?: Rhetoric or reality?', *Long Range Planning*, **25**, No. 1, (1992), 81–9.

Coulson-Thomas, C., 'The competent director', Corporate Administrator, *Administrator* (July 1990), 12–14.

Coulson-Thomas, C., *Transforming the Company: Bridging the Gap between Management Myth and Corporate Reality*, Kogan Page, 1992.

Coulson-Thomas, C., 'What the personnel director can bring to the boardroom table', *Personnel Management* (October 1991), 36–9.

Coulson-Thomas, C., and Wakelam, A., *Developing Directors*. A survey, funded by the Training Agency, undertaken by Adaptation Ltd with the Centre for Management Studies, University of Exeter, 1990.

Coulson-Thomas, C. and Wakelam, A., *The Effective Board: Current Practice, Myths and Realities*. An IOD discussion document, 1991.

Crystal, G., 'Do directors earn their keep?', *Fortune International* (6 May 1991), 56–8.

Crystal, G., *In Search of Excess, The Overcompensation of American Executives*, Norton, 1991.

Davies, A., *Strategic Leadership: Making Corporate Plans Work*, Woodhead-Faulkner, 1991.

Demb, A. and Neubauer, F-F., 'How can the board add value?', *European Management Journal*, **8**, No. 2 (1990), 156–60.

Demb, A. and Neubauer, F-F., 'Subsidiary company boards reconsidered', *European Management Journal*, **8**, No. 4 (1990), 480–7.

Demb, A. and Neubauer, F-F., 'The boards mandate mediating corporate lifespace', *European Management Journal*, **7**, No. 3 (1989), 273–82.

Demb, A. and Neubauer, F-F., *The Corporate Board: Confronting the Paradoxes*, Oxford University Press, 1992.

Dobrzynski, J.H. *et al.*, 'Taking charge', *International Business Week* (3 July 1989), 36–43.

Drucker, P.F., 'The bored board', in *Towards The Next Economics and Other Essays*, Heinemann, 1981.

Dyer, W.G., *Team Building, Alternatives and Issues*, Addison-Wesley, 1977.

Farmer, A.F., 'Accountability and the board of directors', *Chartered Institute of Building Society Journal* (May 1983), 52 and 53.

Fearnley, H., 'Window dressing or watchdogs', *Financial Weekly*, No. 536 (10 August 1989), 16–18.

Federation of Small Businesses, *The Penalties of Being in Business*, December 1990.

Garratt, B., *Creating a Learning Organisation: A Guide to Leadership, Learning and Development*, Director Books, 1990.

Goold, M. and Campbell, A., 'Non-executive directors role in strategy', *Long Range Planning*, **23**, No. 6 (1990), 118–19.

Gordon, R.A., *Business Leadership in the Large Corporation*, Brookings Institution, 1945.

Greanias, G.C. and Windsor, D., *The Changing Boardroom*, Gulf, 1982.

Grindley, K., *Managing IT at Board Level: The Hidden Agenda Exposed*, Pitman/Price Waterhouse, 1991.

Gupta, L.C., *Corporate Boards and Nominee Directors*, Oxford University Press, 1989.

Hambrick, D.C., 'The top management team: Key to strategic success', *California Management Review*, **30** (1987), 88–108.

Hambrick, D. and Mason, P., 'Upper echelons: The organisation as a reflection of its top management', *Academy of Management Review*, **9**, No. 2 (1984), 193–206.

Harper, J., 'Developing competent directors'. Paper presented at Institute of Personnel Management Annual Conference, Harrogate, 1991.

Harvey-Jones, Sir J., *Making it Happen*, Collins, 1988; 2nd edn, Fontana, 1989.

Heidrick & Struggles Inc., *The Changing Board*, Heidrick & Struggles, 1987.

Henke, J.W., 'Involving the board of directors in strategic planning', *Journal of Business Strategy*, **7**, No. 2 (1986), 87–95.

Holton, V. and Rabbetts, J., *Powder in the Boardroom*, Report of a survey of women on the boards of top UK companies. Ashridge Research Group, Ashridge Management College, 1989.

Horovitz, J.H., 'Strategic control: A new task for top management', *International Studies of Management and Organisation*, **III**, No. 4 (1979), 96–112.

Howe, E. and McRae, S., *Women on the Board*, Policy Studies Institute, 1991.

Houlden, B., *Understanding Company Strategy: An Introduction to Thinking and Acting Strategically*, Blackwell, 1991.

Houston, W. and Lewis, N., *The Independent Director: Handbook and Guide to Corporate Governance*, Butterworth Heinemann, 1992.

Institutional Shareholders Committee (ISC), *The Role and Duties of Directors: A Statement of Best Practice*, ISC, 18 April 1991.

Institute of Chartered Secretaries and Administrators, *Good Boardroom Practice: A Code for Directors and Company Secretaries*, The Institute of Chartered Secretaries and Administrators, February 1991.

Institute of Directors, *Guidelines to Boardroom Practice: Companies in Financial Difficulties*, Direct Line, No. 94, January 1991.

Institute of Directors, *Guidelines for Directors*, 4th edn, Director Publications, May 1991.

Institute of Directors, *Directors' Personal Liabilities*, Corporate Governance Series, No. 6, Director Publications, June 1992.

Jenkins, B., 'Companies in need of a code', *Boardroom Agenda*, Issue 1 (February 1992), 18–19.

Kakabadse, A., *The Wealth Creators: Top People, Top Teams & Executive Best Practice*, Kogan Page, 1991.

Kenward, M., 'Should the boffins come on board?', *Director*, (July 1991), 56–9.

Koontz, H., *The Board of Directors and Effective Management*, McGraw-Hill, 1967.

Korn/Ferry, *Boards of Directors Study UK*, Korn/Ferry International, 1989–92.

Kotter, J.P., *A Force for Change, How Leadership Differs from Management*, The Free Press, 1990.

Lindon-Travers, K., *Non-executive Directors: A Guide to their Role, Responsibilities and Appointment*, Director Books, 1990.

Lorsch, J. and MacIver, E., *Pawns or Potentates: The Reality of America's Corporate Boards*, Harvard Business School Press, 1989.

Loose, P. and Yelland, J., *Company Director: His Functions, Powers and Duties*, 6th edn, Jordans, 1987.

Mace, M.L., *Directors: Myth and Reality*, Division of Research, Harvard Graduate School of Business Administration, 1971.

McDougal, W.J., *Corporate Boards in Canada*, Research report, University of Western Ontario, 1968.

McDougal, W.J. (ed.), *The Effective Director*, University of Western Ontario, 1969.

Masterman, R., *Creating an Effective Board*. Paper delivered at Institute of Personnel Management 1991 Annual Conference, Harrogate.

Margerison, C.J., 'How chief executives succeed', *Journal of European and Industrial Training*, **3**, No. 3 (Monograph: 1980).

Margerison, C.J. and Kakabadse, A.P., *How American Chief Executives Succeed: Implications for Developing High Potential Employees*. An AMA Survey Report, 1984.

Mills, G., *On the Board*, Gower/Institute of Directors, 1981.

Mills, G., 'Who controls the board?', *Long Range Planning*, **22**, No. 3 (1989) 125–32.

Monks Partnership, *Disclosing Board Earnings in Company Annual Reports*, Monks Partnership, 1992.

Monks, R. and Minow N., *Power and Responsibility*, Harper Business Books, 1991.

Mueller, R.K., *The Incomplete Board*, Lexington, 1981.

Mueller, R.K., *Directors and Officers Guide to Advisory Boards*, Quorum Books, 1990.

Mumford, A., Honey, P. and Robinson, G., *Director's Development Guidebook— Making Experience Count*, Institute of Directors and Department of Employment, September 1990.

Mumford, A., Robinson, G. and Stradling, D., *Developing Directors: The Learning Process*, Manpower Services Commission, 1987.

Norburn, D. and Schurz, F., 'The British boardroom: Time for a revolution?', in B. Taylor (ed.), *Strategic Planning, the Chief Executive and the Board*, Pergamon Press, 1988, pp. 43–51.

Pearce, J. and Zahra, S., 'The relative power of CEOs and boards of directors associations with corporate performance', *Strategic Management Journal*, **12**, No. 2, (February 1991).

PRO NED, *Research into the Role of the Non-Executive Director*, PRO NED, July 1992.

Revans, R.W., *Action Learning*, Blond & Briggs, 1979.

Ryan, C.L., *Company Directors: Liabilities, Rights and Duties*, 3rd edn, CCH Editions, 1990.

Sadler, P., 'On shaping the balance of power', *Director* (March 1992), 25.

Sadler, P., 'The painful path to competence', *Director* (September 1991), 23.

Steiner, G.A., Kunin, H. and Kunin, E., 'The new class of chief executive officer', in B. Taylor (ed.), *Strategic Planning, the Chief Executive and the Board*, Pergamon Press, 1988, 23–33.

Sullivan, T. and Bottomley, P., *Boards of Directors Study UK*, Korn/Ferry International, 1991.

Syrett, M. and Hogg, C., *Frontiers of Leadership*, Blackwell, 1992.

Taylor, B. (ed.), *Strategic Planning, the Chief Executive and the Board*, Pergamon Press, 1988.

Taylor, B. and Tricker, R. (eds.), *The Directors Manual*, Director Books, 1990.

Tricker, R. I., *Corporate Governance: Practices, Procedures and Powers in British Companies and their Boards of Directors*, Gower, 1984.

Tricker, R.I., 'Should the chairman also be the CEO?', *Accountancy*, **99**, No. 1122 (February 1987), 109–10.

Tricker, R.I., *The Independent Director: A Study of the Non-Executive Director and of the Audit Committee*, Tolley Publishing Company, 1978.

Tushman, M., Newman, W. and Nadler, D., 'Executive leadership and organisational evolution, managing incremental and discontinuous change', in R. Kilmann and T.J. Covey (eds), *Corporate Transformation*, Jossey-Bass, 1988, pp. 102–30.

Vance, S.C., *Board of Directors: Structure and Performance*, University of Oregon Press, 1964.

Vancil, R., *Passing the Baton: Managing the Process of CEO Succession*, Harvard Business School Press, 1987.

Van Sinderen, A.W., 'The board looks at itself', *Directors and Boards* (Winter 1985), 20–3.

Wakelam, A., *The Training and Development of Company Directors*. Report for the Training Agency, Centre for Management Studies, University of Exeter, October, 1989.

Weisbach, M.S., 'Outside directors and CEO turnover', *Journal of Financial Economics*, **20** (1988), 431–60.

Wright, D., *Rights and Duties of Directors*, Butterworths, 1991.

Zahra, S.A., 'Increasing the boards involvement in strategy', *Long Range Planning*, **23**, No. 6 (1990), 109–17.

Zahra, S.A. and Pearce, J.A., 'Determinants of board directors strategic involvement', *European Management Journal*, **8**, No. 2 (1990), 164–73.

Index

Further titles in the McGraw-Hill Training Series

THE BUSINESS OF TRAINING
Achieving Success in Changing World Markets
Trevor Bentley   ISBN 0-07-707328-2

EVALUATING TRAINING EFFECTIVENESS
Translating Theory into Practice
Peter Bramley   ISBN 0-07-707331-2

MAKING MANAGEMENT DEVELOPMENT WORK
Achieving Success in the Nineties
Charles Margerison   ISBN 0-07-707382-7

MANAGING PERSONAL LEARNING AND CHANGE
A Trainer's Guide
Neil Clark   ISBN 0-07-707344-4

HOW TO DESIGN EFFECTIVE TEXT-BASED OPEN LEARNING:
A Modular Course
Nigel Harrison   ISBN 0-07-707355-X

HOW TO DESIGN EFFECTIVE COMPUTER BASED TRAINING:
A Modular Course
Nigel Harrison   ISBN 0-07-707354-1

HOW TO SUCCEED IN EMPLOYEE DEVELOPMENT
Moving from Vision to Results
Ed Moorby   ISBN 0-07-707459-9

USING VIDEO IN TRAINING AND EDUCATION
Ashly Pinnington   ISBN 0-07-707384-3

TRANSACTIONAL ANALYSIS FOR TRAINERS
Julie Hay   ISBN 0-07-707470-X

SELF-DEVELOPMENT
A Facilitator's Guide
Mike Pedler and
David Megginson   ISBN 0-07-707460-2

DEVELOPING WOMEN THROUGH TRAINING
A Practical Handbook
Liz Willis and
Jenny Daisley   ISBN 0-07-707566-8

DESIGNING AND ACHIEVING COMPETENCY
A Competency Based Approach to Developing People and Organizations
Editors: Rosemary Boam
and Paul Sparrow   ISBN 0-07-707572-2

TOTAL QUALITY TRAINING
The Quality Culture and Quality Trainer
Brian Thomas   ISBN 0-07-707472-6